The Umbrella Garden

The Umbrella Garden

A PICTURE OF STUDENT LIFE IN RED CHINA

MARIA YEN

Adapted from the Chinese by
MARIA YEN with RICHARD M. McCARTHY

GREENWOOD PRESS, PUBLISHERS
WESTPORT, CONNECTICUT

Library of Congress Cataloging in Publication Data

Yen, Maria.
    The umbrella garden.

    An enlarged and revised version of the author's
Hung ch'i hsia ti ta hsüeh shêng huo.
    Reprint of the ed. published by Macmillan, New York.
    1. Students--China.   I. McCarthy, Richard M.
II. Yen, Maria. Hung ch'i hsia ti ta hsüeh shêng huo.
III. Title.
[LA1133.7.Y372 1978]   378.1'8'0951   78-12991
ISBN 0-313-21214-7

Reprinted with the permission of Macmillan Publishing Co., Inc.

Reprinted in 1978 by Greenwood Press, Inc.
51 Riverside Avenue, Westport, CT 06880

Printed in the United States of America

10 9 8 7 6 5 4 3 2 1

Foreword

Most of the chapters in this book originally appeared in Chinese under the title *University Life Under the Red Flag,* published by the Union Press, Hong Kong—a book written to tell Chinese outside the homeland about actual conditions in one Chinese university under the new "People's Government." Foreign friends have suggested that the story might be of some interest to persons who cannot read Chinese. They also suggested that for non-Chinese readers I would have to add a certain amount of new material to provide a proper setting for the events I want to describe. One of these friends, Richard M. McCarthy, has undertaken the task of helping me to expand my original story and rewrite it in English. I wish to thank him as well as the translators of the original manuscript and other friends, Chinese and foreign, who have given me help and advice. However, I wish to make it plain that the opinions expressed in this book are my own and that I alone am responsible for them.

The new chapters we have added to the English version to explain to foreign readers things it was not necessary to explain to readers of my own race have changed my story into a different kind of book. Instead of a simple account of what has happened to our universities under Mao Tse-tung's new government, this has turned out to be a report, if not a complete one, on the Chinese student as such, and how he has faced a postwar world he has had very little part in creating. We students were important to the Communists— how important we didn't realize until they had arrived.

I have tried to write an honest book. Except for the assumed

v

names which I have to use for the sake of security, the narrative is perfectly truthful. Nobody ever counted the exact number, but there is no blinking the fact that a considerable and active proportion of Chinese students studying in Peking in 1948 were working for the entrance of the Chinese Communists into that city. Some were honest idealists. Some were opportunists with a realistic understanding of coming political events. Some, we discovered later, were trained agitators planted among us by the Communist Party. No attempt is made here to analyze the factors which created this student support for the Chinese Communists or to blame anybody. Nor do I try to draw any serious parallels between what I saw happen in China and what has happened in any other country. I have never been in any other country. I am trying to report what did happen to us and then to leave judgment to older and more sophisticated people than myself.

MARIA YEN

Note to the Reader

Whether to call my city Peking or Peiping presents a problem. Since it was the traditional capital of the Empire, it was called Peking, or "Northern Capital," until 1927, when the capital of the Chinese Republic was established in Nanking. It was then renamed Peiping, or "Northern Peace."

When the Chinese Communists set up their People's Republic on October 1, 1949, they gave the city back its old name. Nations which do not recognize the Chinese Communist regime still call the city Peiping. Most people who were born and raised there have always preferred the old name and often called it Peking even during the twenty and more years when it was officially Peiping. For consistency's sake, and not for any political reason, I use the name Peking throughout, except in direct quotations where Peiping originally occurs.

Contents

Foreword		v
Note to the Reader		vii
I	The Eve of Freedom	1
II	Not a Needle, Not a Thread	23
III	Labor Creates a World	32
IV	Sifting the Wheat	42
V	Scraping the Rice Bowl	55
VI	Gray Becomes You	67
VII	Life Managers and Political Shepherds	79
VIII	The Umbrella Garden	101
IX	Sweat and Prayer	111
X	We Close Ranks	124
XI	Who Teaches Whom?	138
XII	The Silver Ear Spoon	150
XIII	The White-Haired Girl	165
XIV	The Bride Saw Red	184
XV	The List of Gold	196
XVI	Decision	215
Epilogue		239

The Umbrella Garden

CHAPTER I

The Eve of Freedom

How does a bride feel the night before she goes to the arms of the man she has chosen?

I didn't look much like a bride in my padded jacket and wrinkled, unfeminine pants that last day of January in 1949 as I stood beside my bicycle outside the main hall on the Peita campus in Peking reading the proclamation posted there. But I felt some of the hope and excitement and anticipation that a bride must feel, because my student comrades and I were on the threshold of a new life too; tomorrow Peking would open its arms to the People's Liberation Army.

We had waited a long time for this—so many years, I thought, it spoke well for us that we could still hope. Years of fighting to keep the university alive in the face of the hunger and repression the civil war had brought upon us. Years of keeping our faith alive by reading the illegal pamphlets that were smuggled in to us. Years of whispering and waiting and, sometimes, when our leaders asked us to, of marching toward the guns of the soldiers defending the government in which we had lost all trust and hope. These soldiers with their caps bearing the blue-sky and white-sun of the Kuomintang still guarded the streets. But tomorrow our People's Liberation Army would march in to take away their guns.

Oh, tomorrow our cheers would be full-throated. Mao Tse-tung's victorious fighters would bring us not just the promise of food and peace, but the bright hope of a new China, young and strong with the power of the liberated masses, standing up to take our rightful place in the world.

And where did we at Peita stand? Up in the front rank where we always stood. We would help lead our people—China was going to need leaders. It was hard to imagine being leaders after what we had survived during the past year, but we were the generation that was going to make over our country. And the smuggled pamphlets had promised that we young women were going to do our share of that leading, too.

I read more details from the proclamation about the triumphal entry. The first detachment would enter the city through the Hsi-Chih Men, the West Gate. Nationalist troops would be responsible for maintaining order until the People's Liberation Army could disarm them. We had not expected such formalities; it would have been more fitting if the new day had been born in a brave show of violence, amid gunfire and the planting of red flags on the city walls.

"Hey, how many times are you going to read that notice! You trying to wear it out?" It was my classmate Fang. Fang's cheerfulness radiated from him. I knew he had written for the underground newspapers; it was rumored that he was even a Party member.

"But it's the great day we've been waiting for," he went on. He put his hand on the handlebar of my bicycle. "Look, comrade, come on along with me. All our friends are over in the men's dorm getting the flags ready for tomorrow."

"Well—my father is worried about what might happen this last night before these Nationalist soldiers clear out. He wants me to go home tonight instead of sleeping here at school."

"Nothing is going to happen," Fang assured me. "The Nationalists know they've been beaten, and they have to be on their best behavior with our own soldiers coming in. Besides, the police have been ordered to stay at their posts. Come on—you females always wait to be coaxed."

I pushed my bicycle after him, grateful that he'd insisted on my coming. At the men's dorm we walked into an excited hubbub where at least thirty students had already gathered in the big common room. Everybody was at work drawing posters, writing slogans on small paper flags, or pasting the flags on sticks.

"Such little flags for such a big day?" I picked up a flag that said "Welcome People's Liberation Army" and wigwagged it teasingly at a girl I knew.

She waved back a pennant which proclaimed "Ten Thousand Years to our Leader Mao Tse-tung." She made room on the floor beside her and handed me a pair of scissors.

"See that fellow over there, the tall one with the thin face?" She nodded toward where the boys had gathered. "He sneaked in through the lines this afternoon from Tsinghua to help us get ready for tomorrow." Tsinghua University, outside the city, had been liberated in December, almost as soon as the siege of Peking had started. This visitor had actually seen our liberators; we shushed one another so that we could hear.

"Sure, we were nervous with all the shooting going on around the campus," he was telling his listeners. "But the day came without the school being touched. And the People's Liberation Army has treated us like brothers. Mostly simple boys from the country. You should see how healthy and strong they are, and how friendly and polite! The Army Cultural Corps has put on some plays for us. The soldiers give us food and do their best to help us. Really, wait till you see for yourself—like brothers! Here, let me show you something." He felt around in his padded jacket and unearthed some brightly printed pieces of paper.

"*Jen min piao*—People's Bank Notes!" Hands grabbed for the money.

"This is what we'll use from now on." With the rest of us hanging on his every word, our Tsinghua friend had never felt so important. "Look at it. You see, instead of that toilet paper with the sour face of old Number One on it we've had to use, it shows tractors and trains and productive tools that really belong to the people."

After we finished the flags, we started singing the songs that had been forbidden so long, the songs we would sing to greet our soldier comrades tomorrow. But it was late and I didn't want my father to worry. So I begged off, climbed on my bicycle, and rode home through the quiet streets.

The whole city was waiting. We had all waited for tomorrow. A year ago, this day had seemed a long way off. Could I forget how it had been a year ago, when we knew the hardest waiting was still ahead? We knew then that we would have to endure more hunger and cold as the war came closer, and that some of us would probably be arrested and a few of us might even be tortured and killed. For we Peita students lived under a regime most of us were ready to rebel against; our dearest hopes were with the men the government was fighting.

Peita—a foreigner reading the word might think it just a misspelling of the Christian word *Pietà*, and dismiss the school as just another mission-run university in a backward land. But as a matter of fact Peita was the only one of the Big Four in Peking which was purely and completely and proudly Chinese. Fu Jen was run by foreign Catholic fathers. Yenching lived on missionary funds from abroad. Tsinghua existed on Boxer Indemnity Funds that the United States had returned to China. Peita is the abbreviation of "Kuo-li Pei-ching Ta-hsueh," which means National Peking University. "Pei," the first syllable of Pei-ching, the real Chinese name of Peking, means "north." "Ta" means "big" or "great." Joined with "hsueh," or "study," it means "university." Together the two syllables are pronounced something like "Bay-dah."

We were proud of our freedom from foreign influence; Peita was the great university of China. It was the heir to China's intellectual traditions, and one of the centers from which the twentieth century revolution spread to our nation. In the past fifty years students from Peita and a few other schools have given China the political leadership which in other nations comes from older people.

There have never been very many of us; perhaps that is why we meant so much. When the Japanese seized Peking in 1937, most Peita students and professors packed up and trekked off to Free China, a thousand miles in the interior, to set up a refugee university there. After the war these men and women came back to establish Peita once more. But victory did not bring peace to Peking, the city whose alternate name means "Northern Peace." Nationalist troops, aided by American marines, occupied the city after the Japanese surrender. But most of the surrounding country remained in the hands of the same Communist forces who had held it against the Japs. For a year or so after V-J Day Peking was host to the "Executive Headquarters" of the Chinese-American effort to find some compromise between the old Nationalist government in Nanking and the Communists in Yenan. But at last the truce teams gave up. The American negotiators moved out of the big hospital building we called "The Temple of the Ten Thousand Sleeping Colonels," and the American marines went home.

They left behind a city shabby and hungry and hopeless. Life was a struggle to keep afloat. Food got scarcer as the war came closer, and money was almost worthless. Most students were supposed to get a subsidy from the government, but more often than not that was in arrears. We had central heating in the girls' dorms, but the men students got only enough coal to keep the stoves in their rooms hardly warm to the touch.

But these personal hardships were not as important to us as the question of what was happening to our country. We had beaten the Japanese, but victory had brought more misery to our people. We watched honest trade die as plundering officials speculated in such imported luxuries as silk stockings, lipsticks and fountain pens and sold the relief supplies supposed to be given to the starving. We watched the soldiers beat ricksha pullers and steal from stallkeepers. Were these soldiers supposed to be our deliverers or our conquerors? We listened to the rumors of corruption among high officials and saw for ourselves the bribes and squeeze exacted by lesser ones. We listened to tales from other cities: "My cousin came back from Nanking last week. He says some of the big shots in the capital don't even know there's a war on. All they worry about is what goes in their bank account. You can see them for yourselves riding around in their big American cars with their concubines in their high heels and foreign dresses."

We listened, too, to the men who told us that China desperately needed a change if we could hope to survive. Three years of watching our rulers flounder with the problems of food and freedom convinced most of us that we had to drive them out and turn to new leadership. And at Peita we were ready to help bring that new leadership into power.

With its life at stake we knew the old government would ruthlessly fight change by every means at its command. We could only win by organization and discipline and struggle; those who believed in the future had to unite to save themselves and our country. Who could unite us? The older liberals whom we admired we also knew were as leaderless as they were courageous, enlisted in factions that pecked away at each other more than they sniped at the common enemy. Except our Communist friends. They were organized. They had discipline. They offered us leadership and the certainty of action. We could only sense vaguely the proportions of the Party underground in Peking, but we saw enough of the results it could produce to know it was there. While others debated, Communist comrades acted. They circulated illegal literature; they pasted up wall newspapers under cover of night telling Peking about the success of their armies. They organized strikes and protest parades. And when the secret agents raided the campus after a student demonstration, it was seldom the Communists among us who got caught.

But what about their ideas? Weren't they rigid and mechanical and intolerant of other beliefs? The friends we suspected of belonging to the Party had an answer to that. "I'm afraid you haven't read Comrade Mao's book *On Practice,* comrade," they said. "That shows that our theory must be wedded to actual conditions. China isn't like some other country. We want to work out a system which suits our own people. The important thing isn't whether we call ourselves 'Communists.' No—don't we all have to fight for the same goals? United action is all that we want, a united front of everybody who believes in freedom and peace. And we'll liberate the masses of our people and make China a new nation!"

So Peita became one of the main headquarters for political agitation and underground work against the old government. Outside the campus, people may have been disheartened and fearful. But inside our walls there was the stir of great events in the air. We spread rumors, argued revolutionary politics, read the forbidden books and pamphlets, and repeated the stories that filtered out of the areas the Communists had taken. By now we called them the "liberated areas."

During the spring and summer of 1948 the food situation got worse, and unrest among the people of Peking grew. Political demonstrations and strikes became our most familiar textbooks. Each demonstration made more followers for our leaders. Some students became sympathizers when they saw how stupid and brutal the government's measures were against such protests. Others who had gone along mostly for the excitement discovered that official snoopers had put them down on the black list as suspected Communists. Once that label had been pinned on them, what else could they do except follow along behind their leaders?

The other side was more frightened of us—or rather of the Communist underground which gave us leadership—than we were of them. Our agitation and propaganda, the slogans we painted on walls, the illegal newspapers we posted at night, and our other "acts of rebellion" provoked the fear as well as the anger of the authorities. They decided to sponsor a counter-demonstration against us under the joint leadership of the Student Affairs Section of the BIS, one of the government intelligence agencies, and the Youth Movement of the Peking office of the Kuomintang Party.

Twenty thousand demonstrators called out by these two agencies, including hired bullies, special agents, and even some genuine students with personal or family reasons for supporting the old regime, assembled at the Tien An Men, the Gate of Heavenly Peace, to march on Peita, headquarters of the "Communist bandits." Firebrand speeches worked the mob up into an ugly mood. In a long column they streamed off toward the university compound. With the biggest, brawniest marchers in front, they tried to batter their way into the Red Hall, a men's dormitory, by frontal assault. But the tenants had received advance warning; they had already barricaded the doors with tables and classroom benches.

Balked, the attackers moved on to the next dormitory and battered down the doors, only to find that the citadel they had conquered was the faculty living quarters. Much embarrassed, they backed out.

Agitators planted in the crowd by the authorities now led it to the west gate of the university. But there they ran into something they hadn't counted on: soldiers armed with fixed bayonets sent there by the municipal gendarmery at the request of university officials. (Perhaps one faction of the city government opposed the raid on the university, or else, quite typically, the government had its signals crossed.) So the mob headed for the president's administrative office at Chung Nan Hai, chanting: "We oppose riots! Down with strikes and violence!" In front of the president's office speakers climbed up in front of the crowd to urge ruthless action against Communist students.

Next on the list was an invasion of Normal University. By now, however, we had alerted all of the other universities in the city of possible attack. The gate of Normal was closed and barred; sentinels manned the wall to give the alarm. Screaming "Down with riots!" the demonstrators surged up to the gate. They drove the sentries off the wall with a volley of stones. They filed off the lock and burst the gate open.

But the first wave of invaders was greeted by a barrage of oil drums filled with stones and cement thundering down the slope at them. They broke and ran, but rallied and pushed through the gate again. From the upper floors of the dormitory the defenders pelted them with paper bags full of choking, blinding cement dust.

In the melee one of the attackers spotted a girl student from Normal standing by the flagpole. "There's one of the Communist bitches! Grab her!" They beat her to her knees and tried to trample her. Two Nationalist Army officers with the mob tried to rescue her. "Stop! It's only a girl! We didn't come in here to beat up women!" The girl tore loose and escaped into the dormitory, her face bloody. Her escape enraged the bullies in the crowd. They turned on the two officers. "They're Communist spies too! Beat the turtle's eggs to death!" One officer kneed in the stomach the man who was holding him and helped the other free himself so that they could both run. A rumor ran through the mob that police were coming, and they melted away.

July saw a worse riot. More refugee students from the Northeast and other areas where the Communists were winning flocked into Peking every day. Some had been evacuated from Taiyuan at the insistence of the government, but no arrangements had been made to take care of them in Peking. Part of this group bedded down in the Temple of Heaven and other shrines; the spectacle of their ragged bedding hung on the walls and the stench of their makeshift latrines offended the sensibilities of foreign tourists "up to take a last look at Peking." Others broke into empty houses and tore up furniture and window frames to build their cook fires with.

When the problem of their plight was raised in the City Council, some of the councilmen argued that it would be extremely difficult to raise money to build the schools the refugees had been promised. Besides, the government was always pestering them for more man power. Why not turn these young ruffians over to the North China Bandit Suppression Headquarters to be drafted into the army? Let them fight instead of studying.

Though the proposal had not yet come to a vote in the council, it was exactly the chance the underground had been waiting for. Peita leaders helped spread the rumor that students were going to be driven into the army to fight the Communists. On July 5th they incited 3,000 refugee students to march on the City Council to present a petition. But when the paraders arrived, everybody on the council had gone home. The students smashed everything breakable and smeared insulting slogans in black paint on the signboard over the gate. Then they marched on to the house of Hsu Hweitung, the head of the City Council. Because Mr. Hsu had already fled to a friend's place after asking the gendarmery to protect his property, soldiers from the 208th Division of the Youth Army blocked the students' advance with rifles, machine guns and a tank.

For two hours the students argued with the officers commanding the troops. Tempers got short; minor scuffles started. Then shooting suddenly ripped out. The students wavered, broke ranks, and ran. Bursts from the machine guns chased them up the street; dozens of students dropped before somebody halted the firing. The official version claimed later that a student stole a pistol from an officer and opened fire first. Others said that a soldier enraged by the jeers thrown at him fired his rifle at his tormentors and that other soldiers had followed his lead. Whoever started it, from now on we students would call it Bloody July Fifth.

Bloodshed made the affair even better for the Communists. They helped us rally in a huge demonstration on July 9th to protest Bloody July Fifth and to honor our comrades martyred by the Youth Army. Though the police and soldiers were tense and hostile, they let us parade in peace, but under watchful supervision.

With the old order falling apart, our classes at the university were not important any more. The political work and demonstrations took time, but even if they hadn't we couldn't have stuck our heads in the sand, lost ourselves in our books while our friends were in the streets helping to change history.

The government black lists of "Communist students" grew longer. Tension and fear descended upon Peita. But suddenly, in the fall of 1948, the university seemed to calm down and take on a sort of tranquillity. It was only because more students left the campus every day.

During a class roll call the teacher might read off four or five names in a row without drawing a response. He'd look up in surprise. "Where is everybody? What's the strike about today?"

Several students spoke at once. "No strike—they've gone home."

"Home? Before winter vacation?"

"That's right. Back home." The students smiled at one another.

I knew what had happened to those who had gone "home." One of my friends, Huang, an intelligent, strong-willed junior, I remember mostly because he always wore a pair of broken spectacles he could never find the time or money to mend. In November, about the time Mukden fell to the Communists, he came to return a copy of Tolstoy's *War and Peace* he had borrowed.

"No, I haven't finished it," he told me. "I won't have time now."

"What's the matter?"

At first he wouldn't say. Then he apparently decided that he could trust me. He told me that his group had information that BIS secret agents had found out about their work.

"Some of us are down in their books for arrest," he half whispered. "I'm escaping to the liberated areas."

"What place? When are you going?"

"Can't tell you. But I'm leaving as soon as they can arrange it."

"Can I come down to see you off?"

"Better not." He laughed. "This isn't a vacation trip. You wait here in Peking. You'll see me again. We'll come back to liberate you."

More than a thousand students deserted the campus by the end of the month. Some were Party members called back to keep them from being arrested and liquidated in the last days of the old government's rule. Others, though they did not belong to the Party, wanted to help hasten our deliverance. They hoped to train for jobs with the new government after the People's Liberation Army had come.

One professor with no clear political stand told fellow teachers:

"What clearer sign do you want that the government is going to collapse! See how many of our students have fled—they are all up in arms against the government. Take a look at our history for the last fifty years. The students have always been the weathercock of what is to come. They have always marched in the direction of the times. The government will fall sooner than we think. The Communists are going to win."

He should have been able to tell that just by reading the newspapers. In the spring the Communists had gone over to the offensive all over the North. From then on each victory was like a blow on a drum. Nationalist troops collapsed en masse in the Northwest. More important, in the Northeast (Manchuria) the 58th Division surrendered the port of Yingkow. Important cities and strongholds in the provinces of Hopei, Shantung, and Shansi fell one after another to the People's Liberation Army.

The morale of government forces reached bottom in the fall. The 92nd Army surrendered; the Communists stormed Tsinan, capital of Shantung, on September 24th. The Manchurian key point of Chinchow fell in October. Then the 60th Army, trapped in

Changchun, the starving capital of Manchuria, yielded. But the fall of Mukden was the worst disaster for the Nationalists. With Mukden fell all of rich Manchuria. And the young military genius, General Lin Piao, turned his Communist soldiers toward Tientsin and Peking.

Our future rolled toward us at a breathless pace. Government troops fell back near Peking as the People's Liberation Army poured through the passes between Manchuria and North China. Foreigners, wealthy merchants, and officials started to flee the city; the west airfield bustled with traffic. The gold *yuan,* the new money the government had introduced as a last gesture to stop inflation, fell in weeks to one-tenth of its first value, and then plummeted down to where simple arithmetic could not cope with it.

The police and soldiers garrisoning the city became even more hostile. We were warned that it was a crime to listen to "enemy" broadcasts. Early in December we heard rumors of fighting near the two airfields outside the walls. On the 14th we heard the big Nationalist guns inside the city itself open fire. The electric news ran through Peita that advance elements of the Communists had been seen near Tsinghua. The People's Liberation Army was at the gates.

On the next day, December 15th, the first shell from a Communist gun arched in over the old walls with a fluttering shriek and exploded on Nan Chi Tze. We wanted our liberation to come on December 17th—the fiftieth anniversary of the founding of Peita. But we had more waiting to endure; Peking settled down to wait out one more siege, the last in five hundred years of sieges.

Like tired donkeys whipped up to one last effort, tattered coolies hunched along under their carrying poles with military supplies for the defenders. More shells landed on the North City; people living there loaded their possessions on carts to move to the other end of town. They bumped into another horde of refugees moving north, for shells had also exploded in the South City. One side of town was as safe as any other; the Communists had advanced to within sight of all four walls.

Late at night, when the noise of carts and army trucks had died, we could lie in bed and listen to the distant hammering of machine guns as the Nationalists fired blindly into the night. Despite the frightened refugees and the periodic burst of a shell a few blocks away, Peita students walked around in a state of cheerful excitement. For us the night was about to end. News of the advance of the People's Liberation Army was whispered in the dormitories and the classrooms. We knew far more than the government newspapers admitted, and we bought them just to laugh at the fear we could read between the lines of the optimistic communiqués they printed. "The Bandit Suppression Headquarters announces another overwhelming victory outside the south wall with 3,000 Communist bandits slain." The reader snorted and tossed the newspaper aside. "The bigger the fear, the bigger the lie. Our comrades will be here any day!"

But the city was still clogged with military traffic—donkeys pulling ammunition and food carts, roving bands of infantrymen all wearing the familiar white sun badge of the old government. Their big, khaki-colored army trucks still hooted our bicycles aside in streets around Peita, and their drivers leaned out to curse us as they careened by.

"The soldiers are here!" To a Chinese this cry has always meant that the bandits, the looters, were here. People heard that Fu Tso-yi's troops were well disciplined. But who could believe that these bitter men infected with defeat could be kind or mild? Because it would be too late to take precautionary measures after they robbed you, prudent householders closed and barred their doors. Wiser families posted big red seals on their gates to announce that they were dependents of this or that army unit, hoping to keep away marauding soldiers. But the soldiers came just the same and hammered on the gate with their rifle butts.

Inside, the confused inmates shouted: "We're all army dependents here! Better go next door!"

"You son of a turtle, open this gate! We're here to fight the Communist bandits for you and you want us to sleep in the street! Open up or we'll break your gate down. Hurry up! Do you want us to shoot it open?"

With the gate about to cave in, the head of the household sent a trembling servant out to negotiate with the invaders. "This house belongs to a regimental commander in Hsuchow," the servant shouted, trying to bluff the invaders. "Go someplace else!" He opened the little door in the gate a tiny crack. "Go around the corner, masters. There's a fine big house there, and only two or three people living in it!"

"So this is the home of army dependents," one of the biggest soldiers jeered. "So much the better: we have dependents too! We'll move in first and our dependents will come along later." Without more palaver the soldiers barged in with their carts, donkeys, and equipment. The only things they forgot to bring were rice and coal.

With the soldiers grabbing all the supplies they could lay hands upon, our food problem became bigger than ever. Because the flour-grinding machine in our mess hall broke down, we began to feed on Indian corn. Students who had been able to wolf down a catty (about 1.3 pounds) of Chinese bread or three big bowls of rice or noodles a day could choke down little more than a bowl of the gritty corn meal. It took more time to force down half a bowl of the meal than it did to eat three bowls of rice. Our jaw muscles ached after every meal; our teeth had to do the grinding that a machine normally did.

With our corn we tried to get some vegetables every day and sometimes some scraps of meat or fish. One day the school butcher returned from a trip to the Chao Yang Men market to report that the vegetables and the hog carcass the school had ordered had been stolen by soldiers on the way back. So we had to content ourselves with chewing on fried salted vegetables with soybeans or salted roots.

We had trouble getting from one part of the city to another with troops constantly marching back and forth and forced-labor gangs building pillboxes in front of public buildings and at street intersections. To add to the traffic snarl streets leading into Hatamen Street were closed off while a swarm of workers sweated in the cold to build an airstrip in the heart of the city to replace the two fields abandoned outside town. Sometimes the heavy guns emplaced in the parks shook a whole section of the city when they replied to the Communist artillery.

Several shells burst on the street connecting Red Hall with the other men's dormitories. Another shell struck the dormitory and wrecked one of our rooms. The two students who lived there happened to be out, so they escaped death. Rumors passed around that the shell had really been fired by Nationalist troops in the South City in order to stir up trouble against their sworn enemies, the students. As proof our leaders told us that the missiles were of small caliber and could have come from antiaircraft guns. Besides, they said, the People's Liberation Army would never bombard Peita, which was not close to any military target we knew about. Luckily, most of the shells came in the daytime. With Peking living by candlelight, the nightly curfew made it increasingly hazardous to wander around after dark. We heard stories, in fact, of how trigger-happy patrols roaming the city had opened fire on their own military cars dashing through the darkened streets.

When the electric lights and water were cut off, we went into action as planned to protect the school from the looting and violence we feared from the defending soldiers. Our men students strengthened the defenses they had already prepared. Girl students sealed up one of the two doors into our dormitory with bricks. The other door we locked at sunset and piled chairs and desks against it to hold back any attackers until we could call help. Special agents, we had been told, might try to break in at any time.

Our leaders divided us into self-defense platoons to stand guard every night. Each platoon stood three watches: from eight to midnight, from midnight until four, from four to eight in the morning. Each platoon had four sections. One section stood sentry at fixed posts, another maintained a roving patrol around the wall, a third maintained liaison inside the buildings, and the last kept in telephone contact with other universities.

My first turn to go on watch came on a moonless night from midnight until four. I was so worried about falling asleep on watch that I went to bed before sunset. The more I worried, the wider awake I got. Night came. I heard the big door bang shut and afterward I could hear nothing but an occasional sharp-spoken challenge as the patrols met each other outside and identified themselves. I dozed and woke at eleven. Beside me Wang Mei-tien was breathing hard in her sleep, almost snoring. I envied her; my brain seemed as active and sleepless as it would have been at ten in the morning. I gave up, threw back the covers, and pulled on my coat. I roused my roommate at ten minutes to twelve, just before the messenger came to call us. We tiptoed out of the silent dormitory.

In front of Red Hall we lined up for a whispered roll call, two persons to a team. Each team was issued a flashlight and a club. Mei-tien and I were assigned with another team to man the telephones. The group we were relieving showed us how to call the other stations, told us the password, and wished us luck.

The four of us squeezed into the tiny room, and I closed the window. But an icy draft sieved in along the floor; it must have been near zero outside and quite close to that inside. The telephone buzzed. Mei-tien picked up the receiver.

I waited twenty tense seconds before she took the phone away from her ear. "All quiet. Nothing has happened."

I relaxed enough to feel my lack of sleep and tried to keep from yawning. Inside my wadded cotton jacket I grew warm enough to be on the edge of dozing off. Then a blast of icy air hit me when Lao Ma opened the door and came in from his patrol outside. Struggling with my drowsiness, I asked him to trade posts with me.

Mei-tien gave me our flashlight and I walked outside. To the south a single gun was booming at spaced intervals. I looked up to where the streetlight had been burning, and began to wish I was back inside.

Nothing is going to happen, I told myself. But I opened my eyes wide and strained my ears to listen. I turned to the left of Red Hall. Then I stopped. A black mass of something was scuttling along the wall. It was too big and too grotesque to be a man. I took three short steps and stopped. Why hadn't I brought along the club I had seen Lao Ma lean up against the wall inside? The flashlight in my hand was indeed a pitiful weapon. Then to my horror the blob suddenly split in two. One part jerked crablike up over the wall. The other half squatted at the foot.

Where had the regular patrol gone to? I switched on the flashlight and aimed the beam at the wall.

"Hey! Turn that light off! What are you trying to do!"

But I kept the light pointed until I recognized one of my classmates crouched under the wall. "You scared me half to death!" I hissed at him.

"What do you think you did to us?" His voice mixed anger and relief. "We're on sentry duty here, a half-hour for each shift. It was Lai's turn. But his hands and feet are so stiff with the cold that he couldn't climb up on top of the wall, so I had to give him a boost up on my shoulders."

I looked up. I could see Lai now, squatting on the wall over my head. "What's your time?" I was beginning to lose interest in sentry duty. It must be 2:00 A.M. by now.

"You'd better be patient. Last time I looked, it was only a quarter of one."

"It must be later than that," I said.

"Hey, what is it? What are you doing?" Another guard pounded up to where we were standing.

Explanations. Now I wished something really had happened. I wished that I were anywhere else but standing there with the flashlight in my hand.

Minutes dragged as I walked my beat. The gun boomed away. My hands and feet were slowly turning into lumps of ice. I'd better go back to the guardroom and change back with Lao Ma.

Inside again, my fingers were so numb that I could not unbutton my coat. Lao Ma had to do it for me before he ventured back out in the cold himself.

The next time we stood watch wasn't so bad. Two or three days of sunny weather took some of the bite out of the intense cold. We installed a small stove in the telephone room. We got used to the noise of the guns, the lack of electricity, the nasty-tempered soldiers who shouldered us aside in the streets, the recklessly driven army trucks piled with food, ammunition, or some officer's household furniture. We even got used to the spectacle of the giant silver airplanes settling sluggishly over the rooftops to bounce down on the new landing strip along Hataman Street and brake to a halt just short of the Tartar Wall.

We worried or hoped, depending on the latest rumor. General Fu Tso-yi wanted to surrender. No, that wasn't true. The die-hards really wanted to die—or at least would ask their soldiers to die. Then we breathed easier when we heard that members of the Municipal Council had made a secret trip across the lines to negotiate a peaceful end to the fighting. A few stray students from Yenching and

Tsinghua sneaked in to tell us how their liberators were helping them return to normal. The People's Liberation Army actually encouraged them to come into the city, they said. But the Nationalists sometimes fired on them as they pushed their bicycles across the fields. Fortunately, they added, the aim of the reactionary troops was as bad as ever.

Then newspaper headlines told a few noncommittal details about the attempted assassination of Mayor Ho, who was one of the leaders in the peace negotiations. The newspaper said that a shell was thought to have landed on his house, but we knew that agents of the die-hards had planted a time bomb on his roof. Though the explosion killed his daughter and wounded Mayor Ho, he kept working to bring the city peace.

The defenders went through the motions of getting ready for a last-ditch fight. More pillboxes went up; new batteries of artillery were displayed in the parks. Then, on January 22nd, we read that the two sides had agreed on terms to end the bloodshed. The word "surrender" was not mentioned, but we did not have to read between the lines of the official announcement to know that we had won total victory. We had won; now it only remained to wait as patiently as we could to cheer the comrades who had fought to free us.

It had been an exciting month, I thought, when I stopped the bicycle in front of my own gate. So much to remember during the good days ahead—and when I woke up tomorrow it would be the day when we would actually hold our victory in our grasp.

Nobody seemed to know the next morning exactly what time the first soldiers from the People's Liberation Army would march through the West Gate. To be on the safe side, we all assembled before noon in the field on the campus we were going to christen Democratic Square. We fell into ranks to permit our leaders to count noses and distribute the flags we had made the night before. Then a bicycle courier came back from the West Gate with news that he could see no sign of the troops. We fell out of line and tried to find a place out of the wind to eat the lunches we had brought.

At one-thirty our leaders got us on our feet again with shouts of "Let's go!" Back in ranks we passed the news along that the soldiers were coming at two o'clock. On the way west through the city we sang and cheered, and shopkeepers and householders came to the curb to see what was going on. We shouted at them that the People's Liberation Army was coming, and a few of them tagged along after us. Our leaders halted the column two blocks from the gate.

No People's Liberation Army. We sang one song and then some more. Shortly after three our courier pedaled up as fast as his machine would go. "They're coming!" he shouted. "They're on the way!" Faintly, and then louder, we heard the sound of singing from the west, mixed with clapping and cheers. Our leaders waved down our buzz of excitement. The boy in front of our platoon lifted up his arm, brought it down, and we started to sing:

> " 'You are the lighthouse, lighting the sea;
> You are the helmsman, holding us true on course—
> Brave Liberation Army, sons of the people!
> You are the pivot and the needle of our compass!
> Forever we shall march after you—
> China will be free! Will be free!' "

We ended with a shout and looked toward the west. But the street was still empty. So we struck up again, " 'You are the lighthouse, lighting the sea . . .' "

But louder music drowned out our chorus. A truck with two loudspeakers on top moved down the street. The music from the speakers stopped, and we heard a great voice cry: "Welcome to the People's Liberation Army! Welcome the People's Liberation Army on its arrival in Peiping!"

Then we saw our first People's Army fighter. He was a tommy-gunner, sturdy and vigilant with his gun thrust forward at the ready, its shoulder strap steadying it poised at his hip. Behind him marched a platoon of infantry, clad in mustard-colored uniforms almost like those the Nationalists wore. But these soldiers looked strong and healthy. They were stern and serious, but their faces were smooth and shining and flushed, a very handsome flush.

One girl from Peita ran straight into the marching column with a handful of flowers. She tried to pin the hothouse blooms on the first soldier she came to, but she so flustered him that he backed away as if he had seen a witch. The girl grabbed the next soldier and managed to pin the bouquet on him, and then, embarrassed almost to death, ran back amid the laughter and clapping of her friends.

I looked at the face of the soldier she had pinned the flowers on; he was almost as frightened as the first had been. Before she expressed her joy so vigorously, I thought, my classmate should have stopped to think whether these boys, coming from simple people, would understand or appreciate the way a sophisticated city girl expressed her feelings. I looked at their good young faces strong and reliant under the big fur caps. If all the men in the People's Liberation Army were like this, we could really be proud of our army.

My comrades, I knew, felt the same enthusiasm. The most excited, the declared "activists" and "progressives," behaved as if they were joining their sweethearts after long separation. Their shouts and waving infected everybody around them, and every single one of us from Peita cheered with all his breath.

After the infantry came two jeeps. Then there was a pause. This was a spontaneous sort of parade, I thought, and perhaps the "follow-up" troops had failed to follow up. Across the street I saw two foreigners looking down at us from where they stood on the hood of their jeep. They looked embarrassed and uncertain, I was happy to see. I nudged the girl next to me. "Oh, the foreigners," she said. "Maybe newspaper reporters. Or from one of the imperialist consulates. We don't have flowers or cheers for them today."

More cheering swept along the crowd, but this time it was for our own comrades from Tsinghua and Yenching, parading with banners and giant portraits of our new leader, Mao Tse-tung. Another large portrait paraded by—"Chu Teh, our commander in chief," someone said, and we clapped again. We waved from the curb at our lucky friends who had been liberated a month ahead of us, and they shouted back, waving their flags to show they had seen us.

After a brass band followed a procession of army trucks loaded with soldiers and more Tsinghua and Yenching students. Behind them trailed a few battered civilian trucks filled with members of

ch as the telephone workers, who had a banner
: of their truck reading, "Congratulations to the
peration!"

We waited expectantly, but the civilian trucks were the end
of the parade. Finally we drifted out of ranks, most of us trailing
down the street after the troops. We found one unit preparing to
camp out for the night in the courtyard of a public building. We
thronged around the soldiers to watch them shed their neatly taped
packs and stack their weapons in disciplined, careful pyramids. We
sang for the soldiers, who listened politely, then organized ourselves
to dance the *yang-ko*, the formalized old "planting dance," in the
gathering dark.

Not until we broke up and started for home did I begin to
realize how tired I was. What I wanted most in the world was first
a drink of water, then a bowl of noodles, and then bed. I fell into
step with a friend.

"A long day," he said, "and a lot of walking."

"But it was worth it," I told him. "Our lives are just starting.
I feel that everything we've lived through up to now is just preparation for this moment. It's our revolution—we helped make it. And
it's just beginning today."

When I had my supper and fell into bed, I was as tired from
the excitement and the parading as I had ever been in my life—so
tired that I had trouble going off to sleep. I thought about all the
armies I had seen; even in my short life Peking had had too many.
The armies of the war lords. The ruthless but efficient and disciplined Imperial Army of Japan. The Nationalist troops who entered after V-J Day, shabby and disheartened with so many years
of marching and fighting. The easygoing Americans with them, rich
with equipment we had never seen the like of before and concerned
mostly about getting out of this strange, dirty place and back home.
But I had never seen an army like the People's Liberation Army I
had seen today, so serious and modest, so mild and well behaved.

But how sore my eyes felt from the wind and blowing dust!
And how my legs ached! Let's not think about things any more.
Let's just think how tired I am and how much I want to sleep. No—
let me think about the words we have said to one another so often,
the plans we are going to help carry out, the happiness we are going

to bring to our country. . . . The new People's Government wi.
give us real democracy. . . . Our leaders will not seek personal
ambition or personal profit. . . . We must love the people; we
must labor for the people. . . . And, they tell us— What else do
they say? That we students are the vanguard of the revolution, and
more than ordinary men we must give ourselves for the welfare of
the people. . . . It was going to be good to work for the people. . . .

I could still feel the sandy grit under my eyelids. But my eyes
weren't so sore now. The fatigue all over my body began to dim
my thoughts and then to extinguish them. I fell asleep.

CHAPTER II

Not a Needle, Not a Thread

How would the soldiers behave when they took over the city? Would there be a pounding on the gate and a swarm of boisterous men behind a stuck-up officer insisting that we had to put them up and feed them as our patriotic duty? Would they rush in and make themselves the masters of the house, stealing rice and coal, dirtying the courtyard with their excrement, "borrowing" everything portable that hadn't been buried or hidden?

The People's Liberation Army was supposed to be different. The big parade on February 3rd, when columns of troops, tanks, and guns rolled through the city for nine hours, impressed us as much with the discipline and smartness of our liberators as it did with the power of their captured Japanese and American equipment. But for the skeptical, several questions remained to be answered. It was obvious that these soldiers knew how to obey their officers in a parade or in a battle. But how did they really treat the *lao-pai-hsing*, the "old hundred names," the common people? Did

23

they beat coolies as other soldiers did? Did a young girl have to be very careful to be plain and inconspicuous if they were quartered in her house? Did they steal? From the solemn expressions they wore coming into the city, it seemed quite unlikely.

But soldiers had always taken what they wanted. The reports of the fine behavior of these men could be just propaganda. Could I really believe that they wanted to help the *lao-pai-hsing*? We students all said yes, of course. But privately I wasn't quite convinced that I could let my younger sister go into a room alone where there were soldiers, or ask one of them to watch my bicycle while I went into the post office to send off a letter.

The city watched cautiously while sentries of the People's Liberation Army assumed guard duty in front of public buildings and stood watch beside the traffic police, who had turned in their guns to the army. On walls of houses and public buildings slogans in big red characters hailing the Liberation replaced the old slogans in faded blue paint demanding the destruction of the "Communist bandits." Handsome posters went up showing the invincible might of the people and promising that all China would soon be liberated. Gangs of men began the job of cleaning up the mess left by the defenders. They began to dismantle the pillboxes—in most of which no guns had ever been placed—started to fill in the useless trenches, began to erase the scars left by the construction of the airstrip along Hatamen Street.

A new Military Control Board began to issue orders straightening out city affairs. Not all the officials on it were Communists— staff members of the old government had been asked to remain at their posts. Most of the old newspapers continued to appear. Now, however, instead of calling Lin Piao and General Nieh Yung-chen "bandits," these papers called them "people's heroes." The water was turned on again. And at night, now, the lights burned brighter than they had since the end of the Japanese war.

I quickly got a chance myself to find out what the PLA soldiers were like. Peita students set a movement afoot to contribute towels, toothbrushes, soap, writing paper, and other small necessities to comfort troops guarding the suburban areas. I'd planned to ride along in a truck with some fellow students to help distribute these small presents.

But I woke up in the dormitory with a sore throat and the beginnings of fever the day we'd planned to go. In the classroom we had agreed upon as our meeting place my friend Chang noticed my flushed look. "You look like you're coming down with something, Maria," he told me. "Do you mind if I feel your forehead?

"Huh—I think you've got some fever. Too much excitement, maybe, these last few days. I don't think it would be a very good idea for you to ride around in an open truck in this cold. Why don't you take a day or two off, get away from the dormitory and all this excitement, and spend a night or two at home?"

He walked me to the gate and stopped a pedicab for me. "Get some rest," he admonished me, and the pedicab man pedaled me off. Through the sunny streets I rode, past the posters and the big red slogans painted on the walls. Once we slowed down to pass a team of *yang-ko* dancers from some middle school.

The pedicab stopped in front of my father's house. I really felt ill now; my head was swimming and my legs were wobbly under the dirty robe the pedicab man had tucked around me. The driver realized that I was ill. He let me sit in the pedicab while he rang the gate bell for me.

The door opened. It was a ruddy-faced, young PLA soldier.

"Are you looking for the people of this family?" he asked me politely in a somewhat halting Northern dialect. He smiled at me. "I'll go and find them."

Surprise gave me a short fit of energy. I climbed out of the pedicab and paid the fare. I was just about to stop the soldier from announcing my arrival when our amah came out from within. Seeing me standing by the door, she burst out laughing. "Ai-yah! So it's you, is it? That little soldier said it was a young wife looking for somebody."

An unmarried coed usually resents being addressed as a "young wife," but I couldn't help laughing. Here, I realized, was part of the attractiveness of these simple peasant boys. When a person raised in the country sees a young female without the pigtails of maidenhood, what can he take her for but a "young wife"?

Unfortunately, both my father and mother were out. I climbed into bed, and the amah brought me a cup of hot water and two aspirin tablets. Then I made her sit beside the bed while I asked her how the soldiers had come into our house. "Did they act like the soldiers of the old government, rushing into our place without asking for permission?"

"Well, an officer called on your father and told him he'd heard that you might have a spare room. But they waited for your father to invite them. Anyhow, they're in. But they do keep me hopping— a bunch of young lads like that. 'Ma'am, can we have some boiled water to drink, please?' 'Ma'am, lend me a match.' Oh, they keep me hopping, I tell you."

"Can't you boil some water and give them a box of matches without their asking for them?"

"That's what I'll do." The momentary look of discontent vanished from the amah's face to make room for a motherly smile. "They keep me busy, but they're really good, honest boys. I've lived dozens of years, but I've never seen any soldiers talk so politely to ordinary people like me. Why, when they have nothing of their own to do, they even help me sweep the yard and carry coal and—"

"Ma'am! Ma'am!" They were calling her again.

The amah jumped up, opened the door, and left in a hurry. Alone in the quiet room, I remembered the "Three Rules" and "Eight Intentions" of the People's Liberation Army. The most appealing rule was the second: "Not a needle, not a thread from the people." I liked the "Eight Intentions," too. These soldiers were called upon to be "gentle of word," "fair in business transactions." They were told: "Return what you borrow," "Pay indemnity for any damage you cause." They were warned, "Don't beat or scold people" and "Don't molest women." From what I had already seen, the PLA was observing them all. The boy was right who had said, "I can't see anything wrong about this army." My headache, I felt, was easing, but my legs still felt weak. I had just closed my eyes when the amah darted in again. "I can't decide at all! Tell me, miss, should I lend them our rice?"

I guessed that we probably didn't have much rice left. But I remembered "Return what you borrow."

"Lend them what you can," I told her.

She had just said she would leave the decision to me, but now she wanted to argue about it. "Ai—how can that be done?" She stuck her tongue between her teeth and screwed up her face with worry. Then she hastened on. "T'ai-t'ai said there's no money in the house again—I heard her complaining to master this morning. If we give them all our rice, what do we eat?"

"Doesn't the People's Liberation Army return what it borrows? Lend them something, anyway."

"You students always stand up for the Communists." There was a bit of anger in her, although she spoke laughingly. "Just after they arrived, these young fellows here borrowed twenty-five catties of coal. They haven't returned it yet."

They were calling "Ma'am!" out there again.

"Twenty-five catties of coal is a cheap enough price to pay for our liberation. I said lend them as much as you can. Go on, go back in there and tell them. They've called for you several times, but you've refused to answer them. Any other soldiers than the PLA, and you'd be scolded and beaten. Now go on!"

I drank the rest of the water in my glass, wrapped the quilt around me, and turned my face to the wall to show this was my final decision.

I lay in bed three days and then felt quite well again. So, under the pretext of taking them some boiled water, I went back to the west wing of the house, where the soldiers lived.

Inside the door was a square table and no other furniture. The floor was paved with blankets. Piled against the wall were quilts, rolls of clothing, eating utensils, and jumbles of military equipment I couldn't identify. Six or seven young soldiers were sitting on the floor. The first three to catch sight of me sprang to their feet. "Sorry to bother you, comrade," one stuttered. "Here, we'll take care of this ourselves, comrade." He took the kettle from my hand and began to pour the water into their thermos bottles.

Another soldier pulled down his cotton-padded jacket, bent his head, looked around trying to make up his mind what would be the politest thing to do, and then sat down again. The only man still standing was the boy who had called me "young wife." His face aglow with bashfulness, he mopped at his runny nose with his sleeve, uncertain whether to stand or to take his seat again.

"Please sit down," I said hurriedly.

Without giving an answer, he walked to the table, picked up a large, well worn enameled cup, filled it half full of water, and mumbled, "Have some water, comrade." He shoved the cup at me, then plumped down among his comrades, almost as if somebody had pulled a chair out from under his bottom.

Their agitation at my unexpected visit made me so diffident that I could not tell them what I really wanted to, that I was deeply moved by their simplicity and sincerity. I could only mutter a polite phrase:

"Comrades, we're glad to see you. Please don't hesitate to tell us when you need something. Do you feel at home here?"

I stood waiting for a reply. But they were so covered with confusion and embarrassment that none tried to answer. I suddenly remembered the girl student who had run into their ranks and tried to pin flowers on them the day they entered the city. My desire to talk longer with them vanished. I forced a smile, nodded, and fled from the room. Before I had taken a dozen steps, I heard an outburst of confused talk.

In the yard I met my mother's friend, Mrs. Li, whom the amah was seeing to the door. Mrs. Li was an old-fashioned and rather supercilious lady. Her husband had been a middle-rank government official, but the new authorities had not molested him. With a smile Mrs. Li asked where I came from, and I told her the truth.

"My, how times have changed! A young miss with a good education sending water to rough soldiers and doing it of her own accord—" Mrs. Li clucked and looked at the amah, at whom I threw a resentful look, for she had obviously let the cat out of the bag. "These young soldiers—really, aren't they fresh off the farm! The comical things they've done. You've heard this story of the trouble they've had understanding about electric lights. In this one house some of them wanted to smoke. But there weren't any matches, and no kerosene lamp. So one of them put his cigarette up against a light bulb. He was furious when it wouldn't burn."

Then she went on to tell me another story I had already heard, about the soldiers who wandered around a Western-style house looking for a place to wash their rice. The only water they could find was in the toilet. They agreed it was most inconvenient, but emptied their rice in anyway. But how to get more water? "Pull the chain hanging up there!" Pull the chain, they did. And right before their astonished eyes the rice swirled around once, gurgled, and disappeared.

"Not a very nice story, but—" She giggled.

"Pardon me, Mrs. Li, but did you actually see this happen?"

"Of course not. What do you—"

"Or did you talk to the person who saw all this?"

"I didn't. But everybody has heard the story."

"I know they have. But I haven't talked to anybody who saw it happen. And I don't think anybody else has, either. I don't think you help anybody spreading silly stories like that!"

"Well," Mrs. Li tried to mollify me, "I suppose they're good-hearted young fellows."

"I hear you have some of them living at your house. How are they behaving?"

"Oh, they're honest fellows," she said. "Honest fellows. They're living in our sitting room. When they came in, their company commander insisted on removing all the settees, all the easy chairs, and all the old carved furniture to keep them from damage. We thought it was too much trouble. But he insisted, so we finally let them move everything out of the room except the old pictures on the walls.

"Ai—who would have thought that those boys would damage a T'ang painting in three days? They didn't know what a treasure it was, of course. The company commander was really excited. He scolded his men soundly and asked what the picture was worth." Mrs. Li forced a smile. "My husband, of course, told him not to bother, that he couldn't possibly pay the indemnity. Even if he could, no money could possibly buy back that picture. But the company commander would not give in. 'We have orders to pay for any damage we have done—and I obey orders,' he told us. Well, as a result we finally had to accept twenty catties of millet in compensation."

"Have they destroyed anything else or taken away any antiques? Their only trouble is that they don't understand the value of things that are old," Amah said to Mrs. Li.

Mrs. Li paused. "Generally speaking, they're very careful. But we did lose a few things."

"Really?" I asked doubtfully. "Aren't they supposed not to take a single needle or a single thread from the people?"

"Well, they haven't taken any needle or any thread," she answered. "But they have used some of our coal."

"Why doesn't the company commander do something about it?"

"He stops it whenever he catches anybody at it. But when he does not see . . . well, we can't always be running to the company commander. And after all, the weather is cold. It's very cold in that sitting room unless the stove is kept going. It seems to me that these soldiers are all good, well meaning boys, and they certainly keep better order than any other army I've seen. Every day they help our servants sweep the courtyard—and they keep it clean as a whistle. Well—" We had arrived at the gate. The amah hurried ahead of us and stopped a pedicab.

I stayed at home two more days, hoping to get my strength back. Then a boy dropped by to bring me my mail. Something new and exciting had happened at school, he said. Some of our former classmates who had fled in the last few months of the old regime had just returned with the PLA. Clad in Communist uniforms, their faces shining with pride, they had come back to visit us. How many? At least a dozen. And three of them were women. I got out my heaviest clothes, dressed, told the amah to bring my bicycle out to the gate, and returned to school.

On the way I saw soldiers on duty beside the police, looking honest, ruddy, and strong. I hadn't planned to stop off and buy anything. But I had an idea. I stopped my bicycle and leaned it against a post near where a soldier stood. "Comrade, would you mind watching my bike for a few minutes to make sure nobody steals it? I'll do a little shopping, but I'll come right back."

He glanced at my student uniform and then at the bicycle. "Okay."

I waited four or five minutes, then bought a packet of peanuts. Back on the street I looked for the bike, and stood petrified. The ruddy-faced soldier stood solemnly on guard with his rifle on his shoulder. He was on duty, but every thirty seconds or so he glanced at the bike to make sure it was still there. Six months ago anybody who passed by and witnessed such a scene would have told himself, "That poor fellow must be guarding a bicycle belonging to the general's daughter!"

CHAPTER III

Labor Creates a World

Back on the campus, I felt I'd been away a month when my friends came to tell me the things they'd been doing. They reported how they had studied the policies the new authorities had announced for running the city, how they had then organized propaganda teams to explain the new policies and the meaning of the liberation to the people, and how they had greeted our old schoolmates returning to school in uniform. "Well, who's come back?" I asked. "What about our friend Wang—you know, the tall fellow from Tsingtao in our Modern History class?"

"Well, he's probably back too. Around someplace, I guess." But it appeared that nobody actually knew. Then a schoolmate suddenly pointed toward the gate. "Say, we're in luck. He's just back. Go over and ask him!"

I spotted a schoolmate in PLA uniform walking in through the gate. Though he looked familiar, I could not recall his name. I remembered only that when he belonged to the History Department he had been lean and pale and argumentative.

We went over to meet him. He shook hands with all of us. Now he looked heavier and healthier. "Here we are," he said. "Liberated at last after all this waiting. It's finally dawn—our day has come!" By now we had heard the expression often enough so that it had lost a bit of its inspiring ring. I smiled back and asked about our old friend Wang.

"Oh, Wang," he said. "You mean the big fellow from Tsingtao, the one who was so clever. He's back too, and with the army. He'll probably go on south with the army pretty soon." He shook his head and started again. "He, uh—"

"Well, how about him?" I couldn't believe that anything awkward could have happened to someone as capable as Wang.

"He—" The PLA man looked a bit brighter. "Oh, nothing, nothing. It was just strange to him at the beginning. Recruits from the bourgeoisie sometimes have a great many defects and have trouble joining the proletarian revolution without some remolding. And the process of remolding is sometimes hard."

He stopped to wipe his nose, and then went on. "When our friend first joined up, he was rather sentimental. And he still is even now. He was sometimes dissatisfied with the old party members and cadres. He raised odd questions in our discussions, and instead of helping himself and other comrades to solve problems, simply muddled them. So, naturally, he's sometimes unhappy."

"How about you? Are you happy all the time?"

"Certainly," he said. "Haven't we worked and fought for this day for the last two years? The new epoch is here; the new tide is here. We must not lag or fall behind." He tapped himself on the chest. "I can feel myself getting stronger and stronger. The country belongs to us—it's time for us to settle down to hard work! I am determined to stand on the side of the people, to battle against the reactionaries until the working people of China and the whole world have been freed."

He patted me hard on the shoulder as if to push me into ranks. "So let's buckle down and work, comrade! Follow the ranks, follow the Party. The fatherland needs you!"

How could we follow the Party? We had heard that all our

new leaders had come to Peking, or were on the way. But where were they? How was the Party going to give us leadership?

The answers weren't long in coming. One morning we read a posted notice that the Democratic Youth League and eight or nine other student political groups which had been supported by the Communist Party from the wartime days of the refugee universities until the Liberation were now to be dissolved. Their membership was to be absorbed by a New Democratic Youth League, which would unify all of the groups which had served the cause in the past.

We got another surprise when the roster of underground Communist Party members at Peita before the Liberation was made known to the public. These hundred-odd underground heroes had kept their identity hidden extremely well; people found that quiet friends they had never dreamed of as being Communists now revealed themselves as veteran Party members. And some of our classmates who had made the most noise about politics weren't really party members. A classmate by the name of Shao Po, reading the list, whispered to me with astonishment, "How come that those guys who used to run around the most and shout the loudest and wave their flags the hardest aren't Party members at all?"

We found that we had four Party members in our own class. I remember that they led us outside to a quiet, grassy corner of the campus one day and told us briefly how the student movement had done its work under the concealed guidance and leadership of the Party. Then they asked us solemnly: "Do you have any criticisms about our work? We're sorry that we had to work so much undercover, but the Party had to protect itself, of course. Do you have any ideas or suggestions about our future work? How do you feel after reading the roster of our members?"

Another Party member took over, and said some of the same things. "For safety's sake, we were unable to identify ourselves openly before. You can understand our motives for that, can't you? We welcome your frank opinions and questions if you have any doubts. Because, by speaking frankly, you will simply show your regard and concern for us."

We appreciated the candor and sincerity these classmates were showing. Their reputations were good; we reassured them that we appreciated their leadership, even during those times when we hadn't been aware of it. The atmosphere was so friendly that the Party members relaxed. Then Shao Po spoke up. "You just said you'd welcome our frank opinions and our questions which just show our concern for you. Well, when the old Kuomintang outfit, the San Min Chu I Youth League, tried to break up the student movement, you guys somehow got everybody to agree that political parties and leagues should withdraw from school and that students should not be under the control of any party. Now how do you explain that today?"

Everyone looked slightly uneasy. But the Party members remained tranquil; they had anticipated such a question. They told us quietly that their attitude had been directed against the attempts of Kuomintang agents to get students on their side, and did not really mean that students shouldn't be involved in politics. Now, since we had already worked so hard to establish the proletarian revolution, we had already proved how much we were interested in the progress of our people and our fatherland.

Shao Po still wouldn't give up. "It sounds logical, but I'm still not sure I understand. In the past you wanted Party and Youth League members to get out of school. Now you want to expand the Party and the Youth League at Peita. It still sounds a little mixed up to me."

Shao Po was in the minority. The Youth League in particular began to expand its activities, and started a large-scale drive to recruit additional members. Classes had resumed again, but most of us were more occupied with the membership campaign and other propaganda activities than we were with who ruled England in 1700 or what happened when two chemicals were mixed together. Mere membership in the Youth League was not enough for many students, who found the thought of going back to classrooms after so much excitement very tame; they wanted what they called "direct participation in the revolution." Some left school to enter the new center for training working cadres, the North China Revolutionary University. Others signed up for the Military and Political University, the Foreign Language College, the Russian Language Academy in Harbin. Many joined the Working Teams for the South, organized to conduct political activities in the wake of the People's

Liberation Army, which was on its way toward the Yangtze River to liberate Nanking and Shanghai.

New recruits for these teams underwent a short course of political training in the city and a month of army life before they followed Lin Piao's Fourth Field Army down south. They seldom had time to write us. When they did, their letters were usually cheerful. They worked hard, they said, but their confidence in the liberation of the whole country was growing daily. These letters had magic when they were passed from hand to hand among those of us who were left behind.

A few of the recruits couldn't adjust to the new life, however. One letter came from a Tsinghua student who had been a well known basketball player and baseball pitcher. His letter said: "This isn't quite what I expected at school. I've found that I've changed. I'm like a machine out of order; I have trouble eating and sleeping. I pant if I run a few yards. Physically and mentally, I'm afraid I'm not fitted for this work. I'd like to go back to school. I put in my application to be released, but it hasn't been approved yet."

A luckier fellow in the law school got released after taking two weeks of training in the city. When he called on us, he was evasive about answering some of the questions we asked him and carefully avoided any direct criticism of the training course. When we kept after him for a more definite statement, he finally admitted, "I suppose I wouldn't have joined if my girl friend hadn't joined up."

Our laughter embarrassed him. "That's nothing to laugh about! A lot of people joined the teams just to follow their lovers." After a moment he went on. "The whole business is still not too well organized, with all these recruits swarming in. To be frank with you, the man who slept beside me turned out to be a thief. I couldn't sleep at night: I was afraid he'd steal my shoes or my clothes.

"It's really a strange mixture of all sorts of people. The higher-ups recognize the situation, but they think they can reform some of the unsavory characters who've attached themselves to us. It's rather comical to be training some of these people to take over the new liberated areas. I, for one, don't believe the cadres can reform thieves. You know, some of these cadres really have rather low cultural standards. They have to repeat ten times to tell us a simple thing. They seem to think that's the only way we can understand it. But we're not children or illiterate peasants."

Most of us who heard this sophisticated young man thought that perhaps he felt a bit superior just because he was lucky enough to be well educated. "He'll have to come down off his throne and mingle with the common people if he wants to get along now," one progressive said. "He'll have to learn that education is no substitute for hard work."

A few days later we heard that Chou En-lai, one of the top leaders in the Communist Party, had paid Peita professors a visit and had spent four hours talking over their problems with them. He had been all sympathy and respect for their position. He paid tribute to their economic suffering under the old government and promised that the Party would improve the lot of educational workers. It was not an empty promise. Soon it was announced that the highest salary for our professors would be set at 1,200 catties of millet a month, the equivalent of about $30, but much more in terms of real purchasing power than our teachers had received before. (The new government wisely had instituted the new system of computing salaries in terms of a real commodity like millet instead of in terms of a paper currency which was likely to become inflated.) It was much more than many Party members themselves were receiving; cadres at the lower level in the new government were only getting between 90 and 110 catties a month.

The basic salary for teachers was set at 800 catties of millet. To get the top salary of 1,200 catties, a professor had to have twenty years of service to his credit and also had to score a grade of 100 on his service record. The grade was to be established by the students and not by his colleagues on the faculty.

This was real democracy, we thought. There was great excitement when the news was given to us that we were going to get the chance to turn the tables and mark our professors on what they knew and how they taught. We all gathered in the compound for the grading ceremony.

Slips of paper were distributed for ballots. When a leader called out the name of a teacher, we all deliberated silently and then put down our marks. Volunteers collected the paper slips. After much hectic computing in front of the group, student representatives announced the average mark. In this way we graded nine professors in an hour.

The new era had really come; this was what we had been promised. Some students were kindhearted. They forgot personal grievances and gave their teachers fair and honest ratings. Some, I regret to say, blew up when they marked the score. One boy even shouted: "You scolded me in the past when I didn't deserve it. You cut down my marks. Now I cut down your millet!"

"Fellow students, you know by now that the schools belong to you," one speaker told us just after the grading ceremony. "But we have much building to do—it's time to go back to work!" Work was exactly what we wanted and what we expected; the enthusiasm created by the first weeks of liberation needed some sort of outlet in action. We knew that the revolution had not been accomplished but was just beginning, that years of building and labor lay ahead before we made the sort of China we wanted.

But study wasn't enough for us then, nor the propaganda work, the marching and the singing. This was the day of the common people, of the worker, the peasant, the soldier, of the *lao-pai-hsing*, or "old hundred names," the names borne for generations by the toilers of China's masses. Those of us who had read some of the Communist doctrines embraced Engels's theory that labor creates the world. Weren't we training ourselves to be brainworkers, working as engineers, teachers, and writers beside our worker and peasant comrades? Chinese students and scholars, we knew, had been criticized as aloof, snobbish, and proud. But it was wrong to be so now; we read a Party member's interpretation of Engels's theory: "Physical labor happened before mental labor. . . . The latter, therefore, is based upon the former and is of secondary importance. We must completely weed out the bourgeois theory of the superiority of mental to physical labor and must realize that physical labor is the most important thing under the sun."

Most of us, to be sure, were not used to regular physical labor. But we had been brought up during the long War of Resistance Against Japan, and most of us, particularly those who had trekked overland with the refugee universities, were used to a hard, strenuous life. Therefore we jumped at the chance to learn the dignity of manual work, to experience what workers and peasants experienced, when our wall newspapers and our loudspeakers invited us to sign up for the voluntary work teams being organized to clear up part of the mess left by Fu Tso-yi's army.

Party members were the first to volunteer; later signers could read their names at the top of the list. A concentrated effort was made next to get women students to enroll. With us signing up, it would be difficult for any of the men to hold back. "Finish the battle, comrades," the loudspeakers exhorted us in the dorms and mess halls. "Help clean up our campus! Unite the theory of work with actual practice!"

The morning the work commenced we assembled by work teams and responded to roll call. To the beat of drums and gongs we marched off behind our homemade banners to the work sites, where piles of dirt had been left by the trenches and air-raid shelters dug during the siege. We were going to fill in the defense works; we wouldn't need them any more. We stood in ranks until we were issued our picks and shovels, and then broke up into individual teams again. We planted our banners atop our own piles of dirt; this was going to be our first production competition with work goals set for each group. When the order was given, we swarmed over the heaps of earth with a will. Our individual pride and our group honor were both at stake. Some students swung their picks to loosen the hard earth. More shoveled the earth into baskets. Others carried the baskets to the holes and dumped them. We shouted taunts across at rival teams. When he noticed a sweating student working extra hard, our team leader called out: "Hey, the rest of you look over there at Wang! He's a real labor hero!" Boys who got blisters or scratches took out just enough time to dab their injuries with iodine, then seized their tools and plunged back into their work to catch up with the rest of us.

"Let's go—let's go! The Third Team has almost finished," our leader chanted. Under our attack the mound of dirt diminished and then disappeared; we scraped the hard ground with our shovels to get the last traces. Around us other teams were finishing their work, too. Finally, sweating and exhausted, but pleased with ourselves, we lined up to hear our chairman make an announcement. "Comrades," he shouted, "we have won the work battle! Every single team has surpassed its quota. We want to award every class a recognition banner." Amid our applause, our delegates went up to receive the pennants we had worked all day for.

The next day every department met to elect its labor heroes. The candidates had already been nominated by the team captains. A few mistakes were made; a few students who had worked the hardest were somehow overlooked. But most who had shown the greatest zeal and energy were voted in. After the balloting the new labor heroes were invited to speak to the rest of us. In their speeches they stressed their embarrassment about receiving such high honors since we'd all worked equally hard. "But," they said, "next time, comrades, we must all show even more strength and devotion to the great rule of life—honest labor."

Later we got a chance to sample the life of the peasants in a bigger labor campaign when we were invited to join in "agricultural production." Students from the Department of Economics were the first to volunteer. Because, when they came back, they told us how much they had learned about the life of the peasants and how much they had enjoyed the day out in the fresh country air, everybody signed up.

We rode out to the field in trucks, climbed down, and lined up to receive our hoes. Then we went to work on the weeds sprouting under the warm spring sun. A few villagers with shabby clothes and muddy feet hung around staring at the unusual sight of students in uniform working away in their fields. One young peasant plucked up enough courage to speak to a couple of us when we reached the end of a row and went back to the truck for a drink of cold boiled water.

"Where are the young masters from?" he asked politely.

"We are from Peking University," we told him with a certain pride. "We came out in those trucks there. We came out here to learn the dignity of labor."

"Unh," he said. He stared at the truck. "I've never ridden in one of those things."

We enjoyed devoting our day to production. In return for our labor we received a great many simple pleasures: the singing in the trucks, the games after work, the smell of earth and plants under the spring sun. This was really sharing in the life of the masses.

When we walked into the Peita mess hall after our day in the fields, the loudspeakers told all of our classmates how well we had done. Warm applause rose from every corner; our proud labor heroes smiled in response to the clapping and the shouts of friends.

I don't know how many catties of millet our work earned— perhaps not enough to pay for the gasoline the trucks burned to take us out and back. I'm sure that sometimes our zealous chopping with the hoes failed to distinguish between weeds and growing plants. But it made us feel a part of the new era, made us feel like brothers and sisters of the toiling masses. This was in truth identification with something beyond our own selfish concerns. It was true; labor was creating a new world for us. But, as I watched the faces of classmates flush with pride when they returned to the mess halls and heard themselves hailed as labor heroes after one day's work in the country, I sometimes wondered if the world it was creating wasn't a world of vanity.

CHAPTER IV

Sifting the Wheat

Who could have imagined that getting enough to eat would continue to be a big problem after the Liberation? Recently a foreign friend in Hong Kong tried to tell me that the chief thing wrong with us Chinese is that we are too materialistic. (He's spent a year or two in Peking, which seems to qualify him as an authority.) "Why, just look," he told me. "Half the time when I watched you students parading or raising hell back there before your Communist friends arrived, the only thing you were screaming for was more rice for yourselves."

I don't think that we are more materialistic than any other people. How could I explain to this foreigner that food is so important to us simply because it has always been so hard to get? Perhaps students in more fortunate countries can take for granted what goes into their stomachs. In Peking we could not.

Besides, in the bitter years after the war food became something more than physical nourishment for us; it became a symbol of our political rights. Remember that students in our country have a far greater political responsibility than students have in the West. True, we form only a scarcely visible fraction of the population; in 1950 China had 134,000 university students in a population of over 450 million, or about three in every 10,000 persons. But these three students have been the articulate spokesmen for the other 9,997.

Ever since the famous May 4th incident in 1919, when a few hundred Peking students protesting the notorious Twenty-One Demands made by Japan upon a spineless Chinese government raised a national outcry, Chinese students have regarded themselves as the political conscience of the nation. (And since 1919, I may add, that conscience has been very much needed.) A conscience is never a pleasant phenomenon for any government, so we have always had to fight jealously to guard our independence against official efforts to muzzle us. Despite such attempts, we have always managed to keep a healthy share of it.

This was true even when many of us had to depend on government subsidies to stay in school. These subsidies were begun in 1937 or 1938, after the Japanese attack, to provide for refugee students. Though the government wanted to abolish such assistance after V-J Day, our nation's economic plight was so bad after the war that the subsidies had to be continued just to keep the schools alive.

We came to look upon the subsidy as the basic right of any worthy student unable to pay his own way, and we viewed any attempt to reduce our aid as a clear and open move to fasten political shackles on us. My classmates thus claimed the right to criticize the very government which was assisting them, or even to work for its downfall. Our leaders encouraged us to ask for more than we were getting and to go out on strike when it wasn't forthcoming.

During the first five or six weeks after the Liberation we were much too excited, much too busy with our parades, our meetings, and our volunteer labor groups, to worry very much about what turned up on the table in our school mess halls. The military administration which had taken over the city simply continued the subsidy we had received from the old regime—with one small difference: we got our subsidy in terms of *hsiao-mi*, or millet, instead of in wheat flour.

We didn't pay much attention to this at first; the quantity of the grain we received was actually more by sheer weight. It did mean that the subsidy was slightly reduced in terms of cash, since wheat flour was worth more than millet, which the Communists had made into the new unit of value for computing the price of other basic commodities. But most of us didn't understand the new price system anyhow. As one of the girls in the dormitory remarked, "Perhaps it is only just that we get paid in the food of the common people." We rather liked the sound of that, particularly as long as wheat continued to be served as the staple of our diet in the mess hall.

Outside the campus, we knew vaguely, prices were sneaking up again—they had fallen just after the Liberation when the siege was lifted and food flowed in again from the countryside. We wondered what had happened to the enormous stocks of grain the Nationalist soldiers were supposed to have hoarded. Some of it, a total of 150,000 pounds, the Communists announced that they were distributing to the unemployed. That sounded like a large amount to us until one boy who was good at arithmetic converted the sum into bushels. Then we heard whispers that most of the supply really was being shipped out to feed the armies marching south toward the Yangtze to liberate Shanghai and Nanking. Well, if that was true, our fighting men needed it worse than we did, we told each other.

Communist students came back from Party meetings to reassure us that the food shortage was only temporary, anyhow. They blamed the price rise on the peasants outside the city, who had sent in too much money to purchase manufactured goods after the Liberation had restored communications between city and country. But the goods weren't there to buy just yet; it would take time to restore the production sabotaged by the reactionary "running dogs."

Now, when I'm trying to earn my own living in Hong Kong, I realize that the whole business of prices was academic for most of us students. Food and lodging came from the government, and our other wants were few enough so that we found some way of supplying them. The complaints about rising prices we heard from our parents, from shopkeepers, waiters in restaurants, or from pedicab boys. Students in the Economics Department naturally kept a professional eye on the cost-of-living index issued by their colleagues at

Nankai University in Tientsin. But even if these economics majors tended to be more conservative than the rest of us, they had to admit that the price climb was not anything nearly so bad as the last wild frenzy of inflation under the old regime.

Then came a blow from the great natural enemy in North China—drought. The spring rains did not arrive on schedule; rumors seeped into the city that the peasants around Peking were going to lose most of their spring wheat crop. A familiar word, "austerity," began to be heard on the campus. "Activist" students who helped out the genuine Party members began to echo newspaper editorials calling for frugality and retrenchment in people's personal lives. "Look at the Party comrades who had come in from years of hardship and sacrifice with the armies to work in the factories, schools, and government," we were told. "If anyone had the right to let their belts out a few notches and enjoy a few of the fruits of victory now that victory was accomplished, it was these people." But we had to admit that they still persevered in their frugal, austere habits, accepting from the people no more than was necessary to maintain their existence. It was true: from what we could see most of the cadres in the government offices as well as those on the campus worked painfully long hours, ate in common messes, slept in dormitories, and devoted most of what free time they had to additional Party activities.

With this groundwork laid, in the middle of the spring semester student leaders in the various departments and classes at Peita began to lecture the rest of us on the whole problem of government subsidies for students. They introduced the subject by talking about the students who had gone over the wall in the six months before the Liberation to go into Communist territory, and hinted that students who had stayed behind should *li-kung*, or "build up merits," too. "In the old society," a speaker exhorted us, "students were naturally the most progressive elements. It was only to be expected that they looked upon subsidies from the government as an innate and inalienable right.

"But we students must realize that when we fought for our subsidies under the Kuomintang, when we staged demonstrations and besieged the dean's office, when we marched in the streets, our goal then was to shove the Kuomintang another step closer to the edge of the cliff, another step closer to the downfall of their reactionary government."

The speaker stopped and smiled at us. "But now the Chinese people have stood up. The situation is entirely different today. Our people are suffering, trying to repair the damage the reactionary government has inflicted on our livelihood. If we don't really need the food, how can we take our people's money and increase their burden?

"Now today, comrades, we students should be determined to serve the people and not to waste the wheat or millet made out of their sweat and toil. When you eat your millet, you must think of the man who grew it. You must take only that which is strictly necessary. Frivolous consumption just because you are a student you should regard as an act of deliberate exploitation against the people. Many of our fellow students here and at other universities have suggested that we abolish the old, unreasonable system of government subsidies of the past and set up in its stead a new and reasonable system of People's Study Aids. We think this is a most reasonable demand. Students of Peita! Let us add our voices to the demand for People's Study Aids! This will be a serious test of all of us, a severe and searching test. Unless you are really poor and have no other way out, don't ask for government allowances. I believe that you, my fellow students, will be able to think this matter through with honor and justice. I believe, my student comrades, that you will all pass this test with flying colors!"

We applauded vigorously and went back to our rooms to speculate about what the People's Study Aids would involve. Three or four days later our student newspaper told us. The new scholarships, the paper announced first, were being established in response to the firm demands of students in all of Peking's universities for a reform of the old, unreasonable system of subsidies which tended to undermine students' self respect. The new study aids, the writer explained, would fall into three categories. Grade A grants would give the recipient 85 catties of millet a month or its equivalent; Grade B provided 65 catties; and the lowest, Grade C, provided 45 catties. Grade A grants, we decided after some hasty figuring, would be roughly the same as the old subsidies we used to receive and would provide for such inescapable miscellaneous expenses as haircuts, and so on. Grade B grants would just about meet minimum food expenses and nothing else. Grade C grants would have to be supplemented with money from the student's own pocket to enable him to exist.

In the private debates which followed the public speeches in favor of the new grants, we decided that most of us could probably qualify for Grade B grants on a legitimate claim of hardship. Even students whose families had funds to support them were in many instances cut off from such funds because their families lived in cities yet to be liberated. Therefore almost everybody picked up one of the application forms which were distributed a day or two after the newspaper announcement. One look at the application blank convinced us that the speaker had told the truth when he told us the test would be a searching one. The questions probed into our background and family status. How many people are in your family? List their names, present places of residence, and occupation. Have they ever been members of the Kuomintang or other political party? Have they ever held any official positions? Where? Which of them are presently earning money? How much? How much have you been receiving from your family every month? Have you ever held employment? How much money did you make? For which category of grant do you wish to apply?

A few of my friends backed out when they saw how much information was required to complete the application. The rest of us filled in the forms and submitted them to our class chairmen. A week went by before our class leaders stood up and announced that it had been decided that we would hold meetings in our classrooms to discuss each application before it was forwarded on for consideration by the general departmental meeting.

These public meetings were our first real introduction to "thought struggle." Of course we had heard about the new technique of reforming a person's old-fashioned conservative beliefs by public, group examination of his background, personality, and thinking. But somehow we had more or less assumed that we would be the accusers instead of the accused, the brain washers instead of the washed. It was a new and unexpected experience, and we went to the meetings with a certain amount of apprehension.

In the meeting I went to, our chairman, who was an activist and a member of the Youth League, began with a speech about the necessity of casting off false dignity to permit our comrades to make an honest and searching examination of each of our applications. Then he shuffled the papers on the table in front of him, selected one, and began to read the application submitted by a classmate I will call Chang. Chang's father, it developed, was a minor executive in the electric power plant in Shanghai, while a brother was a returned student from the United States and part owner of an automobile parts firm. They were clearly as bourgeois as bourgeois could be.

Chang apparently was clever enough to realize it now, and he stood up. "I have been thinking the matter over since I submitted my application, and I've come to the realization that my application was a mistake. Our people have suffered too much. I have made up my mind not to ask for money from our people. I wish to announce my withdrawal."

People scattered around the hall began to applaud, and the rest of us joined in. Chang sat down in the warmth of the approving smiles of students from the Party and the Youth League. The chairman waited for the clapping to end, and announced, "The meeting accepts Comrade Chang's withdrawal." We clapped again. Then he read the next application.

The applicant, one of our most vocal progressives, stood up. "I think my fellow students can see that my financial situation is honestly bad," he told us. "But they also know that I have relatives here in Peking. I won't be able to borrow enough from them to meet all my expenses, but I can make it up by clerical work or maybe by taking a job as a tutor. So I ask that my application be withdrawn too."

More applause and a unanimous vote to permit him to withdraw his application. One of the Youth League comrades got to his feet. "Mr. Chairman, before you read any more applications, I think somebody should point out how well our fellow students seem to be meeting this important test. It speaks well for all of us, I think, that these two comrades here today have voluntarily offered to withdraw the applications which they submitted before they really had a chance to consider their rights and duties toward the people.

None of us who can attend college come from really poor families. We are all of us better off than the average worker or peasant. Personally I don't want a study aid—I can't stretch out my hands to ask for alms from people poorer than I am." We clapped again for him.

The third applicant, Miss Wen from my own dormitory, was a different case. From what we knew about her she really needed the assistance, and she obviously wanted it. But with the speeches that preceded her, she was faced with a dilemma. Perhaps the organizers of the meeting had set a very adroit trap by letting two non-applicants speak first to make it difficult for persons who followed to present a very imposing plea. Those who had decided not to ask for a study aid were showing their regard for the masses. Did it not suggest that those who did apply were not so considerate? Should not people whose fathers or brothers were bourgeois and automatically in some measure members of an exploiting class withdraw their applications? Should not those who had relatives living in Peking look for help from them instead of applying for help from the people? And what about people who could find small jobs to help pay their expenses?

Miss Wen plunged bravely ahead. "I have thought my application over very carefully, both when I submitted it and right now while my comrades have been talking. I don't want to take any help I don't honestly feel I'm entitled to. Fellow students, my need, I hope, speaks for itself. My family is in Chungking, and I haven't been in touch with them for over a year. My father isn't able to work any more and has to worry about supporting my two unmarried sisters. We lost track of my elder brother during the war when we moved inland to Free China from the occupied area. We think that he is in one of the armies, but we haven't heard from him. I don't have any relatives in North China who could help me. I realize now that I don't have any real claim upon the wheat and millet of the people. But if I'm going to graduate a year from now, I am going to have to ask for one of the People's Study Aids."

We proceeded to discuss Miss Wen's application. Several comrades charged her with political indifference. "Not that I mean to suggest that she is reactionary. To the best of my knowledge she is not," one earnest critic declared. "And I think we should admit that she has studied hard. But her work has been devoted to her own ends, to her own narrow personal ambition to achieve what she thinks is her proper station in life. In this way she has exhibited the same apathy toward the great political issues of our people that too many of our fellow students have displayed in the past."

Perhaps some of us would have risen to defend her, but our own applications hadn't been considered yet. Finally one of our Communist friends called for the floor. "Comrades," he told us, "in Miss Wen's case I think the people can afford to be generous. Perhaps she will agree that she might reduce her request from Grade B to Grade C if she can find some sort of work from the university to supplement this aid. But it seems to me that she has been quite frank. She admits that her past life has not produced any positive political viewpoint which would give her any legitimate claim upon the wheat and millet of the people. But the very fact that she admits this shows that she has made a certain amount of progress in her thinking. I am sure that if she studies hard and criticizes her own shortcomings with ruthless honesty she can enter upon a career of true service to the people. I make a motion that we forward her application with a recommendation that she be awarded a Grade C grant."

Students who were regarded as more progressive or who had good friends in the Youth League or the Party were spared some of this public soul searching. The first such student who had publicly displayed his eagerness to "follow close on the heels of Mao Tse-tung" went through the formal motions of apologizing for his application. But before anybody had a chance to agree with him that the grant should be reduced, his Party friend rose to defend him.

"Our comrade has been properly modest and self-critical in presenting his application. But I know that his financial situation is really very poor. He has given much of his time to the people since the Liberation; he has studied hard and made rapid progress in thought. I think he should not try to give up his application. The government has set up People's Study Aids in order to help just such schoolmates. I hope he can continue to work hard so that he can acquire the knowledge to accomplish his present tasks and render good service to the people when he leaves the university."

It took a whole series of such meetings to work through all of the applications. After the first meeting it proved impractical to withdraw your application before the group voted on you even if you wanted to. A few schoolmates faced our questions for a solid two hours or until they screamed with rage: "All right—I give up! I admit I'm wrong. I want to withdraw my application." But although they wanted to give up, their "unreasonable" thought still had to be "struggled against" until we voted formally to reject their applications. Now as we roasted each other on the spit, we appreciated the intelligence of our wiser classmates who had seen what was coming and who had gained much merit by deciding not to submit applications.

The class conferences voted down a number of applications and reduced many others to lower grades at the suggestion of activist students. The surviving applications were forwarded with our recommendations to the next hurdle, a conference of the whole department. A few isolated cases which Party and Youth Corps members attacked severely they nevertheless let slip past these first class conferences. We discovered later on that this was intended to let the persons involved face a more severe "thought struggle" on the next higher level in the departmental meetings.

These departmental meetings were more formal. The chairman first announced which students in the department had survived the first round of examinations in the individual classes and what grades they were petitioning for. Every time he read off a name and a grade, he paused to invite comment. Any student who had comments to make was free to speak out, and the defendant had to rise and answer him. Unless they kept their tempers and spoke carefully and to the point, applicants who were singled out for special "thought struggles" had no possible hope of succeeding, however subtle and eloquent their pleas might be. After these struggles most of the defendants lost their suits. If they happened to be girls, they might sit down with a few irrepressible tears on their cheeks after the strain and heat of the arguments. The boys generally behaved with more dignity, although the very poor ones would sit down with pink cheeks showing their subdued anger and resentment. They might have pleaded that they had left their families, studied hard, and relied entirely on scholarships or government subsidies to carry on their education. Now that they had passed most of the obstacles and were close to the finish, they hoped very much to get a People's Study Aid in order to remain in school. They promised, too, to serve the people some day with all their heart and strength—which last statement unfortunately was a bit too late. It should have been on their lips several months before.

Although they were not a deciding factor in most cases, good academic marks did help. Some of the students who had come from poor families and who could boast of brilliant records in the university were granted study aids although they had been attacked as individualistic in thought and non-positive in action. We thought that the chief reason for these unusual favors was the fact that these students were much respected by their schoolmates, and while not "progressive thinkers" they had never been noticeably reactionary in thought or action. Besides, it was possible that by means of People's Study Aids these academically-minded students could be won over and their unusual talents recruited for the direct benefit of the people.

After this second round our applications went on to the third test: consideration by the All-University Investigating Committee. Some classes and departments, the committee decided, had been too lax in their preliminary investigations and had recommended too many grants in the two higher categories. Therefore the applications were returned, and the classes and departments called new meetings to examine the applications again. The list of names recommended by classes and departments was posted on bulletin boards in the various buildings on the campus for public criticism. Any student who had an adverse opinion about any one of the applicants could privately pass along his information to the committee. The accused would then be summoned to answer the charges made by his unknown accuser. Friends who had to run this gantlet reported that this investigation was the hardest of all. After an intense bombardment of questions from the Party and Youth League officials who sat on the committee, eight or nine out of every ten defendants were compelled to renounce their applications or scale down their requests to a lower grade.

After the three stages had been endured, the results of the applications were posted just like the grades in final examinations. About half of us had been awarded some kind of People's Study Aid. Most of our grants fell into the Grade B, or middle, category. Some of the grants were awarded in the names of two persons—combined mutual-help grants, where a Grade A applicant and a Grade B applicant had agreed to pool their aids and divide them equally. And of course there were a large number of Grade C grants for people who had agreed in the meetings that they should find some sort of job to help support themselves.

Most of us who had survived the test and had won study aids were quite elated. Somehow they carried more weight than the old subsidies, which had been dealt out more or less automatically to appease the students. Not only was our livelihood assured, at least for the holders of A and B grants, but the grants were symbolic recognition of our political reliability and perhaps our future prospects. We echoed the comments of our leaders about the true democracy demonstrated in the distribution of the study aids and the obvious superiority of this new system over the old unreasonable system of indiscriminate distribution.

Some grumbling was heard on the part of students whose applications had been disapproved or reduced to lower categories. They were particularly critical of the awarding of a Grade B study aid to the son of the chairman of the directors of a Tientsin cotton mill. They claimed that he still received a regular allowance every month from an uncle in Peking. (A remittance directly from his father would have been too bold and conspicuous, much too likely to arouse criticism.) Here he was, unsuccessful applicants complained, a rich man's son, reaching out his hands to the peasants and begging for alms. But he had demonstrated himself to be progressive in thought and positive in action like his father, who was considered one of the few genuinely "progressive" bourgeois manufacturers supporting the new government. His Youth League supporters had argued that he had a right to stand on his own two feet without calling on his father for help and thus was just as eligible for help as any of his fellow students.

We realized, of course, that the new system inevitably was

going to produce a certain amount of such bitterness. But most of the disappointed weren't as outspoken as the engineering student who had been rejected because he still prided himself on being non-political. He had told a confidant in a fit of pique, we heard, "From now on I'll beg in the streets before I apply for another one of these study aids."

CHAPTER V

Scraping the Rice Bowl

Girls at Peita never had to give much thought to their figures. Even in a place like Shanghai or Hong Kong, where too many women have nothing to do except eat, go to the movies, and play mah-jongg, it is a rare sight to see a Chinese girl who is as plump and well fed as some of the foreign women you can see in the streets. And at Peita we worried even less about keeping slim when we got a chance to see how the People's Study Aids worked.

At the very beginning the introduction of Study Aids divided the campus into two warring camps. On the right, the discontented and disappointed hinted, in private, at least, that the new government was using food as a political weapon to impose unexpected controls upon students and to test the new technique of "thought struggle" on students whose thinking was inclined to be unruly or undisciplined. On the left, a much larger group accepted the expianations of student leaders and replied that, after all, we students, when we looked at ourselves objectively, were "unproductive elements" supported by the worker and peasant masses. And the worker and peasant masses had the right to nourish those young intellectuals they thought would be most likely to help them.

This difference of opinion, of course, didn't break out into open, public argument. Students who had lost out on the Study Aids were very careful to pick the appropriate time and place to confide their complaints to trusted friends. But discontent over the new subsidies continued to simmer *sub rosa* as the austerity campaign developed and the quality of food served in our dormitories changed.

We had been used to eating wheat flour *man-tou* (steamed bread) as the foundation for our diet, with soup and three small dishes to go with it. One of the dishes sometimes had a little meat mixed in with the rest of the ingredients. Sometimes polished rice was served instead of the *man-tou* as a concession to students from South and Central China, who preferred it to the wheat staple of our northern diet. Two or three times a month we got a better meal with tastier dishes to supplement our very simple fare. Our food couldn't really be called nutritious by any ideal standard, but it was just about enough to meet the minimum needs of an able-bodied person. It happened, however, that our generation had grown up during the War of Resistance Against Japan. In the privations and hardships some of my friends had endured, the treks and wanderings they had survived, lay the seeds of extreme susceptibility to diseases like tuberculosis, as well as stomach ailments and anemia. Appreciating this at least to some dim extent, foreign students and professors at Peita and the other universities in the days before the Liberation would lecture us on the importance of nutrition. "You're throwing away the best part of your food," I can remember one foreign-exchange professor shouting at us. He had the theory that we should eat our rice unpolished and our wheat dark with what he called the "germ" still in it.

We could have replied that more polished rice or more good white flour might also help. What another foreigner, an American Fulbright student, told us was more pleasant to our ears. "You students are one of China's great natural resources," she told a group of us at a university party, "and the government should recognize that by giving you an adequate diet." A progressive student explained to her that while what she said was very true, you couldn't expect a shortsighted reactionary government to realize it. "We're used to tightening our belts, though," he added. "We can wait for a government progressive and farsighted enough to give some attention to our health and our feeding." This was in the fall of 1948, when the People's Liberation Army was winning victories in Manchuria so great that even the Peking newspapers couldn't entirely hide the news, and the more outspoken among us were already talking openly about the fall of the government.

Perhaps the fact that so many of us then ate only their two full meals a day was one of the reasons for our inadequate diet. While the midday and evening meals were served in the mess halls at regular hours, breakfast time was not so rigid. Each month we were handed thirty breakfast tickets, which we could exchange for breakfast between seven and nine o'clock in the morning. About six-thirty the morning bell would ring out to urge us to get up for millet soup. But only a minority could get up in response to its call. Millet soup day after day at seven in the morning, even when it is spiced with salted vegetables, is not inspiring. When we did get up, wash our faces, and join other students headed toward the classrooms with satchels of books slung over their shoulders, we always had to "face reality," as we called it. Across the street was a line of ten or so small street stalls dispensing refreshments: *shao-ping* (wheat and sesame seed cakes), soybean soup, tender bean curd, tough bean curd, fried meatballs, baked sweet potatoes, and persimmons. It was eight-thirty, and your stomach was already complaining about your failure to eat breakfast. Could you "look straight at reality"? Your pocketbook decided. Too often in those old days you did face reality, and turned away hungry. Your purse was as empty as your stomach, and you had to scurry away to class as a member of the "closed eyes" club to endure your hunger until the noon meal.

When you did find yourselves with some pocket money, though, the hawkers' stalls outside the main entrance of the school helped to spice our monotonous diet. Peanuts, melon seeds, fried cakes, fragrant pork dumplings, noodle soup, almond tea—the stalls offered all sorts of snacks ready in an instant if you could produce the money. In the winter we could buy frozen persimmons and, even better, baked sweet potatoes which we could juggle to warm up our chilled hands until the potatoes had cooled enough to eat. Summer brought sweet melons, frozen ices on a stick, soda water, and other aids to cooling off.

Dozens of small restaurants in the neighborhood also capitalized on our distaste for the uninspired food served in the mess halls before the Liberation. They served noodles and pastries, Western-style fancy cakes, peppery Szechuanese food, Cantonese dishes, and so on, and were most popular with men students, who liked huge bowls of noodles and other hearty dishes. When our male colleagues did have money, they would invite two or three close friends to one of these small restaurants, order two or three dishes after inquiring about the prices, add half a catty of hot wine, and spend an evening in very intellectual debate.

Peanuts were the biggest between-meals supplement to our diet, however. They were cheaper than anything else, and fortunately most of us liked them. After lunch or supper Peita girls used to go out in twos or threes to walk on the lawn or rest under the trees with packages of peanuts or melon seeds to share. It gave our teeth something to do, and it did trim the edges off the hunger we sometimes felt after our meals.

Few of us in the old days ever got more than a rare meal in the good restaurants where we could enjoy the roast duck and other Peking dishes. For one thing, Peking waiters have the custom of bellowing out the size of your tip to other diners when you walk out of one of the more expensive places. Although Peking waiters were never rude, it was still a loss of face to have other diners know that you had not been able to give the waiter the customary amount of "wine money." Not many of us in the national universities were very well-to-do. Even in the comparatively aristocratic, privately owned, and foreign-subsidized universities in the city, where students were much more particular about food and dress, only a small fraction had money to throw around. Peking is a quiet and sober old city, rather conservative, and not very snobbish about things that count in the modern world; it used to lack the extravagance and the vanities of more Westernized commercial cities like Shanghai and Canton, and did not provide many places where the sons and daughters of rich men could spend big allowances. These heroes could find no place to exhibit their social valor, and had to compromise with our simpler ways and wait until their vacations, when they could go back home to Shanghai and enjoy themselves.

Despite our grumbling about our food in 1947 and 1948, I suppose that a small increase in the quantity in addition to some planned improvement in the quality and variety would have satisfied the majority of my friends in spite of our heated talk about "food for the people" and "no more hunger." I don't know now whether the Communists really had planned to achieve these goals for us or not. Perhaps drought and the demands of the army and of the countryside did not give them the chance. But the same progressive students who had told us in 1948 that Liberation would solve our food and health problems had to call upon us in 1949 to practice more austerity. As the spring of 1949 came on, the quality of food in our mess began to change. We got more variety, I'll admit; the wheat flour and rice we were accustomed to began to be replaced by coarse grains like millet and ground corn flour. In the different mess halls we now looked down on our plates to find "silk cakes" or bread made out of "eighty-one" flour. "Eighty-one" flour, I should explain, was a rough variety obtained by grinding eighty-one catties of flour out of one hundred catties of wheat, which meant that many of the impurities which ordinarily would have been thrown away were now retained.

The "silk cake" was so called for satirical reasons; it was manufactured out of steamed corn flour plus a little millet meal mixed in. It looked very much like sponge cake coming out of the kitchen on a tray. It looked somewhat like sponge cake when it was set in the center of our long table. But it tasted not at all like sponge cake in our mouths. This rough-grained compound, which only usurped the beautiful name of "cake," was something of a punishment to schoolmates from the South, who were used to soft white rice. Some of them declared they'd rather eat unpolished *kao-liang* grains than the imitation sponge cakes.

In response to the official exhortation of "Don't waste the millet of the people" conveyed to us by the Youth League, more of us began to get up for breakfast. For breakfast we still drank millet soup, with a dish of diced, salted dried vegetables to season it. In fact millet soup actually became much more popular. As my roommate remarked, "Millet soup every day gets tiresome, of course, but it does go down easier than anything else we get." The dishes served at our noon and evening meals continued to get worse as the new government called upon people for a greater display of austerity. At least it was real austerity that we practiced; we remembered the periodic "austerity" campaigns under the less efficient old regime when everybody practiced austerity for a week or two until "face" was established for the government and then promptly forgot about it. The greatest loss to our diet at this time was cooking fat, which we depended upon for much of our protein in the absence of regular dishes of meat and other proteins. As time wore on, we ate more and more boiled cabbage, boiled greens, boiled bean sprouts, boiled turnips; fried dishes became a rarity.

The food retained the same physical bulk it always had, and prevented our stomachs from clamoring for solid victuals. But at the same time the deterioration in quality whetted our appetite even more for supplementary delicacies. Wheat cakes and peanuts could not normally be counted as treats. Yet now I saw my friends hurry to open their paper sacks and jars as soon as they returned to the dormitory from the dining hall, dig out peanuts and wheat cakes, and munch away with a voracious haste which would have astonished those male schoolmates who admired their dainty manners in public. After several months of austerity we managed to frighten ourselves into believing that the loss of edible fats from our diet was seriously impairing our health. When we could afford it, we chipped in to buy a jar of lard, which we kept in the room. We weren't accustomed to eating cheese or butter, which are strictly foreign, but we began to spread thick layers of lard on the wheat cakes we ate after dinner in an effort to keep our weight up.

We were worried about our health. The addition of the new political classes to the curriculum and the extra meetings and *hsueh-hsi* (study) sessions meant that we had more work to do, even those of us who didn't belong to the Party, the Youth League, special propaganda teams, and other new political organizations. We were young people who could take a lot, and pride and hope in the future kept most of us going; but the circumstances didn't help those of us who had a tendency toward tuberculosis or the other diseases latent in the student group.

I remember one afternoon in June, just before the end of the semester, when Peking had turned hot. Perspiring, I hurried back to the Gray Mansion, the girl's dormitory, after lunch, hoping to spend the rest of the afternoon inside, away from the sun. I stopped outside Chien Tien-fang's door, rapped twice, and then tapped again once to show it was I. Without waiting for an answer from my friend, I pushed the door open and went on in.

Tien-fang was sitting beside her desk on a chair cushioned with two pillows, her perspiring forehead bound up in a wet handkerchief. She looked pale and tired when she turned her head to see who it was.

"Who do you think you are, a princess of some sort, sitting on pillows in such hot weather? No wonder you're perspiring so much," I greeted her, with a joke. She didn't reply, but gave me an annoyed look at my lack of sympathy.

The door opened again. It was a boy student, an officious, humorless little history major. He was so serious about his "progressive tendencies" that he had qualified himself for appointment as leader of the "living circle" in Tien-fang's class. He took a look at his perspiring classmate and inquired: "Miss Chien, have you finished the assigned outside reading for the politics class, that pamphlet by Comrade Liu Shao-chi called *On Class Distinctions?* You know other classmates want to read it too." Though rudeness was absent from his voice, his tone was so utterly flat and emotionless that it was deliberately sardonic, without your being able to explain why it was so nettling.

"Well, you can have it back now if somebody needs it," Tien-fang replied.

"So you still haven't finished reading it? You've kept it for four solid days already." Still the cold, measured voice with no suggestion of any personal rebuke.

"But," she said, with a hint of fire, "you know I have also been sick for four days."

"Where have you put the book? Your other classmates should have been able to read it two days ago."

I watched her eyes moisten and I wanted to speak up in her defense, but she spoke out for herself. "Every one of these last four days I thought I would get well on the next." She looked at him with tearful eyes. "The book is on the bookshelf over by my bed. Please look for it yourself."

He fumbled around, found the book, and took it away. As soon as the door closed, she gave in to her tears. I hurried to the washbasin to wring out a wet towel, and brought it over so that she could wipe her face and stop crying.

"What in the world are you ill of?" I asked.

She dabbed away at her face with the towel. "I've always heard people say how painful this disease is, even if they always make a joke about it. Now I've got it myself. I'll tell you: it's piles. I think it's because of eating the silk cakes and the other rough foods. I'm honestly so scared and embarrassed—I don't want to have to tell other people what I've got. So—" She wadded the towel up between her hands. "These Youth League and living-circle leaders all think I'm not really sick, but simply too spoiled and too petty bourgeois, too selfish and thoughtless!"

"Don't worry about what those people think." I tried to think of something to say, and then said the first hasty thing that came to my tongue. "Piles are painful. And embarrassing. But I hear it only takes a little better nutrition to cure them—more fat, softer foods . . ." I stopped as I realized that my advice would appear to Tien-fang almost as a joke.

"Of course," she said. "I know that too. But a couple of weeks ago, on the open market, I bought a pound of that old canned butter the American army left behind, and took it into the dining room with me. And they kept staring at me with that special kind of self-righteous look. One boy in my group even told me that he thought I was too 'special.' "

The door swung open, and the leader of Tien-fang's living circle was back in the room. "Miss Chien," he announced, "our class has received ten more copies, so I can leave this book here for you again. Hope you can finish it by our meeting on Friday." He looked at her expectantly.

That was enough for me, and I flared up to tell him straight out that Tien-fang was ill and that in our new life we were supposed to keep from making things difficult for our comrades, that we should not treat our fellow students so. I kept my voice calm and deliberately tried to give him a taste of the same flat, self-righteous tone he used on other people. He changed his tone slightly.

"Well, then you'd better take a good rest," he advised.

"I'm certainly glad you're not studying to be a doctor," I shouted after him as he bustled off burdened with his important business.

Inadequate diet also contributed to more serious diseases than the one which so embarrassed my friend Tien-fang. Before the Liberation the tests carried on by the Anti-Tuberculosis Association revealed to the dismay of school authorities that almost one-tenth of us suffered from active tuberculosis, and the percentage did not grow smaller afterward. The most seriously affected were compelled to suspend all schoolwork for a time. Patients whose condition was less serious were confined to their own dormitories and mess halls, but continued to carry a certain amount of academic work.

Serious illness was probably more common among Party and Youth League members than it was among the rest of the students. Many of them had endured the arduous conditions the Party had experienced in its struggle for victory. In fact, so many cadres of the Chinese Communist Party (including important leaders like our Number Two national leader Liu Shao-chi) had contracted tuberculosis from the hardships and privations they had endured that it was almost a "revolutionary disease." I am critical of some other things about these revolutionary cadres and students, but I will admit to a certain admiration for their disregard for their own health and conditions of living. They were confident that "once a person had thought it out," he could not bother much about his personal health in view of more important things. Some of the young revolutionaries who had contracted tuberculosis looked upon it as a sort of badge. They almost deliberately displayed their indifference to consumption. They might cough and break into a cold sweat, but they would tell us "never mind," and refuse to see the university doctor because they wanted to "concentrate on work."

Next on the list of diseases we were most likely to suffer were stomach and intestinal troubles. The roughness of our diet, long hours, and lack of sleep all contributed to these ailments. Besides tuberculosis and digestive trouble, anemia and nervous debility were also quite common. Students who pampered themselves too much when they were ill or suffering from diarrhea were regarded with some disdain by ardent young Party members to whom their own health had been an unavoidable sacrifice to bring about a great era. Self-sacrifice is certainly a virtue, but sometimes a few of us thought that some of our fellows regarded it as an exalted end in itself instead of a means to achieve something else.

In the summer of 1950 the new government apparently became aware of the situation and began to look into the students' health. Investigations were made of student living conditions, and plans to cut down class hours and reduce outside reading assignments were announced. Whether the government woke up in response to the petitions of students, the suggestion of Communist students, or the petitions of parents, I don't know. Perhaps it was only a tardy realization of the fact that we were a "national resource," and all the more so for the new government, which was in evident need of stout cadres and reliable technicians and teachers.

At any rate, the news trickled down to us of the speeches that Peita representatives had heard at a special meeting of the official Cultural and Educational Committee. At this meeting the Vice Minister of Education, Ch'ien Chun-jui, made a moving and emotional plea. "My daughter used to study at the Northeast College of Medicine at Mukden. When she went up there from home, she was in the pink of health and the best of spirits. She has come back home now—afflicted with tuberculosis of the bone. She had so many meetings at the college, so much work, such heavy assignments, she was kept so busy and worried . . ." With the children of such important people setting an example, it wasn't surprising that we sometimes grew less attentive to our own health.

The grumbling about food and health conditions generally took place away from the dining table, in the privacy of our rooms, or in whispered exchanges with a friend in some place like the library. Before the Liberation there had been seven or eight separate mess groups in the Sha-t'an compound. They had been formed more or less haphazardly; you picked out the people you wanted to eat at the same table with, got together, and made out a list to hand over to the mess committee. In accordance with the new

theory of "collective living" designed to promote "genuine democracy," our leaders urged us to adopt a new system after the
Liberation. Seating arrangements in the mess hall were changed to
conform with a student's department and year, so that you sat at
tables with the students you studied beside during the day. This
was undoubtedly a more efficient and time-saving arrangement;
announcements, directives, official requests, and other business of
that nature could be passed down to every student through his
regular department and class organization while he was in the
dining hall. When an issue arose on which discussion, voting, and
resolutions were necessary, we were organized to act without waste
of time, arranged in orderly rows for our votes to be recorded by
our classroom leaders.

Students who tried to avoid politics didn't like the arrangement.
Before, they had generally managed to avoid being buttonholed
by "positive elements" about this or that, and could give zealous
Youth League workers the slip after class and during meals. But
they had to come to meals, of course; so they sat and munched with
patient resignation while they listened to the exhortations and
instructions of our leaders.

In the first week of this new seating arrangement, one of my
classmates did raise the issue of the apparent deterioration of our
diet. With his chopsticks he upended one of the corn-flour-and-
millet cakes in his bowl and inspected it critically before he addressed
the table leader. "I got the impression talking to progressive comrades back in the time of the old reactionary government that when
we stood up and took power we were going to get better food and
more of it. Now I must admit that this silk cake is really just too
rich for my blood."

Without showing irritation the table leader pointed out a few
evident facts. "Our government is still facing a battle," he said,
"and the food we get is just as good as the food which Party comrades in the government or with unions and other organizations
eat. They are working actively for the people and accomplishing
things, and we are still preparing ourselves for service. Are we the
ones who should complain?" Even students who were critical of
the failure of the promises we'd all heard the previous year con-
ceded the truth of his reply. We were all aware of the "three kitchen"

system used to feed members of the Chinese Communist Party. The great bulk of party workers received their meals from the "big kitchen," which served the same kind of fare dished up to us. A lesser number, whose positions were more responsible or whose duties were more demanding, were assigned to mess at the "middle kitchen," which served a bigger quantity and variety of dishes. A small fraction whose poor health or very responsibile position required it dined from the "small kitchen," which served a diet with more appeal to health and taste. And after all, it was genuinely ironic for students who planned to enter the service of the government or of the Party later on to complain now about the same food they would then accept without a murmur.

Part of the muttering about food was inevitable letting off of steam, I suppose. Things hadn't turned out to be quite what we'd expected and what we thought we'd been promised. But food had been a problem before, hadn't it? We could tell ourselves that the government faced drought, had to feed the armies, had to hold grain in reserve to dump on the market at the appropriate times to hold down prices. Later on, during the next school year, after we heard about the damage inflicted by floods and winds late in the summer of 1949, we could remind ourselves of the unpredictability of nature and the stark necessity of saving food for the relief of the famine-stricken areas. With such reasons and with the inspiration provided by news of famous people gathering from all over the country for the formal creation of a new national government most of us could still submerge our small personal disappointments in hope and anticipation when we went back to school for our second semester under the new government in the fall of 1949.

CHAPTER VI

Gray Becomes You

"Still too red."

I shook my head critically, while my friend dabbed at her cheek again with her handkerchief.

Not many of us used lipstick as a matter of every-day practice; nor did other cosmetics—rouge, vanishing cream, or face powder—attract many customers. All the men at Peita and most of the girls declared publicly that a woman really did look much better with make-up. But women students who used cosmetics usually felt that they were doing something slightly immoral. This vague feeling of guilt, however, did not prevent some of us from making tentative experiments.

A friend of mine who was curious to see how much better she would look if she had the courage to paint her face might invite me into her room and close the door. First she would pat on a small quantity of powder, then dab a spot of rouge on her cheeks and try to spread it out evenly. With painful care she would smear a little lipstick on her little finger, daub it on the middle of her lips and spread it with another finger. Then she would pull the mirror closer, examine her image, push the mirror back, and study her face again.

"Oh, it still looks too obvious. Doesn't it?"

"Better wipe some more off. Just a tiny bit," I'd advise.

After a slight scuffing with a hankerchief: "How do you like it now? Can you tell whether I've really used any rouge?"

"It's still just a little bit dark on your cheeks."

My friend, the secret dabbler in beauty, would hold the mirror up and look at her face again. "But if I make it any paler, it'll look like I haven't used any rouge at all!"

Despite such private experiments, the men that we wanted to impress very seldom got a chance to see the results. It would not be in keeping with the Peita tradition. Men and women at our school dressed with more simplicity than students at Yenching and Tsinghua, the wealthier American-supported universities outside the city. Even before the Liberation men students wore in the spring and summer what virtually amounted to a standard uniform: a cotton tee-shirt, khaki trousers, cheap cotton socks, and either black cloth shoes or Chinese-made foreign-style leather shoes. In winter some men preferred the traditional cotton-padded gowns of blue or gray cotton or wool, comfortable, free-hanging, and warm, with cotton-lined black cloth slippers and wool stockings showing below. Others put on heavy Western-style trousers and wool overcoats or second-hand war-surplus American army field jackets which they had bought in the open-air market.

The sharp, dry North China cold also demanded headgear and gloves. These articles appeared in all sorts of strange varieties and odd styles at Peita—not because their wearers had any ambition to set a new style, but because they had to put on whatever they could find. Some of my friends wore Manchurian-style fur hats with flaps that came down to shield the ears; others sported billed caps with earmuffs along with fur-lined leather mittens, or knitted wool stocking caps and wool gloves, again war-surplus stores left by the American army when it left China after V-J Day. If you could stand outside the door on a winter day and watch these boys as they surged out of a classroom, you would be lucky to find more than two or three among a hundred whose clothing exhibited good materials and up-to-date styling. In hot weather Peita men aimed only at coolness. In cold weather they were happy enough just to keep warm. The little money in their pockets had to go for food and books; their families couldn't afford to clothe most of them in the style of Chinese students who go abroad.

We naturally paid more attention to our clothes than the men did. But the male students who came over to visit us from Tsinghua University derived sadistic pleasure out of reminding us that we lacked the sophisticated grace and charm possessed by girls at Tsinghua, Yenching, and Fu Jen. The boys from Tsinghua we regarded as obtuse in many ways, but they were certainly keen and painstaking in their appraisal of their female counterparts. Perhaps they liked to visit us because we were generally satisfied with less. And even for Tsinghua students the price of a meal in a good restaurant for two people was not a thing to be undertaken without some consideration.

In hot weather most Peita women wore cotton dresses of light blue, cut in traditional style, and flat or low-heel shoes. Some girls also had Chinese dresses or Western-style skirts of various designs but comparatively mild colors: blue, green, yellow, and black. Red or golden-red designs were seldom seen on the campus. Without Western trimmings like lace or glass beads, the dresses were very conservative in cut, with collars that fastened high at the throat, short sleeves that just covered the shoulders, no fitting at the waist, and with a short hem that fell one or two inches below the knee. Chinese dresses taper in below the hips and would be difficult to walk in if it were not for the slit up the side of the skirt following the line of the leg. But the slit was conservative, only a few inches high instead of halfway up to the waist as I've seen it in Shanghai and Hong Kong. What the average girl in Hong Kong would spend on one pretty dress, with its high collar almost up to her chin, its tight fit around her waist and hips, its deep slit and the lacy slip sewn inside would buy five or six dresses for a Peita girl. Girls' underwear was usually of cotton and often of our own tailoring.

When cold weather came, many of us wore shorter garments so that we could move about more freely in our heavy padding. Though the traditional winter gown with pads of wadded cotton quilted inside was still popular, it lacked the ornamentation it used to have, the brass or cloisonné buttons, and it was made out of cotton instead of silk, damask, or brocade. After V-J Day more of us wore short padded Chinese jackets and Western-style long trousers, mostly black or blue in color. To the best of my knowledge, this practical if not particularly attractive style came into fashion first in Shanghai in the winter of 1947, when girls at St. John's University took to wearing the costume. These slacks were usually coarse, warm wool; a few girls had even manufactured theirs of United States Army blankets. I've heard the comment that winter always brought on a curious reversal of sex at Peita: the boys put on gowns and the girls climbed into pants to get them through the snappish winter cold. Peking winters are cold, as I have said, cold enough so that I wore worsted stockings inside boots lined with sheepskin in the classrooms, which were sometimes just barely warmer than the weather out of doors.

We would have enjoyed wearing fur, because beautiful fur from the north, Manchuria and Siberia, is cheap in Peking. It wasn't quite cheap enough, though; those friends of mine fortunate enough to have fur coats wore the pelts from sheep, cats, or rabbits. (Cat fur is very common in Peking.) The majority of Peita students wore nothing but cotton, however, thin cotton in the spring and summer, and padded cotton garments in the fall and winter.

Men students liked to cut their hair short, and combed it in the Western style; but it usually stayed well kept and shiny only a day or two after a visit to the barber. A number of boys cropped their hair very short so that each hair stood on end. Although many of my countrymen like to shear off all their hair and shave their heads during the summer months, such bald pates were so unusual at Peita that they could be counted upon to attract attention.

Peita men didn't believe in any niceties of ornamentation. Some of them did wear gold rings, but always as souvenirs rather than as ornaments. Nobody ever tucked a white handkerchief in his breast pocket, for to do so would have provoked audible speculation among his friends about his masculinity. At some schools some of the boys, I heard, liked to use a little cream on their faces at night or to spray a little scent on their clothes. There were no such men at Peita, where fellow students would have looked askance upon such things as clear evidence of probable sexual abnormality.

Girls couldn't help decorating themselves, however. Most of us wore permanent waves or cut our hair straight and short, but some younger students wore two pigtails. A few girls braided ribbons through the ends of these queues or stuck colored plastic hairpins into their hair close to their ears. Or if they had waved hair, they would fasten ribbons on top, with the knots either in front or where they would be covered up behind their necks by hair hanging down in back.

As I have said, the question of whether to use cosmetics was a real problem; most of the girls loved "beauty" in their heart and hoped that people would admire and praise their faces. We knew the boys talked about us in their dormitories and admired the girls who wore lipstick and powder every day. But when one of these girls appeared in person most Peita men would pretend to show no interest at all and would even demonstrate public distaste for her make-up. Needless to say, the plainer girls aided and abetted this distaste.

Natural beauty, however, could be commended by everyone. That was why, back in the privacy of our rooms, we used to remind each other, "A little deeper and the rouge can be detected; a little paler and it won't be any better than no rouge at all." We usually tried to pluck stray hairs from our eyebrows to give them shape and neatness; but trimming eyebrows required so much time and skill, and could be so easily detected, that none of us dared try it. For the same reason none of us tried to wear polish on our nails.

Jewels were not such a problem. Imagine yourself as a fashion designer. Does an imitation pearl necklace match a blue cotton gown, or does it go with a cotton-padded gown of dark hue? Does a brooch of imitation gems look pretty against a padded short jacket of coarse wool? Do earrings go very well with short straight hair or two thick queues? For such reasons ornaments were at a minimum. Once in a while a brooch of blue cloisonné, filigree, or carved camel bone, pinned on a dark sweater, served for decoration. Gold rings were not common. A ring with a real gem in it was like the phoenix's feather or the unicorn's horn—very, very rare.

That is the way a visiting artist might have painted Peita students before the Liberation. Now, wash your brush, pack up your colors, and lay the picture aside. Take out another piece of paper and select a brush two sizes larger. Work up plenty of black on your ink stone, add water to dilute it to gray, and you are ready to sketch.

The most obvious change after the Liberation was the steady increase in gray uniforms on the campus. The Party cadres commissioned to take us over came in gray uniforms. Students who had fled to the liberated areas and who now returned in triumph came back wearing the same new fashion. Some of them even sported pistols into the bargain, decked out with a wisp of red cloth twisted in the handle or at the bottom of the holster. The guns impressed the boys, however, more than they impressed us. The dirtier and more wrinkled the uniform, the more heroic the returned student seemed to think he was. But I don't think this idea was really a part of the Communist philosophy.

Because it was still cold in February, the gray uniforms were winter, cotton-padded suits. At first sight these so-called Lenin uniforms reminded me irresistibly of the clothes worn by children of conservative families, except that the children's loose heavy wrappings were usually in bright colors. The uniforms were not cut to fit; a thin person would wrap his suit closely around his body and move along the floor in it like a partially deflated basketball. It stood up under wear, however, and looked properly austere and businesslike. Before long, many of us began to follow the vogue and put on the padded Lenin suits ourselves. One of the reasons for the popularity of the uniform was its cheapness and durability. The other reasons are left to the imagination.

Many people put these suits on in the first wave of enthusiasm after the Liberation. Later on, when it was announced that the new People's Study Aids would be substituted for the old subsidies, people who hadn't joined the fashion parade got into step and packed away their Western-style suits, if they were boys, or their brighter dresses and skirts, if they were girls, to help pave the way for their applications. You also changed your clothes to show other people that you were beginning to change "positively"—to be labeled "unchanging" was almost as bad as to be called "reactionary." Besides, after we began to hold criticism meetings to examine one another's progress or lack of progress in adapting ourselves to the "new life," wearing a uniform or else the simplest clothes became a routine precaution to avoid attention and subsequent criticism.

Somebody happened to drop a half joking remark, "Cut off this tail of feudalism," and with a wave of scissors the pigtails of the girl students were quickly transformed to straight haircuts just long enough to cover the ears. Some women who had permanent waves also cropped their hair, which then jutted out in back like the hair of naughty little girls who refused to wash or comb their unruly topknots. This infantile hairdo formed a most incongruous match with the serious faces and the heavy cotton-padded clothes when they sat in their lecture halls with such self-conscious dignity.

Powder and rouge became rarer than ever. Behind closed doors, however, women who had habitually touched up their natural color with rouge continued their old practice. After all, they trusted their intimate friends to keep secret their use of cosmetics. In winter most of us continued to use cold cream as a protection against chapping, but not American brands of cream if we could help it.

The unspoken prohibition against cosmetics as a symbol of decadence was lifted for the boys and girls wriggling the *yang-ko* dance at parades and on public holidays. The performers were encouraged to deck themselves in bright costumes and to smear their faces red and white like the heavily made-up actors and actresses of the stage or opera. Men competed with the women in applying a heavy coat of paint to their faces and took an obscure satisfaction in rouging their lips and penciling in marks around their eyes. This, of course, was an attempt at art. But hadn't the *yang-ko* belonged at first to the toiling peasant population? Wasn't dressing up for this dance a "petty bourgeois" idea, then? Or did it mean that the rouge and powder and bright costumes must have also been the idea of the toiling masses? I wondered sometimes as I watched the colorful spectacle whether those students who were trying to learn from, and to keep abreast of, the proletariat weren't still harboring petty bourgeois ideas which they would have to purge themselves of later on.

One of my best friends, who happened to be very fond of pretty things, bought a piece of damask-rose silk at a "cheap sale" at a silk and brocade shop closing out its business. She carried it back to her room, draped it around her figure, compared it here, measured it there, and looked immensely pleased with herself. She was just asking me whether in my opinion she should make it into a dress with short or long sleeves when her boy friend came in. A long-time member of the Youth League he was acknowledged by all of us as an honest, capable, conscientious student. Party members held him in special regard because his thinking was "correct" and his loyalty to the "organization" was without question.

He looked at the piece of material and at the same time recognized the pride she took in it. Without the least trace of embarrassment she asked him with a smile:

"What do you think of this material? Don't I look well in it?"

He stared at the cloth. It was soft and smooth with a silky radiance, elegant with a formal, figured design. Then he looked at the girl and saw her fair, roundish face with its curved chin, her long crescent-shaped eyebrows arching with subtle grace over a pair of lively black eyes, her delicately molded nose, her lips which were a soft red without the help of lipstick. It was an open secret among the girls that he had been in love with her for a long time.

She mistook his silence as a rebuke and unwrapped the material from around her body. I snatched it up again, held it up against her, and snapped out at her friend:

"Well, how about it? Come on, how do you like it?"

By now I realized his embarrassment. And because I resented his timid reluctance to give her the right answer, I kept after him. "Come on, what do you really think?"

He dropped his book satchel on our desk, sat down, and grinned weakly. "Who has time to bother about these things? You girls . . . well . . ." He still hadn't decided what to say. He looked at his watch—if I had asked him the time I know he would have had to look at it again. Then he fluttered the pages of the book lying open on the desk. It was our dictionary, and I'm sure he didn't see a single word in it. "You women," he said. "Really, how do you find so much time to worry about clothes?" He looked at his girl friend again and turned his eyes back to the damask silk.

Despite my resentment, I felt a sudden sympathy for him. From the bottom of his heart he wished to admire the cloth which suited her so well. Yet he felt at the same time that it was his immediate duty to liquidate her petty bourgeois ideas and the same ideas he felt lingering in himself. He stood up, poured himself a glass of cold boiled water, took a gulp, and sat down again. "Now, you should never forget that we are petty bourgeois elements called to take part in a proletarian revolution—"

I cut short what I knew he was going to say. "So we must forsake our own petty bourgeois ideas." I knew the slogans by heart too.

He looked at me sharply as if he wanted to argue. I didn't want to get involved, but I couldn't help hurrying on to strike the first blow. "You don't have to look at me that way. I really can't agree all the way with your theories. The petty bourgeois certainly do worship beauty and like to wear pretty materials. But can you say that workers and peasants do not really care for beauty and do not like fine clothes? In fact it seems to me that the petty bourgeois have contributed as much to mankind as the other classes. Especially in the spiritual and artistic line it seems to me they've done more than the proletariat. Don't most of the scientists, philosophers, musicians, writers, artists, and social scientists come from the petty bourgeois class? Is their search for things like truth and beauty also to be called just a petty bourgeois idea?"

"You should wait until I finish," he cut in impatiently, a little angry. "You ought to know that your view is basically—"

After this "basically" he would try to "give me a hat to wear," that is, pin the label of "reactionary" on me. Once I had the "hat" on, I would have to fight against his rhetoric with all of my resources. Because I certainly didn't want to get taken in in that way, I blurted out as fast as I could: "But I just want to ask you one thing: Are the quests by philosophers, scientists, and artists to be called petty bourgeois ideas too? Should they be completely liquidated?"

By this time his girl friend had dropped the material on the bed. She stood behind his chair and patted him on the shoulder. "You seem to be drifting into bigger and bigger subjects. It's about time for class. Let's talk about all these big, important ideas when we have more time, shall we?" She smiled at him with affection.

Her smile gave me the chance to get in another blow. "If you had just said that we should all resist material temptations like this instead of dragging in the social struggle, I wouldn't have argued with you."

"Would you mind stopping this argument too?" The girl turned to me. "Let's leave it for some other time. I don't mean to deny the value of your argument. But let's change the subject."

By then I was ready to call a truce. If I had kept on arguing, we would have driven each other into real anger and touched off a violent war. After all, any debate could not have possibly led to any agreement because the Communists had already prescribed inflexible conclusions for this boy for everything under the sun.

He stood up and regarded the material peevishly. I felt that he would probably like to resolve his mental difficulty by clutching the damask and tearing it into shreds. If he had done so, however, he would have regretted it, for later she went with him clothed in a dress cut from the same handsome silk to attend various parties in honor of distinguished foreign visitors.

After a few months Peking was a host to swarms of such guests from abroad, most of them Soviet, but a few from the People's Democracies of Eastern Europe. Students were always mobilized to welcome these honored guests and advisers, who made their round of feasts and tours of the campus with much speechmaking and much snapping of photographs. The Party and the Youth League always hinted very clearly in advance of such occasions that the students should appear better dressed, particularly those men and women selected to present flowers, accept banners, and participate in other ceremonies within the range of possible cameras. On these occasions our Soviet elder brothers always beamed upon us with warm smiles in which I thought I read a certain amount of petty bourgeois appreciation.

When the Soviet film team arrived at Peita to film student life as part of a picture they were helping our State Cinema Studio to make on liberated China, we received specific instructions through our living circles to appear neater and cleaner than was our daily habit. Even a little more gaiety, it was said, would not be out of order. When the Soviet visitors saw us, they seemed slightly disappointed. But they had to save our "face," of course. They set up the cameras they had brought with them and ground away to take some scenes of collective student life. For special closeups they focused their cameras on the best dressed, prettiest girls. We felt rather flattered by the attention and pleased at the chance to wear the bright dresses we'd kept packed away for so many months.

In the summer of 1950 we received instructions to appear at a mass meeting in favor of world peace in front of the Music Hall at Chungshan Park. The day before the meeting we were read a directive to go in good clothes. I remarked to one of the men students I knew pretty well, "Huh—I suppose there must be many foreign guests who'll be there who would like to see our picturesque Chinese costumes."

He replied coldly but with a faint underlying thread of satire he knew I'd understand: "The goal of the revolution was to overthrow the bourgeoisie and raise the living standard of our people. We have been liberated for over a year, and we should show the world now that our people are better dressed than before. Besides, there'll surely be motion-picture cameras around. Don't you know these pictures and films will be shown in the People's Democracies and the countries still waiting to be liberated?"

The words of this humorous and quite courageous fellow student made me realize something. The school had been handing out large quantities of Soviet pictorial magazines, *The Soviet Union in Construction*, *The Soviet Woman*, *Ogenek*, and others, to show us how well provided with food and clothes ordinary people were in Soviet Russia. I wondered now whether the pictures of Soviet life were snapshots taken at random or whether they had not been taken on formal occasions like our own when we were asked to put on our holiday clothes.

In the wake of the Soviet magazines and the Soviet visitors and advisers came some Soviet textiles for sale in Peking. We had seen these Russian comrades, all dressed alike in stiff navy-blue suits and black felt hats, invade cloth shops to buy imported wool textiles from Hong Kong for themselves and Chinese brocades and silk prints for their wives. Now we ourselves went into the shops to look over the new materials we had received from our Soviet neighbor. Their designs were sometimes not very harmonious in color: large gold checks combined with small checks of deep purple, for instance, might be printed on a background of dark green. They appeared bourgeois to us, but monotonously bourgeois, "new" bourgeois, with neither sobriety nor real gaiety, without elegance or quiet good taste. In their Western-style suits the Russian engineers and technical advisers we saw in groups on the streets also appeared quite bourgeois to us. Perhaps that is what the USSR has done—created a new bourgeois in the place of the old. But the new middle class appeared to wear its conventional clothes without the ease or the confidence its members will probably acquire as they get more used to their position.

Some of the girls did invest in the new fabrics. Most of us kept away from them because of their high prices as well as their lack of taste. I have a feeling that my reaction was not just personal prejudice. Prompted at one time by a desire to make a small joke, I asked one of my Communist friends whether he thought the dresses made of the Russian textiles were good-looking. He thought carefully. "Well, you'll have to admit they're durable," he said.

CHAPTER VII

Life Managers and Political Shepherds

Suppose, before the Liberation, when I was a sophomore, that you had come along with me to visit a boy who lived in one of the dormitories in the Third Court. With time enough, we could have pedaled our bicycles around the rest of the campus first, and you would have seen how, as it grew more or less haphazardly in its earlier years, Peita had acquired new buildings as it needed them. Classrooms of six colleges within the university—arts, law, science, engineering, medicine, and agriculture—sprawled over five compounds, while the dormitories to house their students were scattered in other enclosures. Each living unit was endowed with its own character and individuality, and even the physical look of each section seemed subtly symbolic of its occupants. Medical students lived in dormitories that were clean and antiseptically neat. Living quarters for engineering students were neat in line, plain and uni-

79

form in design. You and I would not see the college of agriculture. That was off in the suburbs; its attached dormitories were spacious, airy, and quiet.

Graduate students kept to themselves in their small dormitory in Jade Flower Street, secluded and serene. Inside Hsuan-wu Gate, the Fourth and Fifth courts housed most of the freshmen students. Appropriately, these buildings were crowded, with no particular character or individuality. The West Square, inhabited by the science majors, had its huddled rooms or cells neatly arranged in dozens of long rows like a blackboard drawing for a lecture on molecular structure. Like scientific formulas, these rooms always impressed me as being impersonal, devoid of life—but then I was a student of the arts and a natural foe of such scientific precision.

Now we would come to the third Court, headquarters for male students of arts and the social sciences. While the engineering, agriculture, and medical dormitories I have mentioned were all modern, the buildings in the Third Court were old-fashioned European-style structures erected scores of years ago. In spite of their European look, however, they still managed to suggest Chang Chih-tung's adage, "Chinese learning in essence, Western learning in practice." Although it wasn't large, the Third Court was divided into ten units to house men students: the Kung Mansion, Yi Mansion, El Mansion, Hsiu Mansion, Bell Mansion, the East, West, and Back bungalows, Hsiao Chambers and the Assembly Hall (which formerly was used as a dormitory but which was used to house mass meetings during my last two years at Peita). Each of the ten houses clung fiercely to its established "independent personality" and bristled with individualism. Life in the "modern" dormitories was like life in other universities; but life in the Third Court used to exhibit all of the traditional "Pieta flavor."

Inheritor of an ancient tradition, the Third Court was itself antique. It had once been the Imperial School of Translation in the Ch'ing Dynasty. At a corner of the wall north of the main entrance you could have seen a weathered stone tablet inscribed with three large characters identifying the area as the Imperial School. A small river loafed by in front of the gate; most students irreverently called it the "Big Ditch." Along its banks rose small mounds of garbage and refuse, but a few stubborn old willow trees still trailed their long branches over the water. The office of the Master of the Third Court perched on top of the arched-stone passage through the wall. Sitting in this lofty stronghold you could almost sing the melodies from *The Trick of Empty-Walled Town,* a classical opera in which clever Chu-Ke Liang sits calmly and nonchalantly on the wall of a virtually defenseless city, playing on a lute and joking, inviting a huge enemy force to come in. The unusual invitation makes the enemy suspect an ambush, and they withdraw. And from the office of the Master of the Third Court, it was possible to look down and see the "old soldiers," the university guards, joking with each other, the janitors sweeping the floors or just sitting and scratching their feet, displaying all the merits of true "Peking rogues."

Riding up on a bicycle, you threaded your way through these loungers and adroitly scraped by oncoming bicycles and mule carts leaving the compound. Then, if you lived in the Third Court, still sitting astride the bicycle, leaning on one hand against the wall, you halted at the janitor's room to examine the list of names posted outside to find out whether you had been blessed with the receipt of a registered letter or perhaps even a money order. Certainly not—but you were not too disappointed. You pushed down hard on the pedals, the bicycle shot off, and you left the janitor's room behind.

Around the corner the next stop was the reading room, where you could look at the newspapers free. You parked the bike and pulled out the "ordinary mail" drawer assigned to you to see if you had at least received one or two ordinary letters. Then, if there was any money left in your pockets, you could buy a small packet of peanuts from the Student Welfare Department next door to the reading room, sit down at one of the long tables, and pick up a newspaper. When your peanuts were gone, you might walk over to read the "for sale" and "wanted" advertisements posted on the wall. Was anybody offering to buy something you might be willing to spare? Certainly not. Yet you weren't really disappointed. You went out and pedaled your rickety bicycle off to your own dormitory. A few steps away was the bicycle check room; but if you felt energetic enough you might carry your bike into your room. You stepped into the room—well, once you had stepped inside what you would meet there used to depend entirely on the kind of room you lived in.

Some of the ninety rooms in the Third Court were small rooms for two students; others were large enough to hold nine. Most rooms housed five or six men, with each resident entitled to one student lamp, one desk, one chair, one bed made of wooden planks, and half a bookcase. But I knew students living there who had managed to appropriate more furniture from somewhere than they were entitled to. As long as there was room, however, the authorities winked at such things. Some of the rooms even boasted such high-toned furniture as wardrobes and highboys, thereby testifying to the "scrounging" ability or wheedling powers of their owners.

Imagine that you were a boy in the Third Court. Inside your own room you inched your way through an array of furniture as miraculously intricate as Chu-ke Liang's famous maze,* and put your book satchel down on your bed. If it was summer, you took off shoes, socks, pants, and shirt, picked up your basin, and made your way to the bathroom. Under the cold shower you heard your fellow bathers singing together in English or Chinese, sometimes popular songs and sometimes airs from classical operas, which would indeed wash away your cares.

If it happened to be winter, you would pick up your chair instead of your washbasin, and settle down by the stove in the middle of the room, where you could trade stories, highbrow or ribald, ancient or modern, from pole to pole, from China to Peru. If the stove that evening happened to be low-spirited and lacking in vigor, you could only give it a heartfelt curse, rip off your shoes, climb into bed, and wage a "cold war," that is, shiver in unison with your roommates. Or you might swathe your head in a pillow against your roommates' talk so that you could nap until supper-time. The bell roused you for supper and you drifted into the mess hall with your friends, the only time when you met the rest of the Third Court inhabitants in common.

After supper you were free. If you were in funds you might see a movie or listen to a *ta-ku*, or minstrel, accompanying himself on a

---

* Appearing in a story in the classic *Romance of the Three Kingdoms*, this maze was formed by rows of pebbles piled five *ch'ih* (feet) high. Visitors who did not know the way, according to the story, got lost in the maze and heard all sorts of frightening sounds such as thunder, the neighing of horses, and the shouts of advancing troops.

drum. Lacking money, you might window-shop at the Tung-An Market, play ball in the courtyard in the spring until it got dark, join an impromptu chorus, or go off to listen to a wealthier friend's phonograph records. Or you might read, do school work, chat, squabble, play bridge, or even go to bed early. In the same room you might find a reader reading, a serious student studying, a sleeper dozing, a troublemaker squabbling, and a protester protesting—all without conflicting at all. In the same room Tung and Li might knit their brows and discuss Kant, Chang denounce Adam Smith or Marx to Kuo, and Wang might be reading Bernard Shaw. Sitting apart from the others, Cheng might be playing a Chinese flute.

Mutual tolerance, mutual indulgence, and mutual indifference resulted in a strange sort of mutual respect where nobody visibly respected anybody else.

This unrestrained hustle-bustle would persist until after midnight when people went to bed one by one and the Third Court finally sank into silence. Only the lonely cry of a hawker calling out the virtues of the brown pastry or *po-p'o* he was selling to sit-up-lates could be heard far away in the heart of a sleeping city.

In the Gray Mansion, where Peita girls lived, we lay in our beds listening to the same far-off musical cry. With its neat little rooms each holding two beds, two small desks, two chairs and, best of all, a built-in closet, the Gray Mansion was well known for the comforts it possessed. The windows had glass and were fitted with wire screens, a luxury the men students lacked. We even enjoyed central heating, which most of the girls didn't have at home; if a winter wind outside was throwing snow against the window you simply had to turn on the radiator to make it as warm as spring inside. If you were a graduate student or a lucky senior, you could have a room to yourself and rule over a private little kingdom.

Every ten rooms shared a toilet, which usually was washed and scrubbed remarkably clean. For the most part we had plenty of hot water for baths. Each floor had a maidservant whose duties were to sweep floors and prepare boiled drinking water for us. If you handed her a small monthly tip, she would also take care of small chores for you like cleaning desks, washing your laundry, and going out to buy snacks.

These comforts were comforts, of course, only from our own point of view. In 1947 a foreign student from Turkey arrived at the Gray Mansion. A special room had been chosen for her by the university authorities, bigger and sunnier than the rest. But when she took one look, she turned up her nose, frowned, and said in English:

"Why, this is almost like a prison! Tell Dr. Hu Shih"—President of Peita—"that I am going back to my own country."

Whereupon she actually ordered the servants to pick up her baggage again and set off to find a hotel.

In a certain sense, I suppose, the Gray Mansion might have been called a "prison" in the old days when we girls were locked up and guarded like imperial concubines. In the fall of 1948, however, after long negotiations with the dean of students, we won a great victory: the girls' dormitory was thrown "open" at long last. Now the term "thrown open" usually refers only to prisons and art galleries and museums. To compare our dormitory to an art gallery or a museum sounds needlessly sardonic, so perhaps it's wiser to accept the Turkish student's disdainful label for the dormitory that used to be.

To have the dormitory "open," now, simply meant some relaxation of restrictions and permission for male students and visitors to walk into the dormitory during visiting hours. There were, of course, appropriate time limits; between "lights out" in the evening and the morning bell we were locked up safely for the night.

It was paradoxical that this triumph was won at Peita instead of at Tsinghua or Yenching, where the authorities prided themselves on being "Western" and "Modern." But we were individualists, and took pride in being so. We did find out later on that our demands for more freedom for visitors had been privately encouraged by Communist underground workers, who wanted to open up a convenient refuge for themselves. A girl's room, they conjectured, was a safe place to get in touch with your comrades for a meeting. When the police or soldiers searched for a Communist agitator, he now could flee to the Gray Mansion for sure asylum.

After the hall was declared "open," a casual visitor would have seen groups of men and girls sitting together in rooms all along each hall as he strolled down the corridor, but the tenor of the conversation in two adjoining rooms might be very different. One group might be dealing with secret political tasks, plans to inspire a "protest" strike or to transmit information picked up from an unwary friend in the city government. The other group might be occupied with ordinary lighthearted chitchat. Sometimes groups in this second category would boil up a cabbage and meat stew on a kerosene stove. Usually, however, they got along with some sunflower seeds to crack between their teeth or peanuts to nibble on. Once in a while a visitor would find a male student and a girl sitting in a room by themselves, reading or writing, quietly and sweetly companionable. When you walked into such a scene you felt embarrassed, and withdrew hastily like an apologetic but careless intruder.

Which is not to say that the new freedom at the Gray Mansion encouraged "sexual promiscuity." It did give men and women students more opportunities to see each other, and so might have offered more opportunities for improper behavior. But Peita girls were conservative about their personal behavior while progressive in their politics; the vast majority would not have dreamed of cheapening themselves. As for the few dissolute exceptions, nobody can claim that they would have remained innocent even if the dormitory had been preserved as a "prison."

Before the Liberation the Gray Mansion was almost like a large apartment house, except that under certain conditions it was rent-free. Sisters and girl friends of the residents could always move in and live there as long as the young hostess could find space. Such a privilege was especially in evidence during the summer and winter holidays, when there were always more vacant rooms. Stricter measures were enforced after the Liberation. To prevent "secret agents" from hiding themselves among us, any girl who wanted to stay for a few days, whether she was a Peita student or not, had to go through a series of preliminary arrangements with the new "section leader" of the floor. She had to fill out a form, answer a set of questions about her status and background, give sufficient reasons for her request, and finally get two Peita girls already living in the dormitory to guarantee that she wouldn't snoop for state secrets or steal the soap out of the bathroom.

Except for the prompt banishment of the food hawkers who

had set up little stalls outside the main entrance to sell the students breakfast, the physical look of the dormitories did not change much during the first year after the Liberation. (The hawkers were chased away because the school authorities wanted to encourage all of us to get up early enough to eat breakfast so that sleepy students wouldn't waste "the sweat of the people.") But life inside the Third Court, the Gray Mansion, and the other residence halls witnessed a series of adjustments.

Like their male colleagues, girls lodging in the dormitory had always selected their own roommates and then had drawn lots to determine which room they were to occupy, a process designed to avoid arguments over who was to get priority for the rooms with the most light, the rooms closest to the bathroom, and so on. But now it was decided that to encourage more "group-consciousness" students from the same class and department should room together. Our new student leaders drew up the housing lists and took care to ensure that a Party member, Youth League comrade, or at least an acknowledged progressive was assigned to every section of each floor. The new system of assignment probably created more resentment among us than it did among the men, because women naturally have more trouble finding another congenial member of their own sex to live with. When two mortal enemies drew the same room number, they could only make the best of it and move in together. In several cases there were only two girls in the same class and majoring in the same subject. In these cases "the marriage was indeed made in heaven" because there was no way on earth for them to avoid sharing the same room.

Each floor now had a "life manager" to organize what the wall newspapers were beginning to call "communal living." When the life managers took it upon themselves to decide for us what time we got up, what time we went to bed, whom we ate with at what table, and when we had to sit down to review our school work in a group they stirred up noticeable resentment. Later on, the life managers even told us when we were expected to attend certain motion pictures together. By that time, however, even the most individualistic felt themselves firmly cemented to the rest of their group.

In keeping with the austerity drive the school administration retrenched on our coal supply. Each stove in the men's dormitories had consumed an average of twenty-five catties a day in the old days; the supply was now reduced to eight. The radiators in our dormitory still looked warm, but they gave off considerably less heat. In the name of this same austerity the sixty-watt light bulbs were unscrewed from our lamps and twenty-five-watt bulbs substituted. Early in the morning we began to get up for the new physical drill out in front of the dormitories. It was still voluntary, but non-participation revealed to progressive students that you "had not thought things out." Starting at seven o'clock in the morning on the lawn with mass calisthenics, the whole daily routine displayed a new earnestness. The loud chorus in the shower room still went on, but bathers now listened to: "The east is red. The sun is rising—China has produced Mao Tse-tung. . . ." Political activity was even more intense, of course, than it had been in the old conspiratorial days of 1948. But now student political activity was out in the open; instead of plotting against authority we listened to it. Communist students and their followers joined strenuously in the efforts of other students to catch up on their knowledge of Marx, Lenin, Stalin, and Mao Tse-tung and to reform their own bourgeois thinking. If you settled down to do some reading, a student leader was likely to drop by and crane his neck as politely as he could to see whether it was a reactionary volume in your hand. If it happened to be, you might just as well give up any hope of reading any more. With a smile the visitor would interrupt you. "You aren't really interested in that stuff, are you? What's your opinion? You can't think its views are true, do you?" Or he might beat around the bush: "Have you had a chance to read through that reference book for the politics class?" This was intended as a mild hint that you shouldn't be browsing around for your own selfish pleasure.

If your answer wasn't phrased tactfully enough, a series of "spiritual blows," as the Communists called them, would rain on your head. Of course it was all for your own good, but it was annoying. Sometimes you happened to be lucky enough to be holding a Communist book in your hand when one of these political shepherds dropped in, and then they did all they could do to avoid disturbing you. But if you got tired or bored and let fall the book, you opened the door for immediate cross-examination. "Well, tell us what you think. Doesn't this really increase your confidence in the proletarian revolution? Doesn't it give you a deeper understanding of the people's democratic dictatorship? What new discoveries . . ." After the right answers had been dinned into your ears long enough, you could sit there and let your memory recite them back almost automatically as one question followed on the heels of the one before.

It got easier and easier to follow the path of least resistance and parrot back the ideas drilled into you. It was not very intelligent to persist in independent thinking, because voicing any idea beyond the books you read and lectures you attended just led to arguments you were bound to lose. "Independent thinking" was attacked as being equal to thinking "without standpoint." And you had to say something in response to the questions you were asked. Staying silent was as bad as thinking "without standpoint."

In the winter I used to enjoy sitting by the window knitting. The warm sunshine rippled in and caressed your whole body. Beside you on the desk sat a cup of fragrant steaming tea; in a little while it would cool off enough for you to drink. On your lap was the sweater you were working on, so soft, so warm, it was almost an incarnation of the sun outside. Your hands moved mechanically at their work, but your mind raced free, nimble and alive, now sporting with one image, now with another. You imagined yourself as the sparrow outside, perching on a telephone pole in the bright winter sun, scratching your plumage with your beak. When you'd scratched enough, you whisked away to the ragged evergreen tree down in the court.

There on a twig in your mind's eye you saw a fat summer worm . . . but the worm reminded you of a caterpillar, and your mind darted to butterflies fluttering among peony blossoms. You fancied a beautiful woman in ancient costume pursuing the butterfly with a circular fan. You saw her red lips, slightly parted, her long streaming girdle, the folds of her skirts sporting in the breeze. . . . But *whack-whack*, the thump of somebody rapping on your door. You woke and shouted your habitual "Come in, please." In marched the progressive young man who'd been interested in you before the Liberation.

"Knitting again? You always like to shut yourself away in your room like this. Why don't you come on down?"

He came closer.

"A bunch of us are in Miss Li's room downstairs discussing the economic measures we're going to have to practice as part of the New Democracy. You'll want to join in too."

I used to like to waste more time lying in bed amusing myself with light reading. The summer sun was merciless, but you had already drawn the curtains and placed a fan by your side. In fact you'd already taken off your dress and were sitting on your bed, your hair mussed, fanning away and humming fragments of a little tune. Then, the familiar rapping on the door. You jumped up, hastily pulled your dress on over your head, and ran your hands back over your hair in a hopeless attempt to make yourself presentable. In walked the same persistent young man. He looked around the whole room, took in the rumpled sheet and pillow, and discovered the political book on your desk, still unopened. Then he stared at your mussed hair and your sleepy expression.

He sat down, an earnest look on his face. "I've been wanting to have a quiet talk with you. Please sit down."

You obediently brought a chair over to where he sat. He arranged his face into a judicial look. "Now, you appreciate the fact that we understand your family background very well. Your father is a petty bourgeois intellectual. But he comes from small landlord origins. Your relatives might be called 'kindly landlords.' Yet like the rest of this class their designs for exploitation and their feudalistic ideas are very deeply entrenched. Your mother still tends to be an old-fashioned, feudalistic woman who does not ask for liberation and who is afraid of proletarian revolution. Your sisters are largely like you. All this you admitted at your last criticism meeting. Because of your origin, you realize, you should take special care to speed up your own reformation. You should . . ." He settled down into the same rhetoric I'd heard so often before.

All of this was an excellent reason for spending more and more time in the library where the signs still said QUIET! I'm afraid the activists sometimes disregarded even this injunction and whispered lectures to their transfixed victims—I suppose, with their gift for phrase, they would have called it their freedom to whisper.

Some of your time, however, you unavoidably had to spend in

your dormitory. If your roommate happened to be in the Youth League, you might have to face her talk the last half-hour or so before you both fell asleep. Your simple "yes" or "no" wasn't enough. When she was through, she usually asked you for your opinions. If you were too sleepy to have any, or if you hadn't remembered her words very well and you failed to reproduce them back again, you had to face more of her "music."

After a semester of this, more people than myself must have remembered the scornful words of the Turkish student who disdained the best room in the Gray Mansion with "Why, this is almost like a prison!"

Outside the dormitory, however, life wasn't confined to political discussion. The introduction of Western-style ballroom dancing into China was a recent affair, with its popularity limited to the big commercial ports like Shanghai. Very few of the college and middle-school students of Peking knew how to dance in this modern manner, although just after the war, when the universities moved back from the interior, folk dances from the border areas had enjoyed a vogue. Clad in the costumes of the border peoples, in turbans and embroidered skirts complete with flowers, the students had chanted the words and swung round and round, enchanted with the exotic atmosphere and simple steps. The *yang-ko* introduced by the Communists capitalized on the popularity of these native dances.

But under the old regime, only one out of ten Peita students knew anything about ballroom dancing. Private parties were infrequent, and students rarely went to the few foreign-style dance halls Peking had room for. Going to private parties on the occasions when they did get invitations was no problem to men students, who simply brushed up their best clothes before they went out and then walked softly when they returned to the campus later than the accustomed hour. For girls it was different. Before a girl could go, she had to shut her friends out of the room, select her dress and shoes, and put on more powder and rouge than she was used to wearing. As it grew darker, she waited in her window where she could see fellow students walking below in twos and threes. Could she go out now? The twilight was dimming, but it still wasn't dark enough to hide the brilliant dress she'd put on. Should she sit quietly and wait? Gradually the promenaders dispersed and the sky grew so dark that nobody, she was sure, would recognize her now. She stood up, opened the door, and scurried out of her dormitory.

Even at the dancing party she couldn't relax. She did not know how to accept or refuse the men who approached and asked for a dance. Nor was her conversation as witty and refined as she had hoped. She felt most confident when she sat among the few schoolmates who had also come, staring at the greenish-colored drink somebody had handed her, and watching the hands on her wrist watch. Yes, she had to go back early.

Her escort saw her to the university gates and then walked away. Inside the compound she could see only a few dim, leisurely figures strolling about. But the street light by the gate was very bright. All its rays, it seemed, fell directly on her. Pulling some tissue out of her bag, she scrubbed the rouge from her face, and then, choosing the darkest path she could, dashed into her dormitory like a whiff of smoke or a guilt-stricken ghost. Her heart was still thumping noisily when she lay down on her bed.

Girls who did dance would not have been so timid about their skill if circumstances had been different. The old government officially frowned upon dancing parties and periodically announced an "austerity" ban on public dancing, a prohibition which was blandly ignored by more sophisticated officials. More important, the girl who went to dances faced the criticism of her classmates. Progressive students had denounced dance lovers as "too deeply immersed in petty bourgeois consciousness and epicureanism." I can even remember vague threats. "Unless they can make up their minds to reform themselves, these frivolous people will certainly face a reckoning one day. Ballroom dancing! A man and a woman together, couple by couple—pure cliquism! It shows the real consciousness of the depraved exploiting class."

When the progressives voiced these strictures on dancing, they imagined that far-off Yenan, then the seat of the Communist power, frowned upon such bourgeois frivolity. But later they had to perform a curious flip-flop to get themselves back on the right side; from the very same Yenan the Communist Party imported the vogue of dancing. We discovered that its cadres often gave dancing parties—not for the proletarian *yang-ko*, but for "petty bourgeois, epicurean" ballroom dancing, men and women, paired off couple by couple.

The "wall newspapers" began to comment on the new fashion. Ballroom dancing itself, those progressives who were so anxious to hurry back on the right side of the fence pointed out, was not very wrong. As a matter of fact it actually was quite popular among young men and women in the Soviet Union and the new democracies of eastern Europe. If we did not deck out the dance halls in too much splendor, as people did in the capitalistic countries, or spend too much time on dancing, it could actually become a very good thing.

Now that dancing had been declared legal and even beneficial, the first natural consequence was a party given by Communist cadres on the campus. The big classroom in the North Mansion had a good smooth floor. With desks and chairs shoved into one corner and a sprinkle of boric acid crystals scattered on the floor, it made a very acceptable dancing pavilion.

But a classroom remained a classroom; the dancing party, therefore, was labeled a "collective lesson in ballroom dancing." Most of the progressive students invited had previously been disdainful of the art. Now that they had discovered that the Communist cadres could dance and that even Shen Chun-ju, a "democratic personage" feeble with age, was taking lessons, how could they lag far behind? Besides, the wall newspapers had pointed out very clearly that it would be desirable to learn. The revolution was going faster than we had expected; it had already made the epicureanism of the petty bourgeoisie the property of the broad masses, at least as far as the "broad masses" were personified in us.

No paper streamers or other ornaments were hung on the wall at university dancing parties in compliance with official instructions. Students all wore their everyday clothes. Even the most particular dancers only changed to leather shoes with smooth thin soles. Because very few of the boys yet had either the courage or the social experience to approach the girls in front of other people and invite them to dance, the parties became occasions for feminine revenge. At school we had to listen docilely while the boys preached politics at us; now it was our turn to enjoy the pleasant superiority the teacher feels over his students. Therefore in most cases it was the perspiring girl who would leave one man standing alone, walk up to another man and ask briskly: "A dance? You seem to have made some progress since last time. Let's try it again." Or, "We'll do a four-step this time. Your three-step seems to be better than it was." Or, "Oh, come on, it's simple! Have a try at it. Don't worry if you get tangled up and happen to step on somebody."

Does this sound abnormal? Perhaps it was. But most of the expert dancers were women. Men students outnumbered us by far at Peita, and now suddenly almost all of them had become interested in dancing. No wonder we were all in a sweat. And if you didn't want to teach? Why, that showed the selfishness and pride of the petty bourgeoisie!

The music we shuffled and wheeled around to at these parties consisted almost entirely of old "bourgeois" dance tunes. Most of the men, however, had attention only for their inexplicably clumsy feet. Who had attention now to spare for music or beat? If young people from the Soviet Union or from the New Democracies had gaped in through the windows, I am sure they would have giggled. No "democratic" slogans could hide the familiar old bare classroom walls. The chairs and desks were piled in a corner, topsy-turvy. In the center of the room the dancers were pushing and jostling, as badly crowded as the throng in front of the box office of a popular movie. They bumped elbows, stepped on one another's feet, and rebounded off strange shoulders. Chins down against their collars, most boys watched their own steps with deadly intensity. Tugging and pushing their partners, some of them counted half aloud: "One, two, three, four! One, two, three, four—" In the swirl one might often see a man halt abruptly, causing a whole series of collisions around him like the pile-up of pedicabs, rickshas, and bicycles on a busy street when a tram goes off the rails, and comment to his partner with a forced smile, "Sorry—it's all wrong again." The girl who was dancing with him would encourage him as she would coax a reluctant child. "It's all right. Don't think about the mistakes! Don't stop! Just try to follow me."

Awkwardness gradually vanished; after two or three months of strenuous effort, most men really made a great deal of progress. Since they were mostly beginners and very enthusiastic in their desire to learn, they didn't want to let slip any opportunity for practice. Before the Liberation, opponents of dancing had fallen into two groups, left-leaning students and hard-working souls who didn't care about politics but who considered dancing a waste of time and an un-Chinese expression of frivolity. (It was quite true that some dance lovers had really been backward in academic work and irregular in their personal lives.) Now that the leftist students who had joined them in criticizing ballroom dancing in the past had become themselves the boldest and most enthusiastic exponents, the serious-minded felt that they had somehow been betrayed.

They fired questions at their former allies. "You used to attack people for dancing, didn't you? Why do you dance away like this yourself? What happened to your doctrine that a waste of time like this is petty bourgeois selfishness?" Reluctant to admit that their previous criticism had been an unwitting "deviation," but unable to defend their present stand either, the progressive elements invented an ingenious way to forestall further embarrassing inquiries. Before the music began at a formal party, a Party comrade would always stand up to make an announcement, his face aglow with amiability and good fellowship.

"Comrades, we are here this evening to celebrate Sino-Soviet friendship"—or the Liberation of Hainan Island, or the opening of the World Peace Congress, or International Youth Day, or any other near-at-hand holiday. "So we hope everybody will give full expression to the glorious spirit of youth which throbs within him." The Party comrade spread his arms wide as if to embrace the whole crowd at once. "Fellow students, let us enjoy ourselves as thoroughly as we can." He stood now on his toes as if to dramatize the vitality of youth. "We dare to laugh, play, and revel. We are young! The band will start in a minute or two. To show our joy we hope everybody will join in. None of us are experienced dancers; nobody will laugh at anybody else. Come on." He lifted up his arms again. "Fellow students, let's all join in and have a good time for ourselves!"

Dance-loving progressive students had reasons now to vindicate their new pleasure, and swept the "backward" along with their own irresistible enthusiasm. We all whirled about in the pool in the center of the floor; if this was revolution we all enjoyed it mightily, and nobody was left outside to criticize.

Because not even the imagination of these progressive students was elastic enough to use "exercise" as an excuse for the new vogue of dancing, we were frequently exhorted to be sure that we took enough time from our studies to spend some time in the open air in some form of healthful recreation. Not that we needed much exhorting—walking had always been a favorite relaxation for Peita students. Most of us had a habit of taking a stroll after a meal, or when we felt tired out or low in spirits. It might be a solitary walk or a stroll with a close friend. Of course, for the more zealous Youth League members among us the collective life now also embraced taking a walk. If you loitered alone, or with a friend or two, in the Democratic Square or on the lawn in front of North Mansion, one of your more earnest Communist friends might spot you and seek some excuse to keep your company in order to rescue you from the danger of "cliquism." If other business prevented him from joining you then, he might try to study your thoughts as he walked away so that he would be prepared to analyze your state of mind with other Communists in his section to decide why you had taken a walk alone. It was easy to imagine the debate at one of these Party meetings when your name came up.

"I'm afraid she feels hurt by the honest criticism of her classmates. She still has too much of the vanity typical of the bourgeois class."

"Sometimes I think she has no real intention of reforming herself; she always seems to be torn by conflicting ideas," another critic would chime in. "It is the eternal vacillation and compromise of the bourgeoisie."

"It looks like she's still stubborn, still fond of being alone, still negligent toward the collective life, and ignorant of the theories of the proletariat," a third would sum up your character before they passed on to someone else.

Suppose the boy they had seen walking with you had just been accepted as a Youth League member. He came in for even stricter scrutiny because he was more important. "I hope he hasn't become dissatisfied with the policies of the government, the Party, or the Youth League. I hope he's not complaining to her. . . ."

"Do you think that maybe he's not resolute enough in his ideas that he's vacillating? I'm sure he can't be falling in love with her, but . . ." Actually, the boy was just tired of hard work and was out walking alone with you because his other friends all happened to be busy.

I don't have to praise the beauty of Peking, the yellow-tiled Imperial Palace (really a whole enclosed city in itself), Coal Hill, the Pei Hai, Chung-Nan Hai, Sun Yat sen Park, Imperial Temple, Harvest God's Temple, the blue-tiled and exquisite Temple of Heaven, built in the long course of the old dynasties. Even for students who had lived in Peking all their lives and who couldn't afford the expensive imported cameras we saw strapped on the foreign tourists, it was a pleasure to take along a cheap box camera and saunter around the streets looking for a scene which had not caught our eyes before. Picture taking now became more complicated. Before you had adjusted the focus, a policeman or plain-clothes man would be likely to stroll over and inquire what you thought you were doing. If you were tactful and explained in a mild, unassertive way that you had not realized that you were not supposed to take pictures in that place, and if the policeman were unambitious and kindhearted, the only thing you would lose would be the roll of film in your camera. But if your reply displayed sarcasm or resentment, and if the policeman happened to be sufficiently indoctrinated in the service of the people to resent your answer, he would probably haul you off as a "smart aleck student" to the Bureau of Public Security for an educational lecture on behalf of the "people."

One Sunday I went to the Pei Hai, beautiful North Lake, with some classmates. Leaning up against the white marble balustrade beside Yi Lan Hall, with the Jade Girdle Bridge and Chung-Nan Hai in the distant background, we posed as a group for one of our friends to snap our picture. While he was bending over his camera, trying to fix the focus, another classmate suddenly stepped out of the group, looked around, and said cautiously: "Is it all right? Do you think it's safe to take a picture with that in the background?" He pointed off to the Chung-Nan Hai. We looked past his pointing finger and remembered that the State Administrative Council was housed in one of the buildings inside the Chung-Nan Hai park. Our friend had already walked away from the balustrade and, pointing to the Dagoba, or White Tower, announced, "Maybe we'd better go over there."

The Student Camera Club continued to develop films at a reasonable price for students at Peita and periodically exhibited "the best results" in the Democratic Square. Invariably these results were pictures of "significant" scenes: files of Peita students on their way to the May Fourth celebration; the presentation of bouquets to honored Soviet guests; sidelights on daily student life such as collective *yang-ko* dancing, collective choral exercises, group discussions, and so on. It was true, however, that one of my friends who was a camera enthusiast confessed that he sometimes found it difficult to remember which parade was which when he got his pictures back from being developed.

Of all of the scenic beauties Coal Hill, behind the Forbidden City, was closest to our Sha-t'an compound. In the Kuomintang days the university had arranged with the authorities to let anyone who could produce a Peita University badge visit the place free of charge. Coal Hill, the tree-clad man-made hill where a Ming emperor had hanged himself under tragic and romantic circumstances, became almost our Peita garden. In the morning and after school·there were always more Peita students there than there were ordinary ticket buyers. After the Liberation the park was closed for a while for unannounced reasons. Then it was thrown open again; but now everybody had to pay the nominal admission charge, and a new reading room stocked with the new Communist books and newspapers had been set up in the hall facing the main gate.

At the end of the spring term in 1949 every student was called upon to write a paper about his political thinking, with special emphasis upon the remolding of his thoughts and the new ideas he had picked up at *hsueh-hsi*. First, the term paper was passed around among other students in the politics class to give them the opportunity of setting down their comments on the blank sheets attached to the back, then the writer was expected to read the report aloud in class for criticism and self-criticism. In one of these term papers a recent convert to the new faith declared:

"In the old days Coal Hill always intoxicated me by the magnificence of the view and the beauty of the architecture. The golden-glazed tiles glittering in the sun, the vermilion pillars fading with age into softer hues, the curved, mysterious gables seemed to me like immortal works of art where painting and poetry became one.

Every morning I walked uphill from the place where Emperor Szu of the Ming Dynasty had taken his life. All around me were the old pines, graceful and straight, their upward spray of branches fresh with morning dew. When I neared the pavilion at the summit, the matins of the sparrows sounded even more liquid and cheerful. I felt so free, so happy and at peace. . . ."

His voice took on a more militant note. "After I enrolled in the political class, my mind was in flux. My internal conflicts grew until now, at long last, I have finally struggled free of the grip of my old views. When I walk up Coal Hill now, a picture of the corrupt and dissipated life of the ancient emperors leaps vividly before my eyes. All of these pavilions, terraces, mansions, and bowers, I can see now, were built on the sweat, the blood, the labor of enslaved people for the entertainment of the ruling class. The more beautiful the scenery, the more violently it stirs my class hatred. Inflamed with righteous anger, I want to smash such pavilions and terraces, and to smash flat this green hill."

The Communists praised his summary in flattering terms, not for its literary merits, whatever they might be, but for the correct turn its author's mind had taken. Rejoicing in the success of the conversion, they declared that everybody handicapped by the "typical consciousness of the exploiting class" should change in similar fashion, for only in the eyes of backward people could such buildings resulting from exploitation seem pleasing. Perhaps they were right, although we might have liked to bring up the rumors that Chairman Mao was enjoying his own pleasure dome out in the Western Hills.

Several weeks after our visit to the Pei Hai, we got up another expedition to eat lunch on the steps of the White Dagoba on the scenic North Lake. As we lunched and chatted there on the steps, one of us noticed a man sitting by an ancient pine not very far away, with his back turned to us. The girl who first detected him whispered her discovery to the boy next to her; we were sure that there had been no one around when we first arrived, and we couldn't understand how the man could have come so close to us without being discovered. The Youth League man who was shepherding the expedition sensed there was something queer about the intruder. As the conversation died, he burst out with a loud: "Say, you people, last time when our class joined the parade for world peace, why couldn't you manage to hold your banners up straight? They flopped around so much, students behind us said it was almost comical."

The man sat there without stirring. I asked in a low voice, "Do you think there's something wrong with him?"

Nobody answered. So I said again, jokingly, "Maybe he's come here to sulk about his love affair or something."

Our leader shook his head at me to silence me. "We'd better get back a little early today," he told the group. "Remember, we have our Youth League meeting."

While we collected our lunch baskets we watched the stranger furtively. As we stood up, he got to his feet, looked at us without embarrassment and, turning his face away again, lighted a cigarette. We got a good look at him; he was about thirty, had curiously light-colored eyebrows, small eyes, a long face and sharp chin. Was he contemplating the landscape, I wondered, and becoming inspired by hate for the exploiting class? He tagged after us as we left the scene of our lunch.

But he dropped farther behind, until at last the Youth League leader turned around to find that he had vanished. He told us petulantly: "Hunh! What's the matter with that guy? I hinted as loud as I could that we were students, but it didn't register. Then I hinted again that some of us had already joined the Youth League. And he still didn't budge."

"He was certainly in a trance, miles away from anything. Of course, he didn't care what you were saying, League or no League." I was still obtuse and naïve, but, I hope, half intentionally so.

"Well it isn't that." The Youth League leader lowered his voice and spoke to me very seriously. "You see, we have only won the first big victory in our revolution. There are still plenty of counter-revolutionaries around, enemy agents who meet and discuss their plans in obscure corners. That's why we have to plant agents of our own in places like this, to watch out for such people. But that's no reason for him to be so stupid about recognizing that we're just students."

So that was the explanation—the boy from the Youth League was actually in the organization, and understood those things much better than we did. I remembered the people who had followed me around more than once in the parks, but I'd always dismissed them as the usual kind of tramps or loungers who try to follow a lone girl walking. But how many of these eccentrics had actually been "serving the people"? Now I remembered that other day on Coal Hill when I had stood looking at the view below, the golden-tiled roofs of the old imperial buildings, the gray one-story houses of the rest of Peiping, dotted with leafy clumps of fine old trees. I had looked around from the prospect to find a policeman in a black uniform marching toward me. He had looked me over from head to foot and then stood watching me until I got nervous and walked off, trying not to hurry. I understood now. He had apparently suspected that I was a "Nationalist agent" looking for a good corner to bury the time bomb I was carrying around in my bosom.

CHAPTER VIII

The Umbrella Garden

In trying to describe what happened to Peita in 1949 and 1950, I know that by concentrating on the changes in our life after the Liberation I run the danger of painting the picture in colors that are too dark. More thorough organization of our life did not mean unrelieved austerity by any means. Holidays were administered to us at regular intervals—"administered" is the word I want to use, because these holidays served as a kind of "nerve stimulant" injected deliberately, like vitamins, into what would have been an inadequate emotional life without them.

Red May Day started off the big procession of official festivals during the summer and fall of the Communist year. July 1st came next, the anniversary of the founding of the Chinese Communist Party in 1921. Then we celebrated August 1st, the birthday of the People's Liberation Army. October 1st is the new National Festival, celebrating the official founding of the People's Republic in 1949. Stalin's seventieth birthday, on December 21, 1949, which our papers told us was being hailed as a historic milestone all over the world, was greeted in Peking by two days of city-wide celebration with schoolgirls and schoolboys, university students, and ordinary people parading to the Soviet Embassy for speeches and presentation ceremonies.

Under the big red banners hanging from all government buildings and the smaller flags hanging out over shops and residences, the people of Peking paraded, chanted the slogans which had been printed a day or two in advance in all of the newspapers and, after they had been dismissed from the mass meetings, wandered in the parks, admired the elaborate decorations, and later on watched spectacular displays of fireworks. As he stood shoulder to shoulder with one hundred thousand of his fellow citizens in the new Red Square in front of the Gate of Heavenly Peace leading into the old Forbidden City, and listened to the voices of the speakers up on the balcony coming at him over the loudspeakers, even the reluctant householder who had been sent to the meeting by his street government felt a solidarity, an identity with the people around him, a sense of group power he had never felt before.

Filling the tremendous area embraced by the Red Square with people required detailed planning and painstaking organization. Among the ordinary people in the city, each family was expected to contribute at least one representative to each one of the mass celebrations. Policemen called at each house the day before to note down the name of the person or persons expecting to attend; several hours before the parade leaders selected by the street organization lined up the participants and called the roll to verify that each household was present. Though this means of ensuring that a respectable crowd turned out for each official celebration was carried over from the old government, it was marked by new efficiency in recruiting the involuntary marchers.

The police also continued their traditional job of arranging that the national flag flew from every shop and private house on such gala occasions. Their performance of this duty in the old days, I'm afraid, was often slipshod. On old holidays like the "Double Ten" (the 10th of October, date of the Wuchang uprising in 1911 and beginning of the first Chinese revolution, which used to be observed as our National Day), I could walk for blocks along one of the main streets and see only a sparse sprinkling of national flags, the red banners with the "white sun in a blue sky," discarded now in favor of the red flag with five small gold stars in the corner. But when the new flag was officially adopted just before October 1, 1949, policemen were sent out with armloads of flags and instructions to sell one to each household. The expected rumors arose, of course, about some policemen boosting the price of the flags above the official ceiling, but the cost was so small I'm sure they couldn't have made much profit even if they had tried.

Unlike less favored people, Peita students were not under any formal compulsion to go to parades and meetings. Few students, however, stayed away. We were more thoroughly organized than ordinary residents in the city, and could be counted upon for both discipline and controlled enthusiasm. For days before each scheduled festival, student leaders bustled from one meeting to the next, organizing the rest of us to draw cartoons, paint slogans and flags and pennants, practice the *yang-ko* dance, and rehearse the songs we would sing. It was difficult for any girl to say no when she was asked to help out. If you found a good excuse for turning down the "floor manager" in your dormitory living circle when she asked you to join the special women's chorus, your class leader would drop by the next afternoon to invite you to join the *yang-ko* team he was organizing with the plea that he was still two girls short. It was easier to accept the first invitation that came along, in order to avoid elaborate explanations to other eager organizers who were bound to ask you to help them. At first there was considerable competition among various groups, living circles, and classes to organize the different parts of a parade, but later on things became more efficient as the university authorities assigned each student group a specific task.

Because we were more enthusiastic than other classes of the population, we were invariably assigned a place of honor in front of the speakers' stand at the great city-wide mass meetings. Mass meetings like ours had to have organized noise, and as I've already mentioned we were probably better organized than any other group except for Party members themselves, who were scattered among the people they worked beside every day to encourage applause and cheering. In the parades to and from Red Square our behavior was also in contrast to that of the townspeople, who tended to shuffle along in ragged hit-or-miss fashion, quite apathetic to the urgings of their block leaders. We marched in solid ranks, chanting slogans or singing at the command of our leaders, who marched outside the column, white armbands on their sleeves to identify them. When the parade became snarled up ahead, and one unit bumped up against another's heels, the townspeople were likely to break out of line and sit on the curb or cluster around the itinerant hawkers of tea and peanuts until the police could shoo the vendors away. But we stayed in the center of the street when the column stopped, and performed the *yang-ko* for the onlookers, who gaped at our gyrations with what we hoped was some appreciation.

Certainly the *yang-ko* was the most colorful part of the parade. Its methodical drum beat and cymbal clash, *Chang, Chang! Chichang-chi!* formed the basic rhythm of the new People's festivals as long caterpillars of students threaded through the streets to the emphatic beat. Anybody could follow the basic step, three steps forward and a single step back, with the sole of the foot striking the ground first. To punctuate the rhythm we lifted our knees and exaggerated the length of our strides, flailing our arms out ahead of us and back again like the turning blades of a windmill. Thus the customary phrase "wriggling the *yang-ko*." We could perform it either in a long serpentine line, twisting slowly along the street, or around and around in a circle while marchers ahead and behind us halted.

Before the Liberation we never wore costumes while dancing. Even on the most important occasions the men simply wrapped handkerchiefs around their heads, while the women put on sashes. In their uniforms or Western-style pants and field jackets the male students strode back and forth to the sound of the gongs and the drums, wriggling about in their heavy shoes, trying without success to imitate peasant women with tiny bound feet. After the Liberation the *yang-ko* became a gay spectacle; men and women alike put on turbans, short jackets, long trousers, silk sashes around their waists, and cloth slippers—all in bright hues such as red, green, yellow, and blue. We women also covered our faces with thick layers of powder and rouge, painted our cheeks so that they looked as red as over-ripe apples, and drew dazzlingly scarlet mouths with lipstick so that we looked like performers in the classical Peking opera come down from the stage into the light of day. At night, as we danced around bonfires or torches, we did not look so much like peasant women as we did like passionate girls from the southern part of the country. The men, too, smeared rouge on their faces, penciled on heavy artificial eyebrows, and tried to mince daintily in their bright, soft slippers.

Later an attempt was made to make the *yang-ko* take on a more genuinely proletarian look. We were told to appear in clean blue overalls instead of our bright trousers and sashes so that we would look like factory girls, and men students were asked to wrap clean towels around their heads to make sweat turbans such as peasants wear in the fields. Then we cut imitation hammers, flails, sickles, hoes, and other tools out of cardboard to brandish aloft to show our identity with the working masses while we danced. City-bred boys who couldn't tell a stalk of *kao-liang* from a sheaf of wheat cut huge slices out of the air with their cardboard sickles, while we girls swung our hammers with a violence that would have demolished anything they might have landed upon. To any real workers or peasants in the crowds who watched us, we must have looked singularly innocent with our new, spotless overalls and our flimsy paper mockeries of tools. But we enjoyed the show and danced with a will, although we still would have preferred the theatrically bright clothes we had made for ourselves just after the Liberation.

Some of the innovations we made in the planting dance eventually ran afoul of the Communist sense of moral propriety. In June of 1949 an editorial in the *Chin Pu Jih Pao* (Progressive Daily) clucked piously about the "excesses" which had appeared in the *yang-ko*. The Municipal General Labor Association had already ordered workers under its control to drop several practices in celebrating the dance. Such traditional characters as Buddhist and Taoist priests could no longer be represented because they were "feudalistic and superstitious." Men dancers were ordered not to dress up as girls, while more moderation was called for in the use of cosmetics both by men and by women. Our leaders called these rules to our notice, and our performances began to show more restraint.

Although it seldom rains in Peking, the organizers of parades and meetings ran into an unusual streak of bad luck with the weather. In their first big formal parade, in February, 1949, the troops of Lin Piao had brought the countryside along with them in the form of a choking dust storm carried on a blustery wind which somehow managed to insinuate the yellow grains inside your eyelids and up inside your nose. The mass meetings we attended that spring and summer seemed to call down upon our heads either a drenching rain or, worse, a ghastly and depressing drizzle which seeped in through your clothing without making you decently wet. Students who had worked for days to organize a good show stood in their sopping wet shoes behind their red flags, which dripped higgledy-piggledy on their poles. The red lanterns that we had pasted together so carefully the rain now reduced to bamboo skeletons like unclean bird cages with forlorn scrapes of paper clinging to the ribs. Our posters with their bold characters brushed on by our best writers turned sodden, and our slogans blurred and then melted as the ink smeared and ran down to the edges.

Superstitious shopkeepers and people from the country among the bystanders who huddled under the rain or the blowing dust storms probably were whispering that the heavens were displeased, that the "mandate of heaven" was being withdrawn from the new government. But we students kept up our stubborn front. We stood solidly and impassively under the downpour, marched with the same discipline we would have displayed under the sun, and continued to sing louder than anybody else, if only to keep our spirits up. Once, in pouring rain, a troop of students over to our left burst suddenly into a loud: "In the liberated lands the weather is fair, and the people—ah, how happy are the people! The People's Government loves its people—and the favors of the Communist Party are too many to be told." If they had careful ears, our leaders on the balcony looking down on us might have heard some slight note of satire in the chorus.

When a shower swept over Red Square and pelted down, it always brought confusion upon the meeting. Once in the square, nobody could leave—unless he fainted or broke a leg. But while no one quite had the courage to violate the formations or disturb the order in the meeting, many people did spontaneously open their umbrellas. It must have made an impressive spectacle to those on the leaders' balcony—thousands of green- and black-lacquered umbrellas blooming like miraculous flowers at the first touch of rain.

In order to show our spirit, however, most of us from Peita refused to carry umbrellas or to cover our heads with our jackets when it started to come down. Instead we stood with our faces up, letting the icy water stream down our backs from our neighbors' umbrellas until our hair and clothing were plastered to our skin. It wouldn't have been proper for us to have taken off our outer garments and wrung them out to dry. But there was usually a breeze after the rain, and the sun to warm us up. By the time the dignitaries high up on the top of Tien An Gate had finished their speeches, our bodies had usually emitted enough heat to dry out our uniforms. Any remaining moisture would certainly evaporate during the parade afterward when we sang, yelled slogans, ran, and danced the *yang-ko*.

Later we might be drafted to go along with our comrades to conduct propaganda in one of the *hu-tungs* (side streets) or to sing around a bonfire for the entertainment of the townspeople. Customarily, it would be about nine or ten o'clock at night before we got back to our dormitory, a long time from the moment when we'd started off fresh and energetic at eight in the morning. We all slept like the dead the night after one of these affairs, and the next day, with aching muscles and tired feet, greeted each other like wan survivors just back from a two-day orgy.

We all realized, of course, that the parades were easier to go to than to stay away from. The individualists, the lazy, the earnest students who turned down the invitations to participate and stayed behind to loaf or study on these holidays were never more than 10 per cent of the student body. They were the argumentative or the indifferent who didn't mind facing the rest of us at the weekly criticism meetings.

One of the few real arguments we ever had in one of these self-criticism meetings happened after one of my classmates named Betty Chang stayed away from the July 1st meeting in honor of the birthday of the Chinese Communist Party. Betty, a pretty, rather vain and shallow-minded girl, preferred the foreign name she'd given herself to her real Chinese one; most of us liked her without considering her very important. Her critics wasted no time in getting down to business.

"In not joining the parade, Miss Chang clearly revealed her free, undisciplined, petty bourgeois way of living. . . ." This was the opening round of the salvo.

But Betty, to our surprise, bristled up. "It's not really that I didn't want to join," she began. Then her voice got heated: "But what's the point of all of this business of meetings and parades and more meetings? We all go and we all spend seven or eight or maybe even more than ten hours standing on our feet or marching or singing. And the next day we're just too tired out to work. Maybe it's just a waste of time, just a drawback to our real work."

In a way this was comical, coming from Betty, who had more time for boys than for books. I was sure that whatever she had remained behind for, she hadn't stayed home to study. She wasn't the ideal spokesman, but perhaps she had a point.

"Waste of time!" The Youth League member who had been interrupted in his criticism of Betty stuttered at this frank heresy. He held in his anger and tried to gloss over it. "But—these meetings have such tremendous educational significance! Waste of time, you say? Why that's—"

"Well, if I spent that ten hours reading I'd certainly get more out of it than ten hours of jostling other people in a crowd." I couldn't imagine Betty reading anything for ten hours, but we all leaned forward to hear the answer.

"That's a very superficial approach to the problem." The Youth League man was doing his best to keep his temper in check, a fortunate thing for Betty. "We know, and you should know, that every meeting we go to has a special significance, and that whatever it is about it always displays the growth and consolidation of the might of the people. Your absence shows that in your heart you do not respect the might of the people, or that maybe you even despise it. Examine yourself, Miss Chang. Check up on your thoughts! Then, perhaps, you'll be able to criticize yourself properly."

The might of the people, of course, could not be offended. Betty could not say that she did not respect it. Though she was in hot water, she refused her chance to climb out. "Anyway, it seems to me there is no need to waste so much time. Just think of it! Every time, tens of thousands of people have to appear, each giving up most of a whole day. Certainly a tremendous number of things could be accomplished in these hundreds of thousands of working hours."

"Let me explain why we must take part in these mass meetings." Our Communist leader had held himself outside the debate until now. "In the first place, as our comrade from the Youth League has mentioned, every mass meeting has a special and important meaning. You must participate in order to convince people that you support that particular meeting. Second, at every mass meeting we should learn valuable knowledge. Aren't the speakers all leaders of our people, possessed of profound political knowledge and rich practical experience? We should congratulate ourselves on having the chance to learn from them, the chance to absorb a small fraction of their knowledge and experience! It is an even greater opportunity than the political courses here in the university, and it should not be allowed to slip by.

"Third, we must understand the direction toward which our new society is tending. Our new society is on the road to over-all collectivism—along with collective production and collective learning we must move toward collective living. Joining a mass meeting of tens of thousands of people can help us develop habits of collective living, make us feel the power and the might of the people when we all stand there together. Think it over—those of you who begrudge your time. Miss Chang, how do you feel about it now?"

Betty was silenced by superior forces. The Communist waited patiently for an answer. Hsueh, the bright progressive whose eloquent summing up always seemed to please our leaders, stepped in to resolve the deadlock. "Under the mighty Tien An Gate," he rhapsodized, "tens of thousands of our people gather before Chairman Mao. The citizens of Peking have collected from every street, from every alley, from every house, from every shop, from every school, from every public building. Red flags are fluttering from the walls, from the lofty stand, from the monster crowd itself. Gongs and drums lend their voices to our songs; gay laughter resounds everywhere; the praise of our leaders is on every lip." It went on and on like extemporaneous poetry. "All of us should want to go just to see the stirring scene. It is reward enough. Doesn't your heart beat faster when you see our people standing there, when you see the discipline, when you see the organization, the whole demonstration of strength? Comrades, when the thoughtful man or woman sees a mass meeting he should realize even more keenly than before that the Communist Party did not come to power by words and promises alone." Hsueh's oration was almost too good; it was a very unwise thing to do if he was trying to pull somebody's leg. But he couldn't have been, I suppose. At least, the other progressives smiled and applauded, and the Party people present looked pleased and a little proud.

Much of what the Party man and the progressive said was true on the face of it. Even for those of us who had begun to surrender to a few quiet doubts, the meetings and the parades offered us a chance to renew the faith. In the impersonal noise and heat of the crowd, we could submerge our doubts and forget our personal difficulties in adjusting to the new life we had entered upon. While the red flags waved, the songs rose, and the gongs and drums beat their rhythms, even the doubters could believe. For us students, standing straighter than the rest, with our faces turned up toward our leaders, there was even a perverse pleasure in our discomfort when the dust storms blew or the cold drain dripped down.

CHAPTER IX

Sweat and Prayer

To be honest about it, Peita was always backward in athletics. We didn't mind; it didn't make much difference to most of us. After all, Peita was a place for things of the mind rather than for things either of the body or the "spirit." Some of us thought that it was almost as admirable to lag behind in foreign-style sports as it was to keep the campus free of the various foreign religious influences evident in several rival universities.

After the victory over Japan, Peita did make a gesture toward the "modern" Western concept of physical education by asking freshmen to devote two hours a week to supervised exercise. The next year, to emphasize the new concern for sports, the school authorities required sophomores to take physical training too. But older students remained free of such compulsion.

The physical-training courses for freshmen and sophomores used to be worth going to just as spectacles. At the first meeting the teachers would toot on their whistles to round up their charges, and then explain to the students clustered around them that university regulations forbade students to miss more than one-third of the classes during a semester. Anybody who did not want to come, of course, might do as he pleased, but it was imperative for him to remember how many times he had cut class lest he miss more than one-third of the sessions and so embarrass the instructor. Mightily displeased with this bad news, his listeners protested with boos and catcalls. The teacher waited until the chorus of displeasure died down and then mumbled, "Well, if you miss a few more I suppose no great damage will be done." Standing there in his shorts and singlet, he looked cowed and discouraged despite his muscles; most of the boys tolerated him as a well meaning but simple-minded acrobat with no real culture.

I don't want to give you the impression that our physical training was an unbearable punishment. By no stretch of the imagination could it be called very strenuous. The ranks were always dismissed after roll call to permit students to divide up for basketball, volleyball, soccer, or baseball—whatever game they liked. If you didn't happen to be in a mood to perspire while chasing a ball around that day, you might sit on a bench on the edge of the field with a couple of friends for a quiet chat. The most your teacher could do was to glare at you with helpless disapproval.

But at the end of each term, we faced the same reckoning we faced in the classes we held in higher esteem. There had to be an examination—just as there has to be an election in the USSR. The men's examination consisted of three special tests of each student's speed and stamina. The baseball throw was the first. A target about one *chang* (11 feet) in diameter was painted on a wall. Each contestant had to back off a distance of four or five *chang* and try to hit the big bull's-eye with a baseball. Each student got five tries. Some of my friends, I regret to say, missed every time.

The second test, basket shooting, required the examinee to dribble the ball from the center of the court down to one basket. After sinking a basket at one end, we had to dribble back to the other end, put the ball through the hoop there, retrieve it, and dribble back to the center of the court while a stopwatch measured the time required. With the whole class to grade, the basketball test usually made the period run overtime. Some students took two minutes or more and racked the onlookers with impatience.

The last event, the one-hundred-meter dash, was the greatest fun of the whole program. On warm days in late spring, the bright sun made the contestants too languid to care about winning. Winter was just as bad; no intelligent man was going to work up a lather of perspiration and then face the chance of taking cold by standing around to watch his friends perspire too. In one race a friend of mine started off the mark at the signal with the others, dressed, like most of his rivals, in his cotton-padded gown and fur cap, with his woolen muffler trailing behind him. One runner wore a foreign-style topcoat buttoned up to his ears, and another had bundled himself inside a wool-lined khaki jacket. Chatting and joking, their hands tucked inside their sleeves for warmth, they made the impatient timer wait so long at the finish line that he could only shake his head in silent despair. The time of the winner, who wasn't my friend, incidentally, was something over twenty seconds. It was some sort of world record, at least, my friend told me when he came back to pick me up.

Peita, remember, was descended from the old "Capital Academy," whose students had been selected by national examinations as candidates for the dignified profession of governing the nation. Like earlier "mandarins in training," Peita students of my generation cherished the "great intellectual tradition," and believed it was below their academic dignity to scamper about like children chasing kites.

Some students at Peita, of course, did not care as much as these young "mandarins" did for personal dignity. Every clear afternoon saw games under way on the basketball and volleyball courts, although only a fraction of the school population played often enough to get any real benefit from regular exercise. It is not quite accurate, either, to say that all freshmen and sophomores joined the physical-training classes. The university doctor was liberal about certifying students as unfit to participate in such strenuous exertion and they were automatically excused.

If you were not interested in the ball games imported by the "foreign devils," you could always join the "Chinese boxing section," where experts engaged by the university taught the Shao-lin and T'ai-chi schools. Chinese boxing is more like "shadow-boxing" than it is like Western-style combat directed against a physical opponent. While energetic, it is characterized more by stylized grace and poise than by actual violence. On winter afternoons you would come upon small groups of students practicing such graceful and deliberate gestures as "scooping up fish" under the tutelage of an expert.

Peita also boasted several athletic associations which regularly challenged teams from other schools to basketball and volleyball contests. The Titan Athletic Club, a survival of more strenuous days during the war when Peita had joined other refugee universities in forming Southwest Union University, met the Tsinghua team periodically in volleyball. But despite our cheers it was more often than not the loser. The North Star Athletic Club was a somewhat larger association, but only a few of its scores of members were real athletes. Instead of sport, the real end of this group was to serve as concealment for underground political activities under the Nationalist Government. When large numbers of Communist and progressive elements deserted the campus and crossed the lines to the other side, during the last months before the Liberation, the North Star Club lost four out of every five members. Therefore the group died a natural death, which was only proper, for it had accomplished its purpose. For a time we also had a T'i-ch'un basketball team, consisting entirely of tall Northerners, quite well versed in the game. Later, however, the North Star Club "infiltrated" and absorbed this team as its own creation.

With the Liberation, healthful physical exercise rapidly began to play a more important role in our lives. Our new leaders exhibited a concern for building healthy bodies by mass exercise never dreamed of by our school authorities in the old days of *laissez faire* —or rather of *may-yo fa-tse*, or, "Well, it can't be helped." Perhaps the new emphasis upon physical conditioning was partially in compensation for our more restricted diet, and certainly the vast majority of students didn't appreciate it. But, undeniably, it was good for us young "mandarins" to sweat like ordinary people.

Before things really got organized systematically, the most

popular new form of exercise was the drum dance, which is not to be confused with the *yang-ko*, or planting dance. The drum dance involved a double row of men and women students, clad in short garments, lined up on the Peita drill field. Drumsticks poised above red-painted drums hanging from our waists, we thumped away on the stretched parchment drumheads, took a stride, wheeled about-face, and turned again in imitation of our physical-training instructors. After a year's training, however, few of us could play a complete series of flourishes. Most students knew only the simplest, elementary theme: *Thump, thump! Thump, thump, thump!* "You there—about-face!" *Thumpety, thumpety, thump!* "You—kick out your leg and land out on your foot!" Or, as an extra flourish, you kicked your leg high while you reached around down under your thigh and gave the bottom of the drum a hearty whack. It was scarcely swanlike, but it was energetic. One of our leaders commented to me with enthusiasm that it was "fine discipline for getting us to do things together. Rhythm, you know, is a group thing, a cement to bind us closer together." It was the only time I heard anybody waxing poetic about the drum dance.

Later on, all Peking schools were officially called upon to institute a more systematic method of mass physical training with the announced goal of hardening the bodies of students and building up their strength to prepare them for active service for their government. This was our introduction to arm-waving group calisthenics performed at the shouted commands of a drill leader. The most unpopular fact about this innovation was the time appointed for our drill. We were called out in front of our dormitories at seven every morning for a session before most of us were really awake, so that we went off to our first class feeling the dried perspiration sticky inside our clothes.

The stretching and arm swinging, the push-ups, the hopping and bending and squatting at the call of our leaders were described as "new Soviet-style physical conditioning." While these contortions did superficially resemble the exercises conducted in other armies, we were told, Soviet scientists had added new "progressive movements" to the repertoire which were largely responsible for ensuring that the soldiers of the Red Army were in better physical trim than troops in more backward nations. This was not the best propaganda in the world for us; there were mumblings of, "But we're not in the army yet."

For our younger brothers physical training was reorganized in the middle schools to make sure that graduates would be in better shape if they were called into the nation's expanding military forces. Baseball, which had been fairly popular after the war, but still sec ondary to volleyball and soccer, was neglected for a while by the new authorities as an American game. But it was soon revived when the authorities discovered in it certain "military values." New stress was put on the baseball throw with a missile shaped like a crude grenade substituted for the old softball. Track and field now emphasized the steeplechase for endurance and the running broad jump and high jump for agility. New tests were introduced in rope climbing and ladder scaling, useful for any later military training. Such strenuous feats were reserved for the men, of course; girls joined in the drum dance and in the group calisthenics but were excused from the quasi-military types of activity. At Peita we women did practice marching for the parades, naturally, and presented a militant spectacle which made a fine subject for photographs sent abroad for foreign consumption.

Sometimes we heard of more spectacular sports practiced by the army: motorcycle racing, bayonet races, leaps from high platforms, and parachute jumping. Somebody in the dormitory whose home was in Hankow read a letter to us from her brother telling about the exhibition staged at a sports show in that city by the postmen, who formed a gigantic bicycle brigade. They must have practiced for days to accomplish the feats they performed: with pennants flying from their handlebars they circled around holding hands in a serpentine chain to form the giant characters reading "Kung-ch'an-tang Wan-sui," literally, "The Chinese Communist Party, Ten Thousand Years"—our equivalent of "Forever!"

Like physical recreation, religion had never played an important role in the lives of Peita students. Just as a few zealots pursued a ball around a tennis court, so a few zealots pursued the welfare of their souls, while the rest of us looked on with comfortable indifference. In fact, it was popular among freethinking students absorbed in political issues to dismiss religion as a "curious mixture of cowardice, reformism, and escapism," a long phrase, but only a mouthful for an enthusiastic young revolutionary.

Most of us were more tolerant, although we naturally looked upon ourselves as intellectually superior to the devoted followers of assorted religious faiths on the campus. One of our native religions, Taoism, which has degenerated from its great days, we regarded as a remnant superstition fit only for uneducated peasants. Belief in Buddhism could seldom be found among our students. To admit "I believe in the Buddha" would have sounded almost as incredible as "I believe in Zoroaster," and would have provoked the same amused smile.

We had a scattering of Moslems in our midst, who clung to their peculiarity of preparing their own food and eating apart from the rest of us. On holidays, when we were served better dishes, they would not even deign to look at the fragrant potted pork, which I think we probably cook in more tasty fashion than anyone else. I heard that the followers of Mohammed had their own doctrines, commandments, and institutions. But they carried on no organized religious activities at all on the campus, attempted to win no converts, and would never explain their faith to other students who were curious. If we kept on asking why they followed the precepts of Mohammed, the first and last reply we got was simply: "My ancestors were Moslems. We've believed in it for centuries."

Among the rival Christian sects, the Catholics could have given the same answer, for their faith had often been passed along from generation to generation. They knew, however, a complete catechism of replies to our questions, and made a point of having ready answers on hand. Every Sunday morning they declined all invitations to go bicycling or to walk to the Pei Hai, set aside their favorite reading, and went off to church. They were devout, but for most of them their religion was centered in their own souls.

The Protestants were perhaps more active in campus affairs. But their number was so small that they could not hope to have any real influence upon the rest of us. They did have a fellowship, which failed to arouse any marked attention among the non-Christians. The Christians, I suppose, were individualists, and thus could not communicate to the rest of us the emotions they said were deep in their souls.

This was the status of religion at Peita. The situation was quite different at some of the other schools, as we discovered when we visited friends at those universities under the influence of missionaries from abroad. Besides the religious subjects, some of the other courses were tinged with a religious point of view, and some classes were taught by ordained priests or clergymen. Though students who objected to the religious tinge to their studies were not punished, the school authorities did not give up their quiet attempt to gain converts. Non-religious students, therefore, gradually abandoned their hostility. A certain predictable share of them, in fact, would eventually be converted and accept baptism. Although there were not many extracurricular religious activities to capitalize on students' free time, visitors noticed an imperceptible religious atmosphere pervading the campus—a picture of Jesus or a religious motto hung in the waiting hall, an image of the Crucifixion or a portrait of the Mother of Christ in rooms in the Catholic schools. The old servant on the floor of the dormitory my friend lived in at Fu Jen University was gentle, courteous, and obliging. With a cross swinging from his neck, he would tell you while sweeping the floor how much he had suffered before baptism and how the Christian God protected and blessed him now. The celebrations during Christmas and Easter were big events at these schools. We didn't believe what our friends believed, but we granted them the right to their faith and acknowledged their honest happiness in celebrating the feast days of their religion.

Most of these Christian friends were as anxious to display their advanced political stand as the rest of us when the Liberation came, while they greeted with satisfaction the provision in Mao Tse-tung's Common Program providing for "freedom of religion." A few of these saintly souls had read the passage in Chairman Mao's *New Democracy* which stated, "We Communists may form a united front with some idealists or even followers of religion for concerted political action, but we certainly cannot approve of their idealism or their religious doctrines." They felt, however, that they could reconcile their own faith with their support of the new government which promised so much, particularly since prominent "progressive" church leaders had hailed its coming in glowing terms. Therefore they continued to go to mass meetings and parades to pay homage to our new leaders, and then trotted off to church on Sunday.

They enjoyed a six months' period of grace before they were forced to defend their faith. But at the end of this interval, at special symposia organized at Peita to study "the religious problem," the faithful heard their religion become the target of attack for the first time.

Lenin's famous dismissal of religion was quoted: "Religion is the opium of the people. Religion is a kind of spiritual gin in which the slaves of capital drown their human shape and their claims to any decent human life."

After more quotations amplifying this, the verdict of the party comrades present was announced. "Religion is unscientific, superstitious, reformist, unrealistic, effeminate, dope for the people. . . ."

At the second symposium a student speaker explained the religious activities tolerated in the Soviet Union as an illustration of the truth of Lenin's dictum.

"Now, although a few chapels still survive in the Soviet Union, and quite a few people, I admit, do go there to 'worship,' as they call it, these devotees are all old and ignorant." He paused to let this sink in. "This simply shows that the older generation has not managed to shake off the influence of the old society and that religious and reactionary ideas have not been completely wiped out of their minds. The new generation, however, is different. They have received the Marxist-Leninist education of the new era—and they certainly will never believe any more in religion. Therefore—" Now the climax was at hand. "Therefore, when this group of old people die, religion will disappear for good from the Soviet Union."

An ovation came from Party and Youth League people scattered among us in the hall.

On the same evening my friend from Fu Jen University took me out for a stroll so that we could talk about what we were being told. (This was in 1949; a year later, in 1950, she would have been afraid to trust me or anybody else with private doubts and questions.) She had read in one of her religious magazines, she told me, how the Soviet attempt in 1924 to weed out religion, to close the churches, and burn the devotional books had run into so much resistance among the peasants that worship had not been stamped out. The article also claimed that Stalin had been forced during the last World War to open up some long-shut churches in order to hold the loyalty of the people he ruled, and that young soldiers and workers had knelt beside old people at the services. Why, she asked, did Stalin have to throw open the chapels and let people sip "this spiritual gin for the slaves of capital" again? After all, thirty years ago, when the Russian Communist Party seized power and imposed the Communist brand of education in all Russian schools, the "old people" of today hadn't been so very old. Why, after thirty years in the "new society," did they still disobey the will of their beloved leader and persist in observing their religious faith? Why hadn't Stalin, with the power we knew he had, been able to suppress or exterminate religion altogether?

I didn't know why. Perhaps some people were built so that they had to believe in something more impressive than themselves, whether it was Buddha or Christ or Mohammed or Mao Tse-tung or Stalin. It was a complicated question—that was about all I could think of to reply—perhaps even more complicated than her religious magazines would admit. "Well," she persisted, "if religion is really the opium of the people, it seems to me conditions in Russia can't be as good as they say they are if Stalin has had to open up places where people can smoke it under state guidance."

I wasn't prepared to be as candid as she was. "I've never been to Russia," I said. "All I know comes from what I've read in the magazines and what we hear at school."

"But if religion is what they call it, escapism, it means there must be something that religious people are escaping from?" She was determined to come to some sort of answer. "What I'd like to know is, what are they escaping from now in the Soviet Union?"

While we walked, I repeated again that I didn't know enough about the Soviet Union to have a scientific opinion. "But perhaps the will to believe is something you can't stamp out. You can only try to channel it to the right object. And the will to escape, too; you can only provide some more attractive way of doing it." We settled the matter by stopping at the next hawker's stall and buying a handful of peanuts wrapped in a newspaper.

My private opinion, I suppose, was that in thirty years of trying, the Soviet leaders had learned that the religious impulse peculiar to the Russian people could not be completely exterminated and that all-out persecution might actually promote its existence underground. But our own leaders were still in the 1924 period.

Thus the signal was given for the descent on organized religion. The period of cooperation was over; organized religion was now recognized as a possible competitor of the state and was scheduled to be broken up and then reorganized. Foreign imperialism could scarcely be blamed for the purely Chinese secret religious societies which had branched off from our own traditional religions, but they were rooted out now with a violence that dismayed us. Newspaper publicity told how leaders had preyed on the superstitions of gullible followers, how they had committed illegal acts, how leaders had raped and stolen, how popular demand had forced the government to take ruthless action against them. (We also speculated that perhaps these societies had been resisting some of the policies of the government in the rural areas.)

The Buddhist and Taoist faiths were already under attack as superstition and as a means of exploiting the masses. We began to hear reports about the confiscation of temples and the forced return of monks and nuns to secular life. Stories began to appear in the newspapers about nuns voluntarily abandoning their seclusion to engage in production on behalf of the masses, just as the prostitutes were said to be reforming themselves through productive labor. It seemed a little incongruous to bracket nuns and prostitutes, but perhaps it was the Communist intention to so lump together all groups engaged in "unproductive" activities.

The foreign religions came in for their share of abuse. Catholicism was the chief target as the single largest organized group. Priests and sisters were accused of incredible crimes, with foreigners sentenced and deported and Chinese sent to prison. Many missionary schools were "taken over" in the name of the people. Control of administration at Fu Jen Catholic University was taken out of the hands of the Catholic authorities. Out in the country, we heard, missions were losing their churches. The government unsheathed a new weapon from its arsenal, the weapon of freedom of anti-religion. If you must argue that people had to have the freedom of faith and religion, well, all right—they had to have the freedom of anti-religion, too. When mobs were incited to invade rural churches, to loot them and then to set fire to them, the local military government refused to interfere. After all, didn't the authorities have to sympathize with these attacks since they represented the will of the masses? The authorities certainly had to safeguard the right to violence if they intended to uphold the freedom to oppose religion.

In the face of this campaign, even the few religious groups which had once shown some signs of life at Peita withered now into complete silence. The more courageous and the more devout continued to attend services and to practice their faith. But the services were reduced to dim, flickering affairs in candlelight, attended by a handful of the really dedicated. Catholic priests and sisters were compelled to move off the campus. Choirs were disbanded; after all, if these people wanted to sing, plenty of other opportunities would be provided. Some Christian students lashed out into furious denunciations of their former thoughts and actions in an effort to get back into official favor, declared their resolution to learn from the people, and their determination to cease serving the imperialists and their cultural aggression. Such people were not greeted with enthusiasm, particularly since some of us knew that behind their own doors they continued to kneel and pray. As far as we were concerned, they were the real "rice Christians," who followed the trail of rice back to the state. There would be a place for them, they recognized, when it became evident that the state would allow some religious services to continue as window dressing—as long as the services were conducted as political classes which would subordinate religion to "serving the people."

We non-Christians had mixed feelings about the whole campaign. We didn't like many of the foreign missionaries, whom we regarded as opportunists leading a more comfortable life than they could lead at home, while feeling smugly superior to us and our culture. Others, of course, had been quite good teachers and doctors, even for those who accepted their professional services but not their faith. These people were lumped in among the others without discrimination, and in some cases, I suspect, actually attacked more violently because their reputation among us was good. We did find it hard to swallow the stories about the nuns and the thousands of babies they murdered. The orphanages, we knew very well, had been a convenient place for mothers to abandon their weak or unwanted children. It wouldn't have taken much effort on the part of the nuns to slay such babies, many of whom were in a dying condition when brought in. However, we were aware that the story was not intended for us, but for the ignorant, who, as the ignorant must be in other lands, are credulous of old-wives' tales about ogres and monsters from foreign nations.

Apart from this somewhat detached dismay, the campaign against religious faith touched us only as stories in the newspapers and pictures in the magazines. But the new physical hardening program was different. It involved everybody, and nobody liked it, except those stern individuals who prided themselves on the physical rigors they could endure. But it must have pleased one group of people at least. It must have given the instructors we had harassed for so many years infinite pleasure now to stand in front of us and watch the dignified young "mandarins" who had taken twenty seconds to stroll 100 meters a year ago flailing their arms desperately and bobbing up and down, red-faced and sweating, to the shouts of demanding drill leaders.

CHAPTER X

We Close Ranks

"Shall we make Peita into a recreation hall, perhaps a rendezvous for a few men of culture, or a training center for revolutionary cadres?" This question was asked by Ho Kan-chih, one of the Communists' favorite authorities on Marxism. It is a rhetorical question; it answers itself.

Despite all the changes in our daily life, it took us some time to realize what the People's Study Aids, the self-criticism meetings, the political classes, the increasing regimentation of our everyday existence were intended to turn the university into. Not many of us realized that the first semester under the Communists was little more than a period of exploration which gave our new leaders a chance to learn more about us.

But at the beginning of the new school year, in the fall of 1949, things began to take on clearer shape. The Communist cadres sent to Peita had enjoyed six months' observation in which to select those students likely to help them, and from experience with living groups, self-criticism meetings, and other testing grounds they were ready to apply effective techniques for coping with natural independence of youth.

To carry out their plans for us, these cadres had to gain control of three phases of our life: what we did in our regular academic classes, what we did in the new political classes, and what we did with ourselves outside the classroom. I have already described how students who lived in the dormitories were assigned very early in the game to living circles consisting of from five to ten students from adjacent rooms. These circles were linked in turn into "floor groups" which themselves made up a dormitory union. All these individual dormitories next were organized into the all-dormitory council which could control all of the living circles we started with.

Control over us during regular class periods was imposed by breaking each class down into "mutual-aid circles" of five to ten students. Over these circles stood the class organization responsible for all students of the same year majoring in one subject. Each class organization had a full set of officers: an administrative manager and his assistant, a study manager, a welfare manager, and a business manager. These officers got their orders from the departmental council formed of the four classes in a particular subject or department. This council had another set of officers, of course.

Several modifications of this pattern appeared when the authorities organized the new political classes. Since these subjects were "universal" (that is, compulsory for all students), the classes were enormous, usually containing about two hundred students drawn from several departments. The classes were divided into sections, and the sections into squads, each under the command of a chairman and vice chairman. Down at the bottom again, each squad was divided into mutual-aid circles.

The mutual-aid circle was something like a Party cell except that it usually included only one Party or Youth League member. Perhaps I should say, rather, that it was more like a squad of soldiers with six or eight privates and one stern corporal. For the Party or Youth League member naturally ran things. He called meetings and did his best to answer the questions that popped up during our discussions. He also had to check up on us to make sure that we had all given enough time to our required outside reading. His most important duty, however, was to maintain a close watch on the personal life of each member of his circle and observe vigilantly the development of his thinking. He had to make detailed reports in writing on the daily activities of each one of his charges, a responsibility he could not afford to take lightly.

In no way did the new student organizations resemble the old clubs and class unions, which had been little more than an arena in which ambitious and popular students scrambled for the prestige that election to class office would bring. Instead, these new organizations were part of the machinery to weld Peita students into a tightly disciplined group ready to play whatever role it was called upon to take in the People's Democratic Dictatorship. All of our officers were chosen by the new system of "democratic centralism" instead of by the old-fashioned means of popular vote. In theory democratic centralism was supposed to enable the individuals at the bottom of the structure to register their will through a chain of bigger and better organizations until their mandate reached the top of this inverted pyramid of power. With Party and Youth League men in all strategic posts of leadership, we found out that it meant in practice that commands could be very efficiently transmitted down from the top.

It required time and hard work to hammer this machine together; but once the gears were all meshed no individual student could hope to escape his obligations as a citizen of New China. Suppose you were a third-year student in the Department of Western Languages and Literature living in one of the men's dormitories. To begin with, you would belong to your mutual-aid circle within the junior class. You would be a member of the junior class organization, of course, and a member also of the all-department union. That takes care of your regular academic studies. Now in your political classes you would belong to another mutual-aid circle. You would also have to go to meetings of the squad made up of three mutual-aid circles. To discuss really important matters your squad would join four or five others in a section meeting.

When you went back to the dormitory in the evening, you might have to attend a meeting of your living circle with your next-door neighbors. You also belonged to your floor group and to the dormitory union. Like all Peita students, you would have to join the Student Union. If you did not want to be accused of "isolationism," it would be a good idea to join the department chorus. If you belonged to the Youth League, you belonged to your cell, your branch office (one in each college of the university), and the main "trunk" office. Count them up: you belonged to exactly thirteen different groups. Of course, if you were at all active, you might also belong to the Library Club, a special political discussion group or something else.

The Communists introduced the new political classes ahead of any really thorough attempt to reform the old academic curriculum. Perhaps the theory was that after we had been heavily dosed with Marxism it would be much easier to enlist our cooperation in pushing the reforms through. At first we gave only nine hours a week to our political studies, three hours to lectures, three hours to group discussion, and three hours to homework. In addition, we were also called out on Saturday morning to hear special lectures by political big shots who came to the campus to elaborate on what we were supposed to be studying.

We were expected to take painstaking notes of what each of our political teachers told us and to carry our notes to the mutual-aid circles for discussion. Some of our teachers, I am afraid, spent more time discussing "historical materialism" (which turned out to be their own revolutionary experience) than they did "dialectical materialism," which is the heart of Marxist theory. Perhaps they were timid about discussing theory until it had been more clearly defined for them. But I can assure you that they were most eloquent in describing their own contributions to the revolutionary struggle.

The Saturday-morning lectures by important visitors were always held in the Democratic Square, the only place offering enough room. We plumped ourselves down on the ground and sat taking more notes under the vigilant eye of our leaders. The truth is that the same set of notes could have served very well for all of the lectures, for each visitor brought us the same standard set of remarks approving the economic, political, and cultural aspects of the New Democracy we were so lucky to have. By the time that Ai Szu-chi, the man whom many regard as the leading official custodian of Communist theory in China, spoke to us about "Prospects for Our New Democracy," most of his listeners could have kept pace with him sentence by sentence just by reading back the notes from the last lecture.

Then we began to listen to radio speeches; each lecture hall had two receiving sets assigned to it. The radio lecturers were supposed to answer questions submitted to them by the students through the Committee for Political Education.

Sometimes the answers to our questions were not as detailed and informative as might be hoped. One well known speaker told us, for instance: "Some students have written that they cannot understand how cultural aggression has been committed against China by such imperialist nations as England and the United States. Are not missionary schools a typical example?" Without more ado, he went on to the next question.

Another speaker told us: "Someone asks whether the union of the Party with the bourgeoisie and petty bourgeoisie doesn't actually amount in effect to the Party exploiting the wealth of the bourgeoisie and the knowledge of the petty bourgeoisie. The answer is *no*."

Next week, we secretly hoped, somebody would be brave enough to ask him *why* the answer was "no."

All of the things we heard in the classroom and over the radio we had to discuss again in the mutual-aid circles. We quoted portions of our notes back and forth at one another under the gaze of our leader, who had to make sure that we all chimed in. After a bit we could chant the phrases almost without thinking.

Then the time arrived when the priests of our New Democracy thought that we were well enough indoctrinated to assist with a systematic overhauling of the academic curriculum. From the beginning, I suppose, our leaders recognized that a complete reform would not be easy. For one thing, they faced inevitable inertia on the part of students who thought that it was splendid to change what everybody else was studying but that the courses in their own department should not be tampered with until after they had been safely graduated. And, of course, any reforms were bound to arouse resentment among the professors, who had a vested interest in what they were teaching and who would be most reluctant to abandon materials they had been using in their classrooms for ten or fifteen or twenty years.

Therefore, the reformers moved in with a certain amount of caution. They could, they knew, use a three-pronged attack. First, they could simply establish brand-new courses containing what they wanted; second, they could cancel or abolish old courses as "reactionary"; or they could preserve the title of an old course, but completely change the content and viewpoint. I saw all three of these methods in operation.

The first semester after the Liberation, the 1949 spring term, had seen only one new academic course offered to the student body as a whole, "The History of Social Development." Unlike the recognized "political studies," this course was not "universal" or compulsory. But it was taught by our friend Ho Kan-chi, the Marxist scholar who had been made an important officer in the new North China People's Revolutionary University, and because most of us guessed that it would help toward graduation the enrollment was enormous. The course was somewhat disappointing. It had been advertised as a survey of the whole process of social development. But "Professor" Ho spent most of his time berating the old government and eulogizing the Communist Party.

A fair number of old courses were abolished during the first semester, with the Department of Social Science and the School of Law as the chief sufferers. Virtually all of the law courses were found to be "reactionary," and so were dropped from the curriculum without any discussion. This was rather unfortunate, of course, for our law students, who found themselves facing a semester with nothing much to study as well as a future in which the place of "old-fashioned" law appeared somewhat uncertain.

Changes to the "new stand" and "new viewpoint" in courses retaining their old titles were more far-reaching, if more devious. Some of the scientific and technical courses escaped purging this first time around. But the Departments of Economics, Social Sciences, Philosophy, and Western Languages and Literature were hard hit. In fact the latter had found it necessary to distribute hastily printed translations from *Mao Tse-tung's Thought* to use as reading material in the English prose class instead of Harold Laski's long article "Freedom in Danger" and other writings of Western liberals. In the social science classes the changes were even more startling. Professors who had lectured for years about the advanced political and social ideas of the West now had to do an about-face and condemn the "false democracy," "reformism," and "devouring capitalism" of the Western nations. "Why didn't you tell us this before we got so far along," some of us upperclassmen were tempted to ask.

But the changes to be made during the fall semester of 1949 were destined to be much more systematic and far-reaching. After much preliminary planning and days of drum pounding, delegates supposed to represent all Peita teachers and students met in an unprecedented conference to discuss the basic fundamentals of the whole curriculum. Speakers told us the meeting was historic, and reminded us that Peita stood as a model for all other universities in China. "At this meeting," he cried, "you delegates are going to write a new and glorious page in the founding of our New Democratic culture!"

One of the new and glorious pages consisted of eight unanimous resolutions defining the shape the curriculum was going to take from then on. One resolution declared that courses which did not center around the union of theory and practice must be dropped or have their credits reduced. And, it went on, "Teaching methods should be based upon a spirit of mutual assistance between teachers and students and mutual benefit between teaching and learning."

By demanding that teachers consult with their students regarding reform of the courses they taught, the principle of "mutual assistance" ostensibly gave us the right to help decide what we were to be taught. But by this time our leaders selected by the Party and the Youth League had effective control over the rest of us, which meant that the Party was going to use us to impose the changes it wanted our teachers to make.

In this situation our professors had to act very gingerly. Middle-school teachers giving lessons to our younger brothers and sisters, it was said, had to read the faces of their "progressive" students in order to find out what to say or what to do. Peita professors also had to abandon some of their pride to step down and "cooperate" with us. Depending on the degree of security they felt, our teachers tried one of three methods of consulting with their classes:

a) The most self-confident gave a short talk on the material they planned to cover and their schedule for covering it, and then began at once to go on teaching in their old style without inviting discussion. But before leaving the classroom they remarked, "If you have any ideas, be sure to let me know." They couldn't guess, of course, the future trouble they were storing up for themselves.

b) The less self-confident announced their program for the semester. Then, with a hopeful smile, they asked the students whether they agreed. If not, they invited the students either to speak out at once or to send them notes, signed or unsigned.

c) The really frightened stepped down from the platform and invited their students to air frankly and without reservation their views regarding what should be taught. These professors remained silent during the discussion. To the comments of the students they added only a periodic "Yes, yes," "Quite true," and "Very good idea." Finally, they summed up the general view of the class and tried to devise a teaching plan that would please those students they had identified as leaders.

Let us admit that some retrenchment of the sprawling curriculum at Peita probably would have been a good idea. But now it seemed to mean that we were supposed to cut out regular academic materials to make room for more Marxism-Leninism. Some departments still managed to resist. Professors in the College of Engineering declared that any cutback in their courses would mean that they could not graduate qualified young engineers. In the College of Medicine professors agreed that fewer credits would mean producing doctors of below-minimum standard. The technical knowledge possessed by these faculty members jarred the self-confidence of the Party cadres, who at that point were still timid about their mastery of the natural and applied sciences.

The fate of the rest of the colleges was different. Because their courses could be judged immediately according to the basic principles of Marxism-Leninism, and the cadres were the official custodians of these principles, out the window went the subject matter in such courses to make room for the orthodox theory professors were now ordered to teach. Sometimes a difficulty appeared. Because textbooks written from the approved Marxist standpoint were still very rare, it was decided that students could use the old books from "the new point of view" until new materials could be prepared.

The departments of Chinese and foreign languages posed another problem. Most of the courses taught in these divisions were neither very progressive nor very reactionary; therefore nobody could decide very readily which courses should be pruned out. Students saw their chance here, and pleaded that since they were so busy, some of the more difficult required subjects such as the *Wen Hsin Tiao Lung* in the Chinese department and Shakespeare in the English department should be eliminated. After some argument they were made into electives. New and fashionable courses like "folk literature" were substituted for the courses which were abolished.

The Party officials in charge of reforming these courses did not have any real acquaintance with the great classics they judged, and in the private opinion of the professors they had no understanding of the true values of literature. "Do they want well educated men? Or are they just after cadres who can read, write, run an office, and handle a foreign language?" one professor grumbled. Then an order came down to retrench even more: not more than 40 per cent of the courses in the Chinese and foreign-language departments could treat of "literature" as such. At the same time another order arrived to abolish the old Department of Philosophy. This order of the Educational Ministry, it was blandly pointed out by the Ministry, did not originate with the Ministry. Why, it was simply a response to demands from the teachers and students themselves!

After careful promotion among the students, the organizers of the reform campaign arrived at the point where they thought it would be a fine idea to formalize all of the changes by registering our public approval of the process. A general meeting was called, and a campus leader fired the first gun.

"Comrades, let us take advantage of this opportunity now to discuss the reforms in our studies. We ask you—give us your opinions." He stopped. The other Youth League members also kept quiet to let the non-affiliated students start the ball rolling.

But the first boy who stood up failed to follow expectations. "I really don't think the changes should be as sweeping as the last two government orders have called for. After all, isn't a university supposed to be a place for academic study and research? Is Peita the right place to use materials better designed for a short-term intensive training course?"

"I agree," his friend chimed in. "I don't think these last changes are so good, either. Keeping our standard up is as important as introducing the new materials. In my opinion the university should be kept as a place for training 'higher' talents."

"These last changes are simply too much." The third speaker was even braver. "If all you want to do now is to extend applied political training, why don't you just abolish all the universities?"

Other students seemed ready to line up behind these three critics, and the leader of the discussion sensed the danger. Wouldn't it be awful if more debate led to a petition to restore the old curriculum instead of the expected vote in support of the reforms imposed by the Ministry of Education? The leader hastily gave the floor to another Party member.

"Comrades, I think you are making an unforgivable mistake in clinging so hard to this bourgeois nonsense. The abolition of courses poisonous to the people is our duty as well as our right as students. If your standpoint has changed and you have crossed over to take your stand with the proletariat, you should understand these reforms better than you show today. In fact, some of the statements I have just heard raise a serious doubt in my mind whether we can really get anywhere if we continue this debating. Can't the meeting be adjourned until we have a chance to thresh these points out in our own small groups?" Thus the leader brought the show to a close.

With this spontaneous opposition the undercurrent of resistance to the reforms grew strong enough so that two of Peking's prominent "democratic" personages, Professor Chang Hsi-jo of the Social Science Department at Peita and Professor Chang Tung-sun of the Department of Philosophy at Yenching, went to see Chairman Mao Tse-tung and hinted at their disapproval of the "over-leftist" changes. Chairman Mao was wiser than Premier Chou En-lai, who, it was rumored, had been pushing the reform. He surprised the Ministry of Education with an unexpected personal message: "The proposed changes will be deferred for one year."

For the time being the extremists in the Ministry of Education had to content themselves with the extensive changes in the curriculum which had already been engineered. After all, the most reactionary courses had been banned, and Party doctrine had been injected into remaining subjects wherever they could contain it.

Another resolution which our delegates passed at the "historic meeting" that prefaced the great reform campaign called for the more energetic pursuit of *hsueh-hsi*. These *hsueh-hsi* classes kept our noses to the grindstone, especially after the Student Union passed another resolution ordering us to devote from 54 to 62 hours a week to classroom work and supervised study. Our new daily schedule called for study or classroom attendance from eight in the morning until noon, from two to six, and from seven to ten. Our morning physical drill began at seven, and we had to go to bed at ten-thirty.

More and more emphasis was also put upon "collective study." This was another part of the constant progress we were supposed to be making toward our final goal of "collective living." Few students could find any excuse not to participate, for fear of being accused of "bourgeois individualism." The application of collective study usually involved a group gathered together on the lawn or inside a spare classroom, all reading aloud from the same passage. After each section of a chapter had been read, the leader called a halt to permit discussion. Persons who failed either to raise questions or to supply answers to the questions of others were criticized, politely at first, for showing "an irresponsible attitude toward your comrades."

This system worked well for the slow students; it ensured that they at least read over the material assigned to them. But brighter students sometimes chafed at the reading aloud and the often lamentably simple questions asked by the leader, whose job it was to make sure that everybody understood. They also resented the fact that this scheme forced them to help mediocre students instead of freeing them for extra reading of their own. But who is to say whether the new system was just or unjust? At least it enforced a certain democratic equality by assuring a minimum standard of knowledge for the mediocre while retarding the progress of a few "intellectual aristocrats."

Collective study was most stressed in the Russian Language Department. All loyal adherents of the Party, the students in this class grappled fervently with the tongue of the "Great Fatherland of the Proletariat." You could spot groups of them every day sitting on the lawn chanting aloud the Russian alphabet and the simple sentences they had learned, looking for all the world like kindergarten children learning how to read and write.

Some of my friends expected after the Liberation, now that the millennium had arrived, that the traditional ordeal of final examinations would eventually be abolished. One of the resolutions passed at the "historic meeting" made short work of this hope. It said: "The examination cannot be abolished; but it has already changed in spirit from what it used to be—it is now a check-up and a summary of *hsueh-hsi*."

At first we scratched our heads over this. Hadn't final exams always been a check-up and summary of the semester's work? But when we read the instructions for conducting the semester review, we discovered that the exam had indeed changed its nature. "Regarding the matter of reviewing," this pronouncement read, "teachers may first issue outlines and then point out the important points. . . . Teachers must keep in constant touch with the mutual-aid circles, discover their errors, and solve their problems for them. . . ."

Now we understood. The new system reflected the solicitude of the Party for its own. These classmates were so active with their outside political work that they had little time or inclination for independent study; they could always cover up this possible deficiency by talking a bit louder about the "union of theory with practice." The grades of these comrades under the old system, which put a premium upon individual reading and reflection upon the subject matter, certainly would have suffered. That is why they had legislated so enthusiastically to push the resolution through the meeting. After discussions in the mutual-aid circles, after seizing upon the help of better students in *hsueh-hsi*, after obliging the teachers to "solve their problems," they would not have any reason to suffer embarrassment at the prospect of an examination.

With exams easy to pass but difficult to distinguish yourself in, most good students lost interest in scoring good marks. "When they arrange things like this, how can the authorities expect our students to work hard?" one old professor complained. But instead of blaming the authorities, this venerable sage might have blamed his own lack of comprehension. The authorities did want us to work hard—and now had means of seeing to it that we did so—but they did not want our energies to be concentrated on passing old-fashioned examinations. After all, we were in training as an "élite," destined to take up posts of some responsibility in administering the New Democracy. But our new leaders naturally had new ideas about the training we needed. Instead of spending our time with our books, we got a chance to practice "striking blows" in our discussion groups and self-criticism sessions, in our parades, in the off-campus propaganda work we had to do. Even those of us who didn't particularly want to be, were rapidly being conditioned as competent cadres in the service, perhaps, of the people and, most certainly, of the new government.

Peita was both the testing laboratory and the model for the reform of its sister universities. Our "historic meetings" rapidly produced effects beyond our own campus. We heard with some relish how a professor at Peking Normal, after his classes had asked him several times along the lines of our resolution to point out "the important points" in his course for their benefit, finally puffed out his mustache with fury, and said:

"Can't these young fools find out for themselves which things are important? I have already recited these things to them twice, but still they pretend they are not satisfied. So we cut down our lecture notes again and again. What they really want me to do is to tell them exactly the questions I intend giving them and then tell them the answers on top of that!"

Some of us were uncomfortable in these new circumstances. But I am afraid that we got a certain malicious pleasure out of the discomfort of professors who had always wrapped a gown of academic sanctity around themselves in the past. By now, you see, we were beginning to understand that our teachers had failed to give us the leadership we should have had in the time when we so desperately needed it.

CHAPTER XI

Who Teaches Whom?

Not many of our teachers were like the famous professor at Amoy University who maintained an almost legendary discipline over his students. Every student in his classes had to complete every assignment to the professor's entire satisfaction or he didn't pass. He didn't have to call for silence during his lectures; students didn't even dare to hand notes to each other during class sessions. Outside the classroom he was just as formidable. When students had to call on him at home, they found excuses to linger in front of the door before knocking.

One time, according to a story I'm sure was known all over China, he strode into the classroom and nodded curtly to the students to sit down, for they always jumped up at his arrival. Then he sat down himself. One leg of his chair splintered with a snap, and the professor landed on the floor with a thump. He sat there for a moment with the palms of his hands pushed against the floor, and looked at his students. Not a single titter broke the absolute stillness.

He arose, kicked the debris of the chair out of his way, and delivered his lecture.

Peita students would consider such discipline fantastic today unless the professor happened to be a distinguished government leader or an honored visitor from the Fatherland of Socialism. Teachers and scholars have always enjoyed a solemn kind of respect in China. But teacher-student relations actually had changed radically even before the Liberation speeded up the process. Even before the fall of the last imperial dynasty in 1911, young men excited about new foreign ideas had become impatient toward teachers who could teach them nothing but the classics. Some of these young men graduated and became teachers themselves, but few of them found anything to be as certain about as the rigid old ideas preached by the generation they replaced.

Traditional relations between learner and master grew even more informal during the war against Japan, when whole universities picked up and moved inland. The formality was not restored when the universities returned to Peking after V-J Day. After all, progressive students during the last years under the old government were more interested in politics than in academic work, and a great many other students followed their lead. Professors found it difficult to resist the pressure of organized students, even in those cases when they were not in full sympathy with their political activities. Students skipped class en masse to attend meetings, march in parades, or conduct other political work, and then formed delegations to visit teachers and talk them out of flunking anyone who didn't have time to make up his studies.

Some professors themselves were working actively to bring on the revolution. More held off from actual participation, although they were known to be sympathetic. A certain number tried to remain neutral, and attempted to keep on teaching their own subjects without getting involved in what they rather looked down upon—"politics." Progressive students disdained these last. How could scholars remain aloof when inadequate salaries, inflation, and corruption were threatening to extinguish the scholars as a class?

When the Liberation came, I remember how most professors joined us in the parades and cheering which greeted the arrival of the People's Liberation Army. The Liberation promptly brought them higher wages, at least in terms of the basic commodity unit, the catty of millet; even professors who had been given low marks by their students, and thus had their salaries reduced, made more than before. After the celebrating our teachers sat down to read the new journals and newspapers and to debate with one another what to do to bring what they taught in the classroom up-to-date. Then the excitement died down and classes reopened. Like us, the professors sat down to *hsueh-hsi*, to study what was in store for them under our new leader.

In the first weeks of victory after the new authorities had given us the privilege of grading our teachers and determining what salaries they were to be paid, some of my friends who still had special grudges against some of their instructors declared to anyone who would listen that the Liberation had really emancipated students from their professors. Events proved that this statement was not entirely accurate. The relationship between student and master was adjusted, but only to classify progressive professors with progressive students and backward teachers with backward students. Progressive students got a chance to educate backward teachers, and progressive teachers got a chance to instill Marx-Leninism into backward undergraduates.

There happened to be more progressive students than progressive professors at Peita. After all, we were young and our professors were not; if all non-Marxist doctrines were to be labeled as poison, then our professors had all had twenty or thirty years longer than we to absorb it. Therefore at the beginning we did enjoy a temporary sense of freedom and emancipation. For the first time we got the privilege of telling our teachers exactly what we wanted taught and how we wanted it presented. Now unpopular teachers had to sit quietly and listen at public meetings while we dissected their teaching methods and classroom habits as well as their political views. At first, some teachers tried to argue back, and with their greater knowledge and skill in debate they managed to make their point. Later, this sort of rebuttal proved to be impracticable.

Student leaders who had come back to Peita with the People's Liberation Army naturally helped us to organize the movement to assist our teachers in bringing their teaching and their thinking up-to-date. In our mutual-aid circles they gave us speeches about how essential it was to give our professors a helping hand. "Most of our professors are good men. Many of them are good teachers. A few are really true progressives, and these have stood side by side with us while we marched toward the revolution.

"These last are true comrades. But what shall we say about the rest?" The speaker was older than most of us, a lean, tall Honanese, about thirty years old, who had been studying since early in the Japanese war. I suppose those who are critical would call him a "professional student." He had fled from Peita in the fall of 1948 and had returned to the campus in uniform after the Liberation. "Yes, what about the rest, comrades? We all have our individual criticisms of them, I know. But more important than our personal feelings for them or against them is the basic question of their class stand.

"We know that in all of the years they have been teaching, most of them have been victimized by the poison of bourgeois thinking. Most of them have come from the middle class, and they have tried to cling to their bourgeois position. In a few of them, I am sorry to say, the poisonous juices of the bourgeois way of life have seeped into every capillary, entered every cell of their body." Here, I am ashamed to admit, we all applauded. This was early in the Liberation, when rhetoric like this could still move us.

"Purging out this venom will not be easy, comrades. And our teachers won't be able to do it alone. Truly, they have tried hard in their own *hsueh-hsi* classes, but now we know that is not enough. They will need our help to reform their thoughts, our help to change their way of life. We must respect their knowledge and their ability—I don't have to remind you of that. But if we are to help them, and really help them, we must not tolerate their bourgeois or reformist ideas. And help them we must—for their sakes as well as for our country!"

As a result, all of us agreed that we would extend a polite invitation to all of our professors to attend our political meetings and group discussions. Delegations of students visited the instructors in their offices. We couldn't be sure what the private reactions of all of these thought-poisoned teachers were when we summoned them to learn with us, but they all smiled and voiced polite thanks.

"Thank you for your good intentions. Naturally I do not wish to miss such an opportunity for *hsueh-hsi*."

"It's very kind of you. I'll be happy to be one of you, to reform myself by your honest suggestions."

"Yes, I realize that times must progress. You students have overtaken us. We must try to catch up with you."

Apparently, the rumor about what was in store for them had reached our faculty. We wore triumphant smiles when we came out of the offices where those professors sat who had been stern or short-tempered with us. "Now remember," our leaders told us, "this is the real beginning of *hsueh-hsi* for most of these teachers. Yes, I know, they've all been holding *hsueh-hsi* classes among themselves, but we've discovered that they need to be inspired by your enthusiasm. We must do everything we can to encourage them. In order to help them, we must criticize where criticism is needed, and we must praise when praise is due."

Five minutes before the first joint faculty-student general meeting was to begin, all of us stared unwinkingly at the door where we hoped to see our professors come in. But five minutes after the bell had rung, only two of our teachers had slipped in and sat down in the back row. The meeting was short: the chairman had to throw aside the welcoming speech he had prepared, and to all appearances he couldn't make up his mind whether or not to acknowledge the presence of the two faculty members. Finally he compromised by asking one of the two to comment on a question. "I'm just here to listen and to learn," the teacher said mildly but firmly. The discussion broke up; we smiled at the two professors as we left as if they were reluctant children who had been cajoled into coming to school. But we would have to do something to educate our teachers who had failed to attend.

"Wait and see what happens when the small groups meet," we advised each other. "Maybe they think the 'big class' is just too big; give them another chance." Somebody must have passed down an official rebuke; more teachers attended the more informal discussions. But they were not enthusiastic about chiming in on the actual activities. When the group leader made a pointed effort to bring them in, they were likely to reply with some sarcasm, "Oh, you younger people have a clearer and deeper understanding than we." Or they looked at the ceiling and repeated the words we had heard the first day, "I have come here to listen."

Several weeks later, when attendance by the professors dropped off even from the smaller groups, our leaders called us together to review the results of our invitations and to talk over means of remedying the situation. My classmate Huang, who had gone around with us before the Liberation to cheer up our professors and incidentally win them to our side, summed up the feelings of the Youth League. "When we invited them, they all said they would come. Who would have guessed that they would not be as good as their words? Huh—these old-style intellectuals." He shook his head. "Maybe they're too far gone to be redeemed."

"Maybe it's better to go slow," another classmate said. "Thought reform can't be accomplished in a day, or even in two or three months. The resistance of the bourgeoisie to thought reform in the beginning is inevitable, and we should expect it." He saw the displeasure on the faces of the Party and Youth League members, and added quickly: "That is, as long as we don't relax our efforts and give up. If we keep after our teachers to join our discussions and patiently help them in their struggle to reform themselves, I think we can all make progress day by day."

Somewhat to my surprise, our leaders seconded the idea. "We must go slow; we mustn't hurry or be angry. Everyone please remember: the next time you invite the professors you must be more polite than ever."

It was my luck to be assigned to go with a delegation under Huang's leadership to extend another invitation to Professor Chen. Mrs. Chen opened the door at our knock and asked us in. Treating us like honored guests, she invited us to sit down, brought us tea, and opened a box of candies. Greatly embarrassed, we asked, "Is Professor Chen at home?"

"I'm sorry, he went out a few minutes ago. I don't really expect him back until this evening some time. Do you want to leave any message for him?"

Mrs. Chen was young, soft-spoken, pretty. Her husband must love her dearly and pay attention to her every wish. Looking across the room at her, I had an idea. Why couldn't we ask her to persuade Professor Chen to come to our *hsueh-hsi* meetings? It would be better and less embarrassing than to ask him again directly. So I began:

"At the beginning of the term we asked Professor Chen to come to our *hsueh-hsi* meetings. But for some reason he's missed the last two. We admire Professor Chen very much and I hope—" But I couldn't help laughing nervously here, which bewildered Mrs. Chen. She looked at the other students round-eyed, while one of our comrades picked up where I had left off.

"We hope in the future that Professor Chen will participate in our *hsueh-hsi* side by side with us. This will not only be good for Professor Chen himself, but will also help us. After all, a teacher has the solemn responsibility to teach us."

"Shall we come here ten minutes or so before our next meeting starts?" Huang added. "Here is the timetable for our *hsueh-hsi* discussions." He handed Mrs. Chen a mimeographed schedule. "We gave a copy to your husband when we first invited him, but he must have lost it, or he has the times mixed up or something."

"Thank you. I'll tell him when he comes back. You really have his best interests at heart." Mrs. Chen smiled at us.

Outside the door Huang frowned at me. "What's so funny about asking a teacher to attend our meetings? What's wrong with you? What were you trying to do?"

"I just all of a sudden realized how funny we must sound. Here's the professor, a grown-up man. And we're treating him like a truant boy who doesn't want to go to school. Let's give our teachers credit where credit is due. I believe they can gradually be reformed."

"You think they can be reformed? Well, let's wait and see," Huang said skeptically. "Huh—looks like they won't come to *hsueh-hsi* unless we go and get them ten minutes before the meeting starts. The number of teachers attending the small groups is getting smaller and smaller. Even Professor Chen hasn't shown up after coming to the first two or three, and people claim he's a progressive!"

Our leaders must have reported to their superiors about our mixed feelings toward our campaign to get our professors to attend our political sessions, because, for the time being, the campaign was tacitly slackened. Later we heard that the university labor union had taken over the biggest part of the job of reforming the teaching staff.

Upon the first preliminary reorganization of Peita several months after the Liberation, Professor Tang, head of the Department of Philosophy and former dean of the School of Arts and Sciences, became the first chairman of the executive committee formed to look after our administrative affairs. It was a gesture of respect to this well known teacher. But it meant that Professor Tang had to be progressive in everything he did as an example to the whole school.

When a "proletarian philosopher" was invited to lecture on dialectical materialism at Peita, the bourgeois philosopher Professor Tang had to attend his lecture to learn from him. But the lecture lasted three hours without showing any evidence of coming to an end. Dr. Tang, who was fat and suffered from high blood pressure, got so impatient that he had to get up as inconspicuously as he could and retreat to the lounge. We heard by the grapevine that he had confessed to his colleague that he hadn't understood a word. "I couldn't stand to sit there any longer," the gossip reported him as saying. "I'm going to die as a revolutionary martyr if I keep on studying revolutionary theories!"

Most professors also heeded the demand that they take a greater interest in student life. Our leaders did not overlook many chances to encourage teachers to join in "collective living." When we formed excursions, the teachers always rode along to the suburbs in the same trucks with us. At the picnic site they squatted in a circle with the undergraduates for a quick exchange of viewpoints before we broke up to chat, laugh, stroll, eat, take pictures, gaze at the scenery. We liked the idea of sharing our young pleasures with them.

We played games too. Even when it was just the childish sport of passing around a knotted handkerchief, we urged our teachers to join in, and they had to hunch down in the ring with us amid polite entreaties and cheers. Some students were especially fond of flinging the handkerchief to the most dignified and pompous professors, who usually missed and who had to pay forfeits and endure our jokes.

The dancing party was also a way to promote friendship

between faculty and students. At first, most of the teachers could not dance. But under the twin pressure of politics and "face" they were pulled out on the floor, embarrassed and hesitant, to "catch up with youth."

In a way it was like going back to school again for some older faculty members—and it was probably a good thing for some of them, who had failed to keep up with current ideas. Even after the systematic campaign in the fall of 1949 to reform our teachers, we were not through with them. The process of catching up was a continuous one: after they started teaching the new materials we kept discovering things we had left out of our first suggestions or had failed to think of to begin with. So we offered new suggestions and criticisms at regular intervals at the urging of student leaders, and our professors would try to incorporate them in their lectures.

One department boasted a foreign teacher who proved to be especially agreeable to our ideas. Because I rather liked him, I won't mention his name. But I think some foreign readers would recognize it; he is a man of some standing in his field. In the classroom he was fuzzy and vague and sometimes delightful, as amiable as most foreigners are not. We kept offering him suggestions which he patiently accepted and tried to incorporate in his teaching. His prompt and unmurmuring compliance got to be something of a joke with us; he was rather naïve about politics, and kept telling us that perhaps it was a good thing we had come into our own.

The stresses we inflicted upon this scholar must have been greater than we realized, however. After a particularly complicated series of suggestions had been loaded upon him, his very progressive wife came to us and told us: "Don't offer any more suggestions. What do you want to do—make him go off somewhere and hang himself?" This shamed us into dropping what we had looked upon as a perfectly harmless sport.

Although most professors made steady progress toward reform, our leaders urged us to keep up our diligence in helping them to wipe out their old bourgeois consciousness. "Even after they have a firm grasp of the principles of the New Democracy," Huang warned me, "we have to watch out for backsliding. You don't think it's easy for some of these people who are set in their ideas to forget twenty or thirty years, do you?"

One day I walked over to call on a professor in the philosophy department who had helped me before when I needed it. I found him slightly flustered, in the midst of seeing two student callers to the door. "We'll call on you again when you're in better mood," one of the visitors said.

Professor Hu sat down on a sofa when he joined me in his sitting room. He looked tired and a little bit ruffled.

I had a personal problem of my own that I wanted to get off my chest. But his appearance stopped me. "You look quite tired, if you'll pardon my saying so, Professor," I said. "Perhaps you've been reading too much. Why don't you take a little rest?" This was rather forward, but I did look on him as a friend.

"I'm perfectly all right," he said with some irritation. "I admit I've been busy reading—the political classics—reading very carefully."

"They're very important," I said. "Isn't that your reaction?"

"Of course," he answered me. "I find everything that Lenin said is quite right."

We stared at each other. "Any other books you've read, Professor? How about recommending one to me?"

"Well, Stalin's book on youth is certainly well worth reading. I was quite muddled in my thinking before I read it. Now I feel what a great man he is after I've read his writing."

I knew I had come to the wrong place with my problem.

"Do you happen to know the two students I was seeing to the door when you came?" he asked me.

"I know who they are but I don't remember their names offhand."

"I remember that they're both in the Youth League. Aren't they?"

"They're very active members," I said. "One, I think, is the chairman of a section or something like that."

Professor Hu waited in silence. "What did they say?" I finally asked him.

"Well, they told me that many things could not be explained in the classroom after the country had been liberated. They told me that what they were getting in the classroom nowadays could not satisfy their hunger for knowledge. They hoped that I would explain to them outside of class some time some of the things they heard I used to lecture about in the old days."

"You haven't explained those old things to them yet, have you, Professor?" I hoped that he was wise enough to know that the request of his visitors must be a test arranged by the Party to determine the extent of his reform. If he wasn't careful, he faced the prospect of being framed as a "reactionary."

"Naturally," he said, "I won't do anything against the wishes of the government. I won't spread bourgeois poison behind people's backs. How can I do such things to the Communist Party and to the fatherland? We members of the older generation, I can promise you, will not be submerged by the tide of the times. We know that we have to reform ourselves and drive the poison out of our minds. We know how to change our way of life, how to draw closer to the masses, especially the proletariat and the working masses . . ."

Professor Hu was going to be safe; he was going to pass the test. But I didn't want to listen any more; I excused myself as soon as I could, and left his house with my problem still only my own.

When Professor Hu and his fellow teachers looked at each other as they met on the campus or sat at faculty meetings, I wondered what they thought. No one would ever know, of course. A few teachers openly resisted the pressures and publicly resented such changes as students telling them how to teach. Others, however, took a kind of perverse and painful satisfaction in standing up in public and denouncing their own past backwardness. I think that perhaps a few must have felt at least unconsciously a kind of guilt for not having served us better when they had the chance, for not having given us the kind of leadership and inspiration which might have given better shape to our energies and our hopes.

But from the perspective I have now, away from Peita, I can't blame them too much. They came from a generation that was caught and bent between the old and the new. They began their teaching careers in a day when one revolution was running down and people were discouraged and retreated into scholary backwaters or turned to selfish opportunism just to keep afloat. They had struggled bravely to keep the schools alive during the long war against Japan. Some of them trekked hundreds of miles afoot, moving whenever the Japanese troops came close. After V-J Day they came back with their students to Peking. But with inflation and high prices eating at their salaries and discouragement eating at their spirits, victory hadn't turned out to mean much. So many were tired and disheartened and ready at last to conform. Now I can't blame them too much for not wanting to fight any more.

CHAPTER XII

The Silver Ear Spoon

All through the hazards of the past twenty-five years, the changes in government, the long dreary Japanese occupation, my parents have managed to hang on to a bright red leather chest that belonged to my grandmother. It is all that survives of the old lady; perhaps for my mother and father it serves the same function that an ancestor tablet would serve in a more conservative family. In the chest was a short formal robe or gown which as a little girl I used to take out and admire whenever the opportunity presented itself. It was almost overblown in the richness of its embroidery, an endless filigree of iris picked out in silver thread on a background of blue silk, the sort of formal robe venerable dames wore back in the last days of the Ching dynasty before the coming of the Republic.

The silver embroidery was only the base of the ornamentation, however. Loop upon loop of silver chains hung from the buttons of this short garment. On the chains dangled all sorts of pendants, small fish of carnelian, heads of chrysoprase, miniature images of the God of Longevity carved of white jade. Lower down, in the last rows, hung tiny toothpicks and ear spoons made of silver, mimicking every detail of the full-size originals. These were relics, remindful of the days when gentlemen carried such instruments of hygiene around with them in ivory cases.

I liked to touch this world of miniature objects fastened to my grandmother's old-fashioned gown; they were more exciting toys than I was given to play with myself. But what were the little silver ear spoons fastened to the buttons for? As decoration? Or as useful things to dig the wax out when your ears itched? Both, perhaps, at least while my grandmother was alive. But I must add that as an ornament such an ear spoon is not as handsome as a white jade God of Longevity, while as a useful thing it is far behind a toothpick.

A university, it took me a year and a half to find out, for the Communist Party was just such an ear spoon.

From where I sit now in Hong Kong, I can appreciate with a certain amount of objectivity the problem which must have faced the Communists when they came face to face with a functioning Chinese university. University men, both professors and students, had a traditional prestige which I have heard they do not enjoy in most other countries, and a tradition of independent thinking and teaching. A good many of these professors and students had labored to bring the Communists to power, sometimes at great personal risk to themselves. Because Communist propaganda had promised these university men a leading role in the national life, after Liberation it would appear ungrateful to impose any sudden or drastic changes upon the way of life in universities. And in 1949 appearances were important; the Communist hold upon China was still precarious.

But the complication was that in the new society there was actually no real need for the old-style university. It had already served its historical function of educating bourgeois intellectuals and aiding the revolution. But now there were to be no more revolutions, only a struggle to consolidate this one. The job needed cadres with a high degree of technical knowledge, instead of old-fashioned intellectuals conditioned to the traditional rebellious "liberalism."

The Communists devised a two-part solution for the problem of what to do about the universities. One: The new revolutionary universities created side by side with existing schools would dispense with the frills of incidental, "purely cultural" subjects. The Party and Youth League cadres who were being recruited for the student body already had most of the proper historical and political knowledge. These new training centers could eventually concentrate on the necessary "practical" subjects required to prepare tested and reliable cadres to fill responsible jobs.

Two: The old universities would be preserved as "showpieces," as ornaments, if you will, to reform or indoctrinate bourgeois intellectuals.* China is desperately short on educated man power. And while professors and students might never be as trustworthy as Party cadres captured young and innocent of any other loyalty except to the Party, indoctrination would make them reliable enough to fill positions where they could use their knowledge and skill.

The subject matter taught in most of the courses had to be revised, of course. The core of the curriculum had to be the official classics: Marx, Engels, Lenin, Stalin, and Mao Tse-tung, plus lesser disciples like Simonov in the arts and Lysenko in science, who were currently in vogue. In a sense this establishment of official classics as the basis for a whole university was a curious reversion to the past when scholars all over the country sweated over the ancient classics for years in preparation for the examinations which would qualify them for official positions under the emperor. Rival schools of history, economics, philosophy, literary criticism, and even physics and biology now became bourgeois scholarship and, in the new historical stage, "untrue."

Not that the Communists would abolish them by fiat as a less modern government might have done. It would look much better if abandonment of rival systems of thought were "voluntary" on the basis of self-evident dialectics. And when the Communists quoted Marx and Lenin and Stalin to demonstrate that Marx and Lenin and Stalin were the genuine custodians of truth, most professors appreciated the dialectics and accepted them as such. In the

---

* This was written before the Communist newspapers reported the closing of Yenching and Fu Jen universities in Peking and Lingnan University in Canton, and the "consolidation" of their facilities with those of other universities. I would now modify my statement to read, *"Some* old universities would be preserved."

enlightened new society compulsion would not be an ingredient; old ideas and old subject matter would voluntarily "wither away."

Wither away they did. For too many of us it was a mild, painless sort of leave-taking. Students began to relax in classrooms where the old subjects continued to be taught; a great many teachers abandoned the old system of roll calls. If you stood in well with your Communist and Youth League friends, you enjoyed the tacit liberty to cut classes almost at will. Teachers gave up being stern about asking you to take thorough lecture notes. When you passed scribbled notes back and forth with friends or whispered across the aisle, most instructors pretended to ignore you. If you were really carried away by the conversation, and the noise got out of hand, the teacher might interrupt his lecture to give you a rebuking glance. Pushed to the limit of his patience, he might finally turn to the class with a blunt request, "Will you please quiet down?" But he did not single students out for individual rebukes which might affront the dignity of the Youth League or the Student Union.

Such was the atmosphere that prevailed in the classes whose instructors were waiting for their subject matter to be revised. Discipline in the political courses was different. The lecturers did not hold roll call; but the student chairman of every class and section had to submit a report as soon as class was over listing absences and instances of inattention. These classes were held in the big lecture room, with a single instructor and two assistants sitting in front of at least one hundred students. But the size of the "big class" did not mean informality; spotted throughout the room were the supervisors, Party or Youth League members, who in intensive *hsueh-hsi* sessions had already learned the subject matter by rote. Their primary job was to "help you out."

But to get down to the business of helping us required time. For the first six weeks or so, the size of the class and the dullness of some of the lectures caused some students to regard these classes as something like the lectures on the Three People's Principles we'd all yawned through a year or two before when the old government still ruled us. Some of us passed the time, at first, drawing caricatures of the instructors; a few devoted themselves to copying out lecture notes scribbled in regular academic classes; others passed notes to friends; and the sophisticated settled themselves down behind huge sunglasses and dozed off comfortably to await the end of the period. These examples of disrespect and inattention were brought up finally at criticism and *hsueh-hsi* meetings of the various mutual-aid circles. We talked about the dignity that students should possess and the obligation not to neglect our political education or distract the serious study of our friends. Then we all raised our hands and voted for resolutions calling upon ourselves to listen attentively, take lecture notes, and correct any student who was not paying attention. After these meetings anybody who poked his head in the classroom was treated to the rare spectacle of every student in the big lecture hall glued to his chair, listening and writing like a reverent young monk copying the measured wisdom of his master.

If the lecture had contained anything very substantial, we wouldn't have minded so much our attentive note taking. We were told day after day that dialectical materialism was the only philosophy, the only truth, and that all other schools of thought were heretical or reactionary. But day after day our instructor perpetrated what seemed to us self-evident inconsistencies and errors.

For instance, he told us often enough so that I can repeat the words without thinking: "Under the leadership of the working class we have started a war of revolution against the imperialists, the reactionaries abroad and at home, the comprador bourgeoisie and the feudalistic landlords, by rallying the peasant class and linking up the petty bourgeoisie and the national bourgeoisie. Existence, we know, determines consciousness. The workers are the stoutest revolutionaries because their immediate interests conflict with those of the bourgeoisie. Because of their participation in collective, large-scale production, they have formed such excellent class characteristics as objectivity, firmness, capacity to withstand hardships, and so on. We of the petty bourgeois class, however, are vacillating, ready to compromise, selfish, conceited, slack and indulgent, and we have strong ambitions to climb up in the social scale. We must make up our minds right now to remold ourselves, cast off our bundles, extirpate our petty bourgeois consciousness, stick steadfastly to the proletarian standpoint, and become the stoutest of revolutionaries!"

One of the questions we would have liked to ask him if we had been able, is: "How about the co-existence of *two* stoutest revolutionaries? First you say the proletariat must inevitably by its superior origin be the stoutest. Then you tell us that we students— who are not the proletariat—also can change ourselves into the stoutest. So what you're saying is that of four sisters, the oldest (the proletariat) is the prettiest. But the third sister (ourselves) can become the prettiest too!

"And what about this business of casting off your petty bourgeois consciousness? You said first that existence *determines* consciousness. And now you ask us to cast off consciousness by a conscious act of *free will*. Free will, according to your first statement, just can't exist. If the 'past existence' of the bourgeoisie can not be changed, if its methods of working and living remain the same, how can the bourgeois consciousness change voluntarily without outside compulsion? If you can change your consciousness by being *willing,* isn't this idea of free will, of an undetermined voluntary act, an idealistic, reactionary heresy?"

There must be a flaw in my own argument somewhere. And if I had been permitted to ask these questions in the political class, the instructor might have cleared it up.

Of course, we managed to cover a great deal more ground than we would if what the lecturer said had been subjected to free debate. For instance, he managed to solve China's periodic food shortage in one fifty-minute class. "The theory about a regular food deficiency is nonsense. In fact, our country produces plenty of things to eat. Not only do we have enough to supply our own people; we can also export a surplus to less favored nations like India. Famines used to appear in certain isolated parts of the country because under the domination of the old reactionary government dishonesty and corruption, coupled with a certain disruption of lines of communication, created many serious transportation problems. The Communist Party has always given much thought to transportation and communications. The temporary difficulty we are facing today—the shortage of food—will certainly be overcome!"

Did we have so much food that some of it could actually be exported? It was an open secret, later confirmed in the newspapers, that foodstuffs harvested in our Northeast were rolling by trainload into the Soviet Union. But if we had so much food, I wish we could have seen a little bit more of it. And who had disrupted the rail lines and cut the highways in the old days? The Nationalist Government certainly hadn't cut the supply routes into the cities it held and had to feed. But perhaps it was true that the Party was giving a great amount of thought to transportation. The railroad into the Soviet Union appeared to be in excellent shape.

Are you surprised that these lectures seemed longer than any of the others? To try to make them go by faster, you'd grip your pen and concentrate on the mechanical job of writing until you'd have to put down the pen, rub your hand over your eyes and forehead, and then pick up the pen again. Absence from a political lecture, however, was infrequent. Minor illness was not a very good excuse; it was easier to come to class than to argue with the doctor or nurse who had to sign your sick-leave slip. It was sometimes difficult to look as interested and alert as you were supposed to look, but the monitors were vigilant for boredom or inattention. After class you'd be asked: "You seemed to be restless today, comrade. Do you have some problem?"

In dealing with these monitors, however, women students had one physical resource which nature had denied to men. And some girls would use it without hesitation.

"What's wrong, comrade?" the Party leader would ask in his friendliest tone. "You didn't seem to be at your best in the 'big class' today. You looked as if you didn't feel well, sleepy or something."

"I'm sorry, comrade. I didn't get much sleep last night. It's the time when—uh—you know . . ." And the embarrassed leader would retreat in confusion.

With friends they trusted, some of the former "superior" students once in a while ventured to scoff at the whole process. I walked out of the classroom with one of them one day. "I've been watching you, Miss Yen," he told me. "You don't look too happy when you sit there in class and scribble. But walking out you always carry your notes as though you'd just been given some great treasure, some weighty prize. What do you do with your notes at night—sleep with them under your pillow?"

"I took six pages of notes today. I think you took just as many—" I'm afraid I enjoyed a very human glee that this superior student was in the same boat with the rest of us.

From our classroom we walked directly into the midst of our mutual-aid circle at the dormitory. Even if I had wanted to neglect my lecture notes, the mutual-aid circle would not have encouraged it. The joke about my keeping my notes under my pillow might have been an exaggeration, but it was not a very humorous one. Like every student, I belonged to several of the "interlocking circles," one for my dormitory, one for academic classes, and one for my political classes. As the semester wore on, these circles became managed with such efficiency that I literally had almost no time by myself.

The circle I belonged to in the dormitory also included my roommate and the two girls in the adjacent room. One of the two girls next door, Miss Chang, was a Party member. Most of the circles had a Party comrade or at least an active Youth League member. If a circle, when formed, happened to be without such an activist, the Party would first use gentle means to get one or two of its people into the group. It would try to persuade a member of the circle to transfer to another group in order to leave a vacant place. Then the Party would encourage the remaining members to invite an activist in with the plea that each circle should have at least one person capable of leadership. If this didn't work, more direct methods came into use. Party representatives would talk to circle members alone, attempt to badger them into inviting a new member in, and sometimes attempt to set them against other members of the circle. Sometimes even this tactic would not work. Then the members of the circle could expect a difficult time at criticism meetings, for other students would be more vigilant than ever to single them out for severe criticism. Sooner or later it was always easier to give up than to hold out.

When the circles were first organized after the Liberation, one of the leaders who came in to help us with the task described their purpose: "To make our fellow students better accustomed to collective life, to give them more opportunities to inspire and encourage one another, to make their lives richer and more significant." The circles also served the subsidiary function of making sure that the life and conduct of each student were watched over by three or four of his fellows and that he in turn helped watch them.

Pretending to be "progressive" was extremely difficult under such conditions. Playing a convincing role is demanding enough on the stage; but to play it during your waking hours day in and day out eventually becomes impossible under the constant attention of persons who know you well. In the long run it became easier to play the role you had to play if you managed to convince yourself that you were "progressive," that you actually believed the lectures you heard, the books you read, the public criticisms you had to direct against yourself and other people.

The criticism meetings are perhaps the most important single part of the whole pattern of supervision over the students. (Criticism meetings are not confined to students alone, of course, but student criticism meetings were the only ones in which I ever participated.) Regularly once a week each of my living circles would meet with a few similar circles to discuss the progress or lack of progress of the members. "You have a cousin in Hong Kong who's written to you that they have more freedom of the press under British colonial rule than we have here in Peking. In your reply you didn't succeed in refuting him. You didn't even explain accurately the policies of the People's Government toward the press."

"And you told Miss Wang the other day, 'Ai-yeh, there's nothing else we can do now but keep muddling along like this.' What did you mean by that?"

"In the portrait class you've been using a picture of Vivien Leigh as a model for the painting you're working on. Don't you think that the Western films are decadent and reactionary?"

All of these comments would spring up out of your friends' notebooks to confront you. Overtaken by surprise and indignation, you would not be able to improvise enough excuses to extricate yourself.

So you would have to admit that, yes, you had not paid sufficient attention to your political courses; yes, you were still wedded to the outmoded poisonous theories of the bourgeoisie; yes, you'd tried to escape from reality into the fictional world of popular novels; yes, in your heart perhaps you'd unconsciously envied your cousin in Hong Kong. You had not taken enough interest in the meaningful life you'd been leading and had been neither loyal to the revolution nor firm in joining the revolution. You had been poisoned by Western imperialism. But instead of purging away this poison, you had indulged your selfish bent and had given free rein to your petty bourgeois consciousness.

Besides admitting these faults, you also gave assurance in no lighthearted manner that from now on you would never repeat the same errors. Instead you would *hsueh-hsi* harder in politics and reform yourself down to the soles of your shoes. And you thanked your fellow students for the strict criticism and hearty assistance they had granted you today. You said all these things—and said them with convincing earnestness—or the meeting would never come to an end and you would stand in the pillory for what seemed hours.

The average human being isn't used to examining himself critically. It was hard for us to get used to it, and we'd shuffle out of the meeting tired and resentful and hoping to bury our heads under the covers and fall asleep. But you had your roommate to think of. Seeing your resentment and dismay, she might be silently rehearsing a speech for the next meeting.

"After receiving criticism Miss Yen not only showed no gratitude but even revealed discontent in private—which meant that her confession and her promises to reform were not in good faith. Her judgment is basically wrong, and being a bigot she has no deep-seated desire really to reform herself, but wants to go on antagonizing the people. . . ."

It wasn't advisable to go outside to the park in the open air to walk and blow off steam. Somebody might think that you spent too much time by yourself. The book that might help you cast off your own preoccupations by immersing yourself in somebody else's affairs was the same book that you'd just been condemned for reading, and the books the Communists wanted you to read would only remind you of your troubles. In the end you did nothing. You only suppressed your annoyance as best you could and pretended to be deeply penitent about the past so that the Communists might really believe that you had been affected by the process of criticism. You could only hope to convince them long enough to remain unmolested for a while, unless you were capable of walking up to a comrade after a meeting, grasping his hand fervently, and stammering:

"Comrade, I am really grateful for the accurate criticism you have given me today. It shows your regard for me and for the great Communist Party."

Some of my friends were more adept at accommodating themselves to these new techniques. They became particularly clever at finding the phrases most pleasing to Communist ears. "Really, comrade, when I think of the past—well, it seems so far away now—I wouldn't have dreamed that it was possible for a person like myself to make so much progress in a few months. I'm sure it's due to the help I received. Why, just last meeting . . ." Some of these speakers were proud of their eloquence, and managed to retain a certain feeling of superiority because they were "fooling" the new student leaders.

Criticizing yourself and listening to the members of your living circle discuss your faults was only part of the job. Even if you had walked gingerly the past week and managed to get off lightly at a meeting, you couldn't settle down and wait for the chairman to dismiss you. You also had to criticize your friends. If you failed to speak out with your criticisms, you were asking for more criticism aimed against you. You would be labeled as "irresponsible to your fellow students and to the people, who were giving you your education." Your friends had to be your prime target. It was difficult to find fault with the Communist students and Youth League activists; their discipline had taught them always to be on the alert lest the slightest mistake in their remarks or their conduct bring them penalties from their organizations. Even when a Communist student was wrong, we were not in an ideal position to criticize him in earnest; we could hardly beat the Party members with their own weapons, so we were forced to turn upon one another. The process imposed a very subtle form of humiliation on us. It was my friends I criticized, but sometimes I'm afraid I criticized from a desire for revenge, just because they had criticized me first.

One day a group of us, drawn together by our mutual sense of humiliation, sat together on a quiet corner of the lawn. In ten minutes we were due at our regular criticism meeting. One of my friends idly pulled up some blades of grass, tore them in half, cupped them in his palm, and then flattened his hand out and blew them off with a scornful puff. They scattered in the air and fell to the ground. Another student, who had also been picking at the grass, twisted the tufts he had picked into a thick braid, tied them tightly together, and then blew against them. The braid held together.

Chou Ta-ming watched this by-play. "Why, that's it!" he said with sudden enthusiasm. "Of course. Why can't we get together just as they do? Why should we get blown apart? Why don't we unite and put on our own play too?"

Chou was stubby and clad in a messy student uniform. With his mussed hair and his thick eyeglasses, "Shorty" always seemed to "smell" a book instead of reading it. When he looked at you, he was so nearsighted that he had to strain his eyes as though he were searching for treasure in your features. He was comical, but he was also witty with a humorous brilliance that always made us listen.

"Listen." He collected his thoughts now, and went on. "Before a meeting they always rehearse and prepare everything in advance. That's why we've been drubbed again and again. Well—why can't we rehearse a play too? In the sort of play I'm talking about we must pretend to attack each other. But we must all make sure first that we understand the plot so that nobody will feel hurt when we criticize him."

He waited and looked around to examine our expressions. "How does it sound to you? When the rest of us attack somebody on our side, the accused will make a feeble defense and then quickly admit his error, before they get a chance to get started on him. Then, when they gang up to attack us, we'll unite to defend one another. Now, if we can only work together like that, we won't appear too conceited or too stubborn to accept criticism; but at the same time we won't have to yield so much ground on every point or help to increase their arrogance. Let's try. How does it sound?"

"It'll only give us temporary relief. It's not a permanent plan," someone objected.

"And with the efficient organization we're up against, a little trick like that isn't much use," I chimed in.

Despite our spoken opinions, however, we all felt that a countermeasure of any sort was at least better than nothing, and we proceeded to argue Shorty's idea. Before we could settle on all of the details, time was up; we had to jump up and head for the classroom.

We always sat around in a ring at the meetings so that everyone could look straight into everyone else's face when he spoke. On that day Shorty happened to sit down next to the chairman. It fell very naturally to him, therefore, to fire the first shot in our battle.

In the ten minutes we talked he seemed to have outlined a speech. "Comrades, today I'm going to make a self-criticism. First, I'm worried about my work in the political courses. I have never been absent, whether for lectures or for discussion groups, and I've listened attentively and take part in the talk. In that respect I have made much progress. I've proposed more questions than answers, of course; but I hope that does not mean that I am not willing to help my schoolmates. When you examine it from an objective point of view, it only shows that I know very little about Communist theories, and am therefore not able to help other people. As for the reference books in the political courses, I have read almost all the outside assignments. As far as my daily life goes, all the students here know that I have always led a frugal, regular life, so I don't think I have to say anything more about that now." Finally, he concluded with the usual apology: "There surely must be many other mistakes I have made which I do not yet have the objectivity to discover for myself. So please give me your comments." He gave me an encouraging glance.

I was ready to point out a few irrelevant and harmless errors to give him something to confess to, but a Youth League man struck in before I could. "Our fellow student Chou has recently shown much more marked signs of progress in his political *hsueh-hsi*. That is a very good phenomenon. We hope that he will continue to work hard." The preamble was always carefully doled-out words of encouragement. It was meant to disarm the victim and put him off his guard so that he might, without too much ado, accept the criticism that was coming.

Hot on the heels of the praise a stern *but* always introduced the antithesis. "But a person's political knowledge always depends on his efforts. If you really have listened and studied your notes, if you really have read the reference material with care, you should be able to help your classmates solve their problems of thought. Since you admit you have not given them any help, it shows that you must be either without a sense of responsibility or else too slack in your political studies. Don't you agree?" Shorty wasn't ready to bow yet. "No. I have honestly worked very hard in the political courses. At least I have done about as much as I could. If my thought still isn't correct, if I have often asked questions instead of answering them, I am afraid it is because I am not intelligent enough. I have worked hard, but I still haven't learned much." We all agreed—the Communists along with the rest of us—that Shorty was more intelligent than most of the other students, including most of the progressives. He might be deliberately egging on the Communists, because he knew they disliked half argumentative and half satirical replies most.

And he was drawing blood: the Party comrades all looked deeply offended. They exchanged glances, as if rounding up reinforcements for an attack from all flanks. I hastily stepped in, in the hope of raising Shorty's siege.

"Comrades, fellow student Chou thinks he has done his utmost in his political studies. But"—I could use "but" too— "but Marx-Leninism and the ideas of Mao Tse-tung are profound and inexhaustible fields which cannot be easily mastered in any short time. They are not like ordinary subjects, which represent only parts of the truth, or no truth at all. Truth—the whole truth—is very hard to understand." Here I almost burst out laughing when I saw the nods and expressions of grave approval the Communists put on.

One giggle, however, would have given the whole thing away. I went on, trying to look as solemn as possible: "But truth will certainly be understood at last. That is one of the reasons why we are confident today that we can make ourselves over. Fellow student Chou has worked very hard to learn politics. But his quest has been beset with difficulties. It is quite natural, therefore, that he should regard himself as slow of wit. Some future day, when he sees thousands of people around him turning into new men and understanding truth with ease, he may be able to find self-confidence again. And then his progress will be amazing."

In order to let go of the subject before Shorty had to yield, I ended abruptly and fled on to another topic. To give him some trivial error to admit now, I began to nag at him. "But for his daily life, I think he has been too much given to living alone, too little inclined to mixing in with the rest of us. Comrades, I wish he could build up more of a mass viewpoint in himself and realize the values and pleasures of collective life."

"What you have just said, Miss Yen, is very true." With a flattering smile for me a Party comrade took over my subject. "Fellow student Chou seldom mixes with the crowd—and he always looks bored and unhappy when he does so. He likes to sit and write in the library or read alone in his room. That is because he has the typical supercilious attitude of the old intellectual. He must make up his mind right now to get rid of these defects and stop admiring himself as the lone flower in a desert waste. He must see clearly that the present era is proletarian . . ."

"What an unholy mess I've made for Shorty," I groaned to myself. I had given the Communist the handle for a long tirade. What would Shorty do? Would he give in and admit his mistake? The comrade was still reading off his speech, but I couldn't listen any longer. How could we think that without organization or advance preparation we could match men who were rigidly organized and trained to handle such situations and who always prepared so carefully before a meeting and checked the results so thoroughly afterward?

We would have to be superhuman to win in the face of the odds against us. And besides, our hands were tied by the restriction we had to observe in all of our arguments: we could only defend ourselves with Communist viewpoints and theories; we could not take the initiative and strike back with other ideological weapons. We had to argue about truth with the official custodians of truth. The most we could hope for was to suffer less or to ward off a few of the clumsier nips from the teeth of our sheepdogs.

Chapter XIII

The White-Haired Girl

Drama

The Revolution, we heard back in the days while we were waiting with hope in our hearts for liberation to come to us, was bringing a tremendous burst of artistic creation in its wake wherever it came. New songs, new books, new plays, new films, all drawing vigor and inspiration from the people—these were what students in touch with the liberated areas promised us. The prospect of new vitality in art and literature excited some of us as much as anything else we hoped to get from the Revolution, because for most Peita students interested in such things the old arts were dead. The leaders of the Renaissance of the 1920's had grown old; some of them had gone over to the camp of the reactionaries. Perhaps they had reformed the written language, but they had not reformed anything else. The men we admired now were the forward-looking progressives courageous enough to make their writing into documents of social protest. For the *avant-garde*, which included most of us, the classical opera was decadent; the theater—at least in Peking—was second-rate. Painting had declined into lifeless imitation of old masters or, worse yet, produced monstrous hybrids manufactured by artists with Chinese sensitivity who tried to ape the more obvious tricks of modern Western art. You see, we had strong opinions and even stronger hopes.

The reputation of *The White-Haired Girl*, the celebrated opera of the Revolution, had run on ahead of the People's Liberation Army. We finally got our first chance to see it in the spring of 1949, when a drama workers' group from the new North China University put on a performance a few months after the Liberation. Practically everyone on the campus scrambled to buy a ticket.

It was an exciting and moving experience. Students with any pretensions to advanced appreciation didn't care much for the old-style Chinese opera with its threadbare classical plots and its medieval trappings, but this was brand-new, genuine popular art joined with new technical tricks that made the four hours a series of exciting discoveries. The fact that we had heard all the details of the story and staging in advance only whetted our anticipation. On the night we attended, the hall was full of fellow Peita students; we kept our enthusiasm alight by chanting revolutionary songs and shouting across at each other while we waited for the performance to begin.

But the audience hushed when the curtain went up. Instead of the old-fashioned stage setting with a few gaudy, stylized trappings to symbolize a room in a castle which we normally would see when the curtain rose at the Peking Opera, we saw the interior of an ordinary farmer's hut with its rough furniture, life-like and realistic, with a periodic dab of snow against the papered window to show that it was winter outside. And no lords and ladies with falsetto voices minced out on the stage; instead we found a simple peasant, bent with work and with age, speaking to his young daughter. We listened and learned that he had come to the end of his rope, that his landlord was pressing him for payment of his debt, and that he had no money to pay it. Only one thing could be done to redeem the debt, which as an honorable man he had to settle. That was, to sell the daughter into the landlord's service.

The old father forces himself to sign the paper surrendering his daughter into the hands of his heartless creditor. Then, heartbroken with the enormity of the thing he has had to do, he hangs himself. Some of us were close to tears as we watched the landlord and his hired bully pull the girl away from her father's body to carry her back to the landlord's household. All over the audience we could feel the indignation rise as we watched the girl being beaten and abused like a slave by the haughty women of the household. And the daughter is pretty; the lustful landlord seizes her one night and, despite her struggle, possesses her by force.

The rest of the plot is simple. The daughter becomes pregnant. The landlord promises marriage. But when her time is close, he decides to marry someone else and plots to get rid of this encumbrance by selling the girl into a brothel. When she learns of this, the girl attempts to hang herself, but is found by another servant, who cuts her down and brings her back to life. She decides that she must escape, and she runs away to a mountain cave, where, alone and unattended, she gives birth to her child. For two years she hides in the cave with her baby, only stealing out at night to visit a nearby temple where she manages to filch enough of the food offerings to keep herself alive. In the eternal darkness of the cave her hair grows long and turns pure white, so that the superstitious peasants who catch an infrequent peep at her as she slinks by at night believe that she is a witch or unquiet ghost.

But then the fighters of the *pa-lu chun,* the Eighth Route Army of the Communists, arrive and drive the Japanese out of her native village. Among these guerrillas is the boy who has always loved her. He hears about the ghost with the streaming white locks, and visits the cave to investigate. When he sees the ragged apparition, he raises his rifle and fires. He wounds the girl and pursues her into the cave, and there discovers her true identity.

Together they return to the village to find that the landlord who has treated her so shamefully is to stand trial for collaborating with the Japanese. When the girl recites the crimes committed against her, the peasants shout their unanimous verdict: death for the landlord and his bully. The lovers are reunited as the two condemned men are led away to be shot.

The bare bones of the story don't look very impressive in my retelling. But clothed with the other elements, the singing, the acting, the settings, the simple, moving dialogue, the performance was something else again, a living, organic spectacle which touched off the emotions of everyone who watched it. Not everything was new; the actors still exaggerated their gestures in the old operatic way; and though the music was based on folk songs instead of on the artificial harmonies of the traditional operatic music, the musicians still beat their drums and gongs into a crescendo of crashing sound to herald dramatic peaks in the story. *The White-Haired Girl,* therefore, was close enough to the old arts of the drama and the dance not to disturb too much those who still respected tradition. But its sense of movement was new. The action flowed around in front of the curtain while sets were being changed so that the motion was continuous, and the four hours passed more rapidly than they had ever done at the Peking Opera.

After the villainous landlord had been dragged off by the soldiers for execution, a kind of applause burst out that I had never heard before, as the dammed-up emotion of soldiers and students in the audience gave way. And why shouldn't we applaud? By working for the Revolution, hadn't we helped write the masterpiece we had just seen? The spell lasted out in the night air as the crowd split up again into individuals. "It was wonderful—really wonderful," the boy with me said. "How can they ever surpass it?"

It was a better question than we realized at the time. They never did.

Books

Not in any field have they yet rivaled *The White-Haired Girl,* certainly not in my old field of interest and education, the sphere of writing. I had some knowledge of the old classics and some recognition of the accomplishments of the Renaissance begun by older contemporary writers who cast off the old learned literary language in favor of the colloquial *pai-hua,* which could be more readily understood by the masses. But, like my friends, I had been stirred most by the modern novels and essays of the younger progressive writers who attacked the social cancers of the old society with the tools of language forged by their elders.

To us these men who had been brave enough to attack corruption, political repression, and the poverty imposed on the masses by inept rule were heroes. Many had had difficulties in the old days;

some had actually suffered for their frankness. Therefore we looked
forward to the first "literary evening" at Peita after the Liberation.
I had never expected to see so many famous literary men collected
together in one place—the fine progressive writers Ho Ch'i-fang and
Pien Chih-lin, the other well known writers and poets who adorned
the faculties of the various universities in Peking, and the Number
One Communist Party literary figure at that time, Chao Shu-li. Chao
was the real star of the meeting, and started the evening off with
a sweeping criticism of the great national poet, Li Po, who lived
in the eighth century, because Li Po had made verses for the
feudalistic king and noblemen. Chao was especially critical of the
poems Li Po had set to music in praise of the beautiful royal con-
cubine Yang Kwei Fei. "Were Li Po living today," he thundered,
"he would in all certainty celebrate the beauty of Soong Mei-ling"
(Madame Chiang Kai-shek).

Then Ho and Pien, who had just undergone a special indoctrination course, stood up in turn to talk. Visiting students, who
had walked in from other schools and waited two hours sitting on
the floor to hear their two idols, sat dazed while they heard Ho
and Pien denounce all of their own past work, the books which had
been such inspiration to these young readers. But the books we had
read with such admiration had been saturated with the theory of
"art for art's sake," contaminated with "escapism" and other "decadent elements," we now heard their authors confess. After twenty
minutes of breast beating came the emphatic promise: "I resolve
to wash away my bourgeois ideology. Young comrades, I must start
anew."

Even more embarrassing to listen to were the speeches of the
literary men on the university faculties. All had to speak, but to
save their souls they apparently couldn't think of anything safe to
say except to repeat Chairman Mao's principles of literary creation,
praise them, and then vow their determination to dedicate themselves henceforth exclusively to the service of the people. Were these
the same teachers who had been so knowing and so authoritative
in the classroom, free to range the whole body of literature, Chinese
and foreign, to analyze and criticize the theories of criticism they
had argued before their classes?

We listened now. "In the words of Chairman Mao, literature

must belong to the people. What an author can write can only possess literary value if it is meant for the broad masses of the workers, peasants, and fighters of the People's Liberation Army. Too often in the past have we professors used the classroom as a platform from which to preach the false theories of an earlier time. Too often have we emphasized the abstruse or the precious, which can have appeal only to the limited few. Now, comrades, we are confronted by the immense task of banishing these traditional ideas and false models and of forging a revolutionary literary doctrine which will unite us again with the people." After more self-disparagement, the professor speaking looked around at Chao Shu-li and the other Communist notables sitting in back of him, and said, "I hope that these comrades here tonight, who are richer in experience and sounder in revolutionary thought, will not hesitate to instruct us."

Later visits by other famous writers added new details to the new literary theory. Peita students heard a parade of literary figures; Mao Tun, Ts'ao Yu, Lao Shaw (author of *Ricksha Boy*), and Ting Ling all spoke to us. After hearing the same idea from three or four different pairs of lips, we began to listen mostly just to guess how well the visiting lecturer stood in with the party. The more self-confident and the less apologetic for his past faults the speaker was, the better his current standing. If he put on a dramatic show of repentance, he was obviously still working to establish some sort of case for himself to attract official tolerance. Speakers standing in official favor were free in criticizing the past, but did not dare say much about contemporary literature, perhaps because the inner party council had not yet decided what it liked and what it frowned upon. After all, the theory was that all literary productions belonged to "definite classes" and "definite parties." Virtually everything written before the Liberation, therefore, was under suspicion, since little of it had been specifically addressed to the proletariat or to the Party.

The speeches did teach us how to apply the new literary theories on a rule-of-thumb basis. Pure literary quality for its own sake became secondary. "Appreciation" of literature for sheer style or form was out—one speaker remarked that "appreciation was the business only of the bourgeoisie and the leisured classes." (This speaker had apparently forgotten that Chairman Mao Tse-tung has said that the toiling millions are also gifted with high powers of appreciation.) Literature, instead, was now a tool or instrument. At a conference of literary workers in Yenan in 1942 Chairman Mao gave official shape to the Communist theory in a series of lectures which have been hailed ever since as the Party's literary credo. "In the present-day world," Chairman Mao said at Yenan, "all culture or literature or art belongs to some one definite class or party, and has to follow some one definite line in politics." He went on to make the flat declaration, "Literature has to obey the party." But literature was not to be confined to the negative role of obedience; it had a positive function to perform as a servant of the People's State. Hadn't Lenin described it as "only a screw in the whole machine"? But "tool" or "weapon" is a more dignified term than mere "screw." Only a few of us had ever read Chairman Mao's lectures all the way through. But from the speeches we heard from these famous writers, we learned that the new literature had an inescapable social duty to perform, although the official arbiters who would decide how well the duty was actually being performed were just looking over the land and drawing up the rules.

What then was safe to read in this in-between state while official standards were being established? What a mess it would be if the Party or the Youth League condemned your favorite books as creations of the feudalistic ruling class or as worthless "Trotsky-bourgeois" scribblings without genuine proletarian significance! Most of my fellow students did not fear the risk of being "infected" with this sort of "poison" as much as they dreaded the "help" which would surely be given them if their Party friends discovered that they were being "poisoned." The prospect of such "help" was the chief reason why we tried to be careful in selecting our reading matter. Translations of the modern Soviet novelists were safe, of course; we could buy the works of such popular writers as Fadayev and Simonov. Older masters who had influenced a whole generation of Chinese writers—Turgenev and Dostoevsky and even translations of Gorki—were dismissed as obsolete. In Chinese literature it was all right to read the works of Chao Shu-li, Ting Ling's *Along the River Sang Ch'ien*, and the so-called "collective productions" of young writers, which were hailed as being rich in "party traits."

Virtually everything else, including books the Communists had previously praised as "progressive," was suspect.

Most of the new books were written about workers, peasants, or soldiers; we could find few authors who wanted to write about students, office workers, shop clerks, or professional people. We wanted to read about workers and peasants. But we found out that when we read one book about each class, we could pretty well predict what its fellows would be about. In the books about factory workers, the hero worked very hard and joined an emulation campaign—the Chinese equivalent of the Stakhanovite movement—to step up production despite failing health or other difficulties. In books about farm life, the peasant, after "struggling" with his landlord for land reform, contributed all the grain he could spare to support the front and then joined the army with patriotic enthusiasm. In books about the army all of the soldiers were valiant supermen who thought of nothing but performing meritorious service and becoming people's heroes. In all of these books, the plots were similar, the themes were similar and, curiously enough, even the styles were so similar that most of them could have been produced by the same man.

After a few months of this some of us began to return to those classics, foreign and native, which had not been specifically proscribed. We were dubious, however, about Shakespeare. He had been included in the blanket condemnation passed on all Western literature by enthusiastic progressive students just after the Liberation. Communist students in the Department of Western Languages and Literature pointed out that most of his heroes were kings or noblemen concerned with personal honor or glory. "The only characters from the masses who appear in his plays," we were told, "are made the butt of feudalistic humor." Therefore students who liked Shakespeare had to read him on the sly.

But to the chagrin of the students who had cast Shakespeare into outer darkness, the first shipment of Soviet magazines to enter Peking in the wake of the Soviet Cultural Delegation devoted prominent space to that very author. Featured in one of the pictorial magazines was a series of photographs showing how lavish productions of his plays honored the great dramatist in the Fatherland of Socialism.

His progressive critics began the process of overhauling their past thinking and recognizing their "deviations." To embroider the brocade the famous playwright Ts'ao Yu, when he returned with the rest of the Chinese Cultural Delegation from his visit to Soviet Russia, cited in his speech to Peita students the respect of Soviet literati for Shakespeare and some of the other "more progressive" masters. Shakespeare came back into vogue again; it was no longer the badge of the reactionary to be seen carrying a volume of his tragedies around between classes. We all made a point of attending an exhibition of Shakespeare's works and a photographic display of his life and background at the British Council on the anniversary of the great man's birthday. And to our immense satisfaction the most prominent figures at the show were the same progressives who had denounced England's greatest writer as a "reactionary" three months before.

Music

Listeners to classical Western music declined in number just after the Liberation when the beat of *yang-ko* drums and the chant of the new revolutionary songs were in every ear. "Chi-lai," the great anthem of the Revolution, now had scores of rivals, but it remained on top, for it had been our great national song of resistance in the war against Japan. The Communists had picked it up, like so many other things, and made it their own. It has since been made into the official anthem of the Communist regime and has been banned by the National Government on Formosa. Many Peita students had admired the music of Beethoven, Chopin, Schubert, Mozart, and other Western composers, but we now put our gramophone records away to avoid any accusation that we were lingering in an ivory tower of individual sophistication or somehow slighting the People's Revolution.

Six months after the arrival of the Communists, the Soviet Cultural Delegation came down to hear our new revolutionary music. Communist cadres led us in staging a party in their honor at the Chung-Nan Hai. In the midst of the spacious park our honored guests sat on a platform above us while we sang for them the strident "Song of the New Peasant" to the accompaniment of drums and gongs. Then a chorus of girl students shrilled the brand-new composition "Ten Women Praise Their Husbands." "Ai-yah—it sounds like the ten husbands have been beating them!" I heard an irreverent male murmur.

The foreign guests applauded warmly, as was the fraternal custom, but restrained any smiles of real pleasure. Then they tuned up their own instruments to give us a concert in return. The students looked around at one another after the first selection and then at our leaders before we applauded and shouted for an encore. The first Soviet People's Artist had just played a bourgeois Kreisler composition called "Tambourin chinois," a light little piece of vaguely Oriental-sounding music apparently intended to compliment us. The next number was a soprano solo accompanied on the piano, an air from Schubert, and there was another rustle in the audience. We remembered what somebody had read aloud to us: "Classical music has strayed away from the masses. It has been the pleasure of the exploiting and leisured classes, and has no right to exist under the banners of the proletarian revolution. Vocal and instrumental solos are all individual expressions. They represent individualism and cannot be tolerated within a collective society." The Soviet artists must have wondered at the genuine warmth of our applause when we recovered from our surprise.

In a short speech at the end of the program the leader of the delegation, his face glowing with the welcome his group had received, told us how happy he was to exhibit before his liberated Chinese comrades some of the cultural achievements of the Soviet Union. The ordinary Soviet worker, he told us, had climbed to a cultural level above that of the workers of any colonial or capitalistic country. "He subscribes to *Pravda* and the other papers; he probably belongs to a workers' library. And after work, comrades, he can turn on his radio—his own private radio—and listen to a play or perhaps a symphony of Beethoven."

Workers listen to Beethoven! Our mutual-aid circle leaders faced some discreet but insistent questions for the next few days. So, in the USSR ordinary workers heard the great works of Beethoven! Why, then, were the university students of a New Democratic State, the cultural heirs of the nation, denied a privilege enjoyed by the proletariat in the great Fatherland of Socialism? Why was this music poison to us and nourishment for our Soviet comrades? For once we could all argue on strictly Marxist grounds and embarrass the official custodians of the faith. But by this time our leaders were becoming conditioned to shifting their line when their mistakes, born out of too much early enthusiasm, began to show up. Without admitting that they had been wrong, they allowed that classical composers—or some classical composers—had managed to sense in some mystic way the aspirations of the proletariat. Composers whose works were played in the Soviet Union obviously had possessed some revolutionary sympathies. The gramophone records we had stowed away in hiding came out into the light of day again.

In order to cater to the taste of our foreign visitors, the government invited the violinist Ma Szu-ts'ung and the vocalist Mrs. Kuan to Peking for concerts of the same classical Western music they had always played. But the new native "revolutionary" music remained in first place in the affections of the Chinese Communist Party. The Party allowed classical music to return to the radio station, perhaps for foreign friends and advisers, but gave it no other positive encouragement. All of the official emphasis was on what was labeled "popular music."

This new music ranged from "The Favors of the Communist Party Are Too Many to Be Told" and "Hymn to Chairman Mao" to "Song of the New Woman" and "Brother and Sister Plow the Wasteland." To tell the truth, we didn't hear very many true representatives of the masses whistling these "popular" tunes in the street, but they did echo frequently on the campus. Not only did we hear them every day but we had to sing them too. Before the arrival of the Communists, Peita students had organized a number of "choral societies," which in some cases had been used as a cover to get in touch with fellow students and to conduct underground political activity under the natural camouflage of singing. After the Liberation the choruses swelled in both number and size, and instead of serving as a means of recruiting students for political activity they became a tool for propaganda discipline. Each student was more or less expected to take part in the choral society sponsored by his class, not for the selfish pleasure of hearing himself sing, but for organized propaganda work on and off the campus.

After nine or ten months of singing to student groups, in parades, to audiences of office and factory workers, to housewives, these songs were as much a part of us as our skins. Tunes like "The Favors of the Communist Party" were so drilled into us by constant choir rehearsals that if we hummed any music at all, we hummed them. We heard the new songs any place we happened to be—the campus, the dormitory, the drill field, the mess hall, even in the toilet.

A number of modern Russian songs found their way into Chinese, too. They were not very successful; the translators were either hopelessly clumsy or deliberately satirical. The translations revealed such lines as: "How broad and far-reaching is our fatherland! How numberless its hills and farms. . . . We can go where we like, like masters of our fatherland." Another song stated: "Never have we seen a land where we can dwell in such freedom, never a land where we can dwell in peace like this." But over the halting melody of these foreign importations rang the clear, determined theme of our own leaders: "The favors of the Communist Party are too many to be told."

Films

In the years after the war, motion pictures supplied our favorite entertainment. Peking was not blessed with the modern cinemas one could visit in Shanghai and Hong Kong, and the theaters usually screened old films. That was not really a handicap; most of us hadn't seen any pictures at all during the war and were anxious to catch up. Besides, some of the older films seemed to have more real quality than the occasional new ones that found their way up from Shanghai. When a famous old film was advertised, students sometimes made up more than 80 per cent of the audience, and the cinema often looked like our own auditorium at Peita.

Since few of us had any extra money, we resorted to all sorts of devices to save enough to attend when one of these attractions came to town. Some of the boys I knew actually did their own laundry for a week; or we'd get up early for a couple of mornings in a row to eat the despised millet soup in the student mess instead of squandering our pocket money on rolls and other snacks sold by the hawkers. Those shortsighted students who had already spent all of their government allowance would pester and cajole the rest of us until they got a small loan to buy a ticket. Sometimes the theater would sell special tickets to us at a reduced price, with the Welfare Department of the Student Self-Government Body alert to snap up the chance of serving its public.

When such "superproductions" as *Madame Curie, Jane Eyre, Rebecca,* or *For Whom the Bell Tolls* came along, a ripple of excitement would run across the campus. People living near the university saw us cycling along, gay and exuberant over the prospect of seeing the "superpicture," conversing in groups of two or three on the street or lane leading to the cinema.

Most of us preferred motion pictures to stage performances, not because our cultural level was so low that we couldn't appreciate live plays or opera, but because few such performances were given in Peking. There was always the Peking Opera, of course. But in order to see a performance of its classical art, with its posturing actors and wornout story, it cost three or four times as much as it did to see a movie.

The Peita Dramatic Society, founded by a group of students returned from their wartime years at Southwest Associated University, did attract favorable attention before the Liberation. Actors from the group toured various universities and middle schools in the city with their production of a play called *The Triumphant Return.* Written "collectively" by a group of students, the play described the return of Nationalist troops to a Japanese-held town after V-J Day, and their collaboration with Japanese puppet troops to wipe out the local People's Militia, the only military force which had really fought the Japs. The most memorable scene in the play was a Nationalist officer's awful realization that he had personally shot and killed his own son, whom he had failed to recognize when the son was captured by his troops. Bitterly cursed by his weeping daughter, the officer shot himself too. The dialogue was not brilliant, and the play was rather indifferently performed, but it moved many people to tears.

How to Get a Promotion was another successful effort, produced in collaboration with students from Tsinghua, Yenching, and Shih-ta. This satire was an exposé of the graft and corruption that were sapping the strength of the government. Some of my literary-minded friends even compared it to Gogol's famous *The Inspector General.* The Peita Dramatic Society usually managed to put on short propaganda plays, too, whenever some large-scale student protest was under way to voice our various grievances. Later we discovered that the Dramatic Society had served the same function as the student choruses had served for Party workers. Instead of bothering with entertainment, art, or appreciation, the society had acted as a medium for recruiting underground workers and organizing exchange of information and distribution of illegal propaganda.

When the red flags went up in Peking, the Dramatic Society switched to the new propaganda plays like *Song of the Red Flag, A Problem of Thought, The Character of Moscow,* and *The Russian Problem*. In March, 1949, the second month of Communist rule, the new Cultural Control Committee banned the performance of fifty-seven old-style plays and operas. Some were being proscribed, the official announcement said, because they were superstitious or licentious, others because they insulted the national dignity by showing the invasion of the Mongols or Tatars. Four catered to "slave morality"—however that was defined. More glorified the old days of feudalism, and the official critics dismissed several plays from the stage simply because they were "boring." (I imagine critics in other countries would sometimes like to wield the same power against the last offense.)

The same month, March, witnessed the beginning of the campaign against foreign films, which had previously supported most Peking cinema houses. Open compulsion was still in the future, but theaters were urged to suspend the showing of reactionary films and to substitute more progressive programs. One newspaper was quite blunt about the drive: "Decadent U.S. films are to be ousted by healthy Russian films. Fifty Russian movies are already in circulation in North China and thirteen are to be shown in Peking." A few Chinese films made in our principal producing center of Shanghai were publicly banned as "reactionary."

The theater owners, however, faced a very real problem in keeping their theaters running, since not enough Russian imports and hastily made Communist films were available to make up a full schedule. To their dismay the substitution of progressive films promptly resulted in the loss of most of their audience, and they had to cut the price of their tickets several times within a few weeks to attract a crowd. These price cuts were greeted in progressive quarters as a real step toward making the cinema a true "people's art" available to all the masses. But because the masses continued to stay away, in response to the protests of the hard-pressed theater operators the authorities finally granted formal permission for them to show foreign pictures from non-Soviet sources a maximum of five days a month.

As a result the theaters enjoyed a full attendance five days out of thirty and suffered from a dearth of customers the other twenty-five. The contrast between the full houses for "reactionary" films and the rows of empty seats which greeted Soviet productions was too glaring. The press reported a sudden outbreak of demands "from all classes and walks of life" for complete suppression of all harmful and corrupt foreign films. The response of the authorities was prompt and favorable—"reactionary" films were officially banned, once for all.

A few weeks later we heard that one of the biggest theaters in nearby Tientsin, the Majestic on North Liberation Road, had been sold to the agency distributing Soviet films. It was going to be devoted exclusively to the showing of imports from the USSR. Its new name was the Moskva.

Peking audiences refused to flock to Soviet films not exactly because they disliked the Communist Party or the Soviet Union, but because one Russian film would satisfy a man so well that after seeing one of them he did not care to see another one for many days on end. A whole scroll of solemn, weighty themes was unfolded: *The Story of Madeline, The Rainbow, Chapaev, The Cub of the Tiger, Maxim's Youth, Defense of Leningrad, The Battleship Potemkin, The Eastbound Train.* A few, mostly older films made before the war, were well done and inspiring. Most were dull, even to Peita students, who were as progressive as any other group in Peking.

When one highly advertised film, *The Young Grenadier,* came to town, the administrative manager of my class asked us to stay an extra five minutes so that he could make a speech about it. He praised its educational significance and pointed out that the officers of the Student Union, acting in accordance with the principle of "democratic centralism," had already made arrangements for us to see it in a group at half the regular price. Everybody who wanted to go, he added, simply had to sign his name and then give the money for his ticket to the "functional manager" of the class. I had already seen several similar films, so I put my books back into my satchel and started to leave the classroom without bothering to add my name to the list; but the assistant manager caught up with me before I had managed to escape out the door.

"Didn't you sign?"

"I just don't feel like seeing it tomorrow." I walked on down the hall toward the stairs.

But he fell into place beside me. "Miss Yen, I hope you'll try to take this seriously. You know, we can no longer bother about our personal interests these days. Today—" He suddenly seemed to remember that he had used "Today, the proletarian revolution—" on me several times already. He began again.

"I realize that perhaps you are not especially interested in this film. But for that very reason you should see it and receive benefit from it. Every student who has acquired any serious enthusiasm for the revolution should, as a matter of course, be keenly interested in a classic film like this."

He stopped. I knew he was simply waiting for my reaction so that he could decide what tack to take. I also knew that if I argued with him and told him what I really thought, we would both waste our time and, what was more serious, I might get into trouble. I mustered up what I hoped was a friendly smile.

"I don't think I'm any less interested than you are. I saw *The Rainbow* just a few weeks ago. It was a fine picture; it affected me so much that I'm afraid I actually cried. And ever since I walked out of the theater, I have been turning the picture over and over again in my mind, using it to overhaul my old ideas. I've made up my mind not to see foreign films again, but to try to seek more benefit from Soviet pictures. Of course, I realize that my own standpoint is not firm enough yet. But while foreign films just dragged me deeper into habits of bourgeois thought, the Russian films will change my political ideas and help me hold more steadily to the proletarian standpoint."

After my speech I felt like slapping my own face.

"That's fine." He stared at me askance. Perhaps he had detected my insincerity, for the smile had left his face. "But if that is true, why then don't you want to go with us to see *The Young Grenadier?*"

I was stuck, committed to my lie now, whether or not he had detected my real feelings.

"Well, I'm just not in the mood to see it now—I've been feeling rather out of sorts these days. I certainly won't miss it when there's another chance later on—I'm sure it'll have a very long run."

"You'll go there alone, or with your family, won't you?" He seemed to believe me again. The hostile look in his eyes vanished and the smile came back. "But I've noticed that you have never really enjoyed mixing with your classmates in something like this. If you go on this way, you will never feel or think with the crowd. It will really be a serious handicap in your self-reformation. Why don't you see it with us? Just try it!"

Once again he glowed with the same youthful vitality he had displayed when urging people to dance at the first dancing party. "You will love collective life. You honestly will! Help us build up a collective spirit. You will love it! And you'll also love this film!"

So, in the end, I wrote down my name—not because I was really convinced, but because I wanted to test my love of Soviet films and my love of collective living.

It was a special noontime show. The Democratic Square was crammed with filmgoers looking for their individual classes. Finally we lined up, responded to roll call, and marched off to the Cathay Theater singing the "March of the Democratic Youth" at other pedestrians, who turned to stare at us. In front of the theater we halted in line to permit each class to enter the hall, row by row. Across from us some street urchins watched with open mouths. I wondered if they envied us.

A leader yelled "Law Department!" and the various classes in the Law Department marched straight on in. "History Department!" The history classes moved along in an orderly line. Group by group we filed into the theater until we were all seated. I had a good seat near the middle aisle; some of my unlucky classmates who drew seats behind pillars whispered angrily down the row at the functional manager, who had booked the tickets.

Out went the lights. The customary portraits of Marshal Stalin and Chairman Mao Tse-tung flashed on the screen. Frantic applause. Then a burst of military music, and the feature started.

It had been dubbed with Chinese dialogue, but the dubbing was not very good. I don't know who had supplied the speaking voices, Russians or else Chinese speaking some outlandlish dialect; and the tones and the emphasis were strange, to say the least. It was the story of how a heroic Soviet youth, steeled by his Marxist faith, triumphed over wounds and betrayal to wipe out a whole group of German fascist invaders. The story may have had merit, but the merit had no opportunity to emerge in the face of the annoying technical defects.

Glowing statements of faith in the cause which should have rung with conviction were read as if the Chinese or Chinese-speaking Russian had had his doubts. Strongly emotional passages were enunciated with exasperating calm; praises sounded like curses; sad events were reported lightheartedly. True feeling was in the script, but the speakers applied it in exactly the wrong places. When we heard the flippant tone of the young soldier's stern declaration, "I will sacrifice—I swear to sacrifice to the death for my fatherland!" it was difficult to feel inspired. When I saw another young grenadier run to a fighter who had just dropped with a bullet in him and exclaim, with a treacherous sneer, "Stay quiet, comrade—I'll carry you on my back," I was really worried for the wounded hero.

The casting was outlandish, too; there were obvious inconsistencies between the appearance of some of the actors and the parts they were supposed to play. Plainness and simplicity are fine, but they should not be confused with ugliness. Some of the actors, to our Chinese eyes, at least, were actually comical. Their serious lines did not move the audience in the least; in fact, their speeches sounded like travesties. The leading actress lacked any beauty and charm that we could see. She was supposed to be a spy, to whom a German officer, bewitched by her breath-taking beauty, was supposed to give away military secrets. I am not surprised that the Germans lost the war.

As I sat in the dark and watched, I looked for the inspiration we were supposed to get. I wondered why the courage of this Russian youth was supposed to be any more praiseworthy than the courage our own youth had displayed in our long fight against Japan. Why did these acts of gallantry I was watching have more educational value for us Chinese because they were performed by a Russian?

Finally, after a long time, the hero made his last speech, the film ended in a triumphant peal of music, and the lights went on. We filed out, slightly dazed from the crowded, stuffy atmosphere. Everybody was busy praising the film as loud as his voice could carry. "Rich in technique." "Rich in educational significance." "The best film we've seen since *The Rainbow*."

I nudged a friend I trusted, who had just finished praising the film to the leader of his mutual-aid circle. "Was it really that good?" I asked.

"Well," he replied with a warming smile, "of course it all depends on your proletarian standpoint."

He walked off with me back through the afternoon sunlight toward the campus. And threading our way through the dispersing crowd, I rather envied the classmates who had been placed in seats behind pillars.

CHAPTER XIV

The Bride Saw Red

"What about relations between men and women back there under the Reds?" This was the question the doctor asked me after he had finished examining me and had prescribed some very expensive medicine for the chest cold I had gone to him with just a few weeks after my arrival in Hong Kong. "I hear the Communists are very loose in their morals, aren't they?" He looked pleasantly titillated. "Why, they say a girl can become pregnant without even knowing who the father—"

"All I know is this," I cut in. "Maybe there's some immorality in the army. I haven't heard about any myself, but perhaps things like that are inevitable. But they behave quite differently in schools and offices. There's no immorality there. Not at all!"

"But—but—" he stuttered. "Yes—certainly! That's quite true, I suppose. And since the Communists came, the roads have been restored and there's more food. Of course. Uh—all that's quite a boon to the people."

I had a hard time holding back my smile. His abrupt about-face meant that he thought from my emphatic denial that I was a progressive or even a Party member sent into Hong Kong to spy on complacent businessmen like himself. But I was only trying to be honest, for love and what foreigners call "sex" don't play a big role in the lives of young people in New China. Anybody who tries to tell you anything else is only trying to cater to your taste for the lurid.

Naturally, Peita students were aware of sex, even before the Liberation, and just as naturally found one another attractive for that reason. Most of us went walking with boys, were taken to the films from time to time, while a few girls attended dances and other affairs. Best of all, though, was boating. Almost anyone could afford to hire a boat on the Pei Hai or on Lake Kunming. In the fading afternoon of a late spring day there was nothing better than to float slowly along among the light green duckweed and the dark green lotus leaves supporting the buds that would blossom later on in the year to cover the whole surface of the lake. As it got darker you could watch the lights go on around you while a soft breeze came up to riffle the water. It was very pleasant, especially if you knew that you were going to be treated afterward to a feast of tiny, spicy *chiao-tse* (meat dumplings) at the open-air restaurant not far away.

At the films we did admire Ingrid Bergman and Gary Cooper and Charles Boyer. But remember that we Peking students were conservative about our personal lives even if we were progressive in our politics. Besides, we usually had more urgent things to think about—and in 1948 the job of building for the future seemed more important than our personal indulgences. A few really advanced students had read the old Communist dictum about the act of love being no more important than a glass of water when you are thirsty, and I suppose were prepared, in theory at least, to be bold and unconventional as soon as the Liberation brought them the opportunity. But these venturesome souls folded up their plans when they saw what the realities were going to be. For life became even more earnest after the Liberation; there was more to do and less time for personal relations to become the most important thing in a man or woman's life.

I remember a boy and a girl in my department who were both

candidates for entrance into the Party. They were friends and comrades; they had work in common and they often met. But any rendezvous was always for official business. He talked over with her whatever business they had and left her as soon as they had finished; they were both busy and happy in the first months after the Liberation, and had no time for long conversations, certainly not about personal matters.

Suddenly the boy realized that he had fallen in love with her. This was a complication, for he was serious about becoming a good Party member and was afraid that his longing for her would disturb his work and his *hsueh-hsi*. Things hadn't come to the point yet, though, where he thought that he had to talk things over formally with the Party. Instead he sought out his closest Party friend and had a long and serious talk with him. "If it's that serious," his friend told him, "we'd better take straightforward measures." The two of them agreed that the only thing to do was for the aspiring lover to get his peace of mind back by wooing her hammer and tongs and getting it over with. "Wage an offensive against her. You're both good comrades. You can only win, not lose. Let love and work go hand in hand!" his friend declaimed to him.

So, the next afternoon, when she was busy writing in her room, the boy rapped on the door. She welcomed him, asked him in, and invited him to sit down. "If you've got any important business, maybe I'd better stop and put this work away," she told him.

He stared back as if he hadn't even heard her. Uneasy under his stare, she began to repeat what she had said. As she began to speak, he jumped out of the chair, seized her hand awkwardly, and blurted out an unceremonious, "I love you—please accept my love!"

She was astounded. She had never had any experience in love, and she certainly had never expected this rash comrade, whom she knew only as a fellow worker, to be her first suitor. She pulled her hand away from his nervous clutch, stood up, and stepped back. "Well, I—I don't know you well enough yet. . . ."

He kept straight to the point. "Please take my love; I want you to. Why are you so bashful?" It sounded like both command and reproach. "We're comrades, aren't we? We've passed through the same hardships and the same tests. We've worked side by side. We have the same faith and the same standpoint. I don't have to tell you what attitude we should take toward love. Anyway, we are comrades. Our work has brought us together, and you have already learned the most fundamental and most important thing about me. Please accept my love!"

She still could not find an adequate reply. After a pause she could only say: "Give me some time to think. Let me think it over and—"

"What is there to think over?" He could not relinquish the attack. "Haven't we vowed to remake ourselves, to throw off the old bourgeois consciousness? This isn't the day and age for a man to devote his life to running after a woman, or for a woman to put on false coyness or false airs. Let us love frankly, love without fear. Only that can be proletarian love, the real love of revolutionists!" Crushing one's comrade with the ringing title "proletarian"—the last and best weapon.

But she answered again that she had to have time to think about it, that it was a very important decision for both of them. He took the matter up with his Party friends; after all, it was of concern to the Party. After some frank discussion, all agreed that the two, if she could return his love, would make an ideal couple. They had both "thought things out" and would become Party members very soon. They had both been very loyal in the service of the Party. If they could love and encourage each other and work hard together, they would be very helpful to the Party. Whether they were compatible with each other in other respects was a personal affair, and the Party did not discuss it.

With the support of his friends, the boy visited a female comrade and had a long talk with her. He hoped, he said, that she would have an intimate talk with his beloved, tell her about him, and advise her not to stick to the old bourgeois ways of love-making. "This is a time for revolution. We can't waste too much time on writing letters, seeing romantic films, visiting parks, drinking tea together. We have to learn to display our feelings frankly. It is not proletarian for a new woman, and especially an intellectual, to put on a pretense of shyness." The female comrade carried his message to the girl.

Not knowing what to think, the girl appealed to her Party superiors. They told her that she could accept his love. Of course, if she did not really like him, they didn't expect her to force herself to accept him. Until that time, she replied to her Party superiors, she hadn't been able to develop any feeling for him stronger than comradeship.

But, all smiles, less than two weeks after this incident he passed candy around to his friends—a generally accepted method of announcing one's engagement at Pieta—as a token that the two of them had declared their love. Her girl friends scurried off to her and teased her to admit whether it was true. It's premature, she said at first. But they coaxed her still more, and finally she confessed bashfully that in the past few days she had begun to feel proletarian love for him. Yes, she thought, yes—she could accept his love. For a week or two we kept up our teasing. But we got used to seeing them together in their spare time, and after a month or so they seemed like people who had been married for years.

We wondered, however, whether she had actually found true love for him or whether she had been conquered by the magic key "proletarian."

Love sometimes did get in the way of the more serious business of service to the people. Earnest young comrades at times, I think, used their political mission as a half deliberate device to improve their acquaintance with girls. If a boy belonged to a singing propaganda team, he could find excuses to ask a girl he admired to join. If she refused, he could point out solemnly that "your refusal to join mass activities shows that you stand aloof from the masses and that you still cling to petty bourgeois notions." If he was a very bad dancer, or pretended to be, and if she was unusually good—that is, according to his notion—he could always ask for lessons so that he could be together with her often. If she appeared reluctant, he could always be self-righteous again. "So-and-so doesn't like to help her fellow students, but is still supercilious and snobbish."

Or it was just as easy to catch her walking alone, fall into step with her, and strike up a conversation about the principles of the revolution. If her mind wandered during the political classes, he could ferret her out after the meeting was over and comment gravely: "From the questions you asked, I'm afraid that some wrong ideas still stay in your head. These bourgeois things have taken deep root and are growing rank in your thinking. You must make up your mind to pull them up by the roots, completely and ruthlessly." Then, with a look of deep concern: "When you have time, I think we'd better have a good talk. I'll be glad to spend some time to help you liquidate these confused ideas. How about tomorrow?" Quite obviously, her mind couldn't be remolded in a short time. And she would need help from now on to make sure that she didn't backslide.

His face would beam upon her complacently when he heard her criticize herself in the self-criticism meetings. "Basic changes have already occurred in your mind," he would tell her afterward. "I hope you keep on exerting yourself like this in *hsueh-hsi* and forge right on ahead. Don't fall behind the rest of us; you have to keep up the pace. I think we'd better keep on with our conversations— don't you?"

Sometimes the shoe was on the other foot, when the girl was the Party or Youth League member and the boy was just a progressive or even politically indifferent. Instances when the wooed was more positive in thought and action than the wooer were very rare, of course. Most such wooers were rapidly frightened away. But when it did happen, the girl would either reject her suitor altogether or promise to accept his love if he worked hard and got his name on the "list of gold." The list of gold used to be the list of candidates who had passed the official examinations in the old imperial days and thereby became eligible for appointment to government office; but now, of course, the list of gold was the list of those applicants who had been accepted into the Youth League or the Party.

Instances where one of a couple was in the Party and the other outside were always discussed with frankness and in detail at Party meetings. Anyone who concealed his romance would be accused of being "too bashful to confess," of "showing feudalistic consciousness," or of "having secrets which cannot be made public and which therefore must be inconsistent with the standpoint of the proletariat." When you had confided your love affair, the circle would talk it over and then give you suggestions. Though you certainly didn't have to accept their views, as a member of the Party you were concerned about your "political career." If your *ai-jen,* or lover, was seriously backward in thought, the Party or Youth League might ask you to sever your sentimental ties; but more often it would impose upon you the duty of influencing and remolding him or her. If you could change his thinking, you could proceed with your affection.

The happiest face I ever saw on a human being I saw on a girl friend of mine who loved a boy who had graduated a year ahead of her and who had been assigned work in a small town to the south. She was already a Party member; he was still trying to prove himself worthy of the honor. Despite her devotion to the Party, she worried about her personal problem quite often and sometimes wept alone in her room. After a walk with me one day she came back to the dormitory to find the gateman waiting at the door with a letter for her.

"From him?" I asked.

"Yes," she said. "I'm afraid he's getting terribly discouraged. I'm almost afraid to read his letters any more." She waited until she got to the room to open it.

But when she read the first sentence, her gloom turned to the brightest look of joy I've ever seen. She read on, and then danced about the room as if electrified. "Oh," she said, "they've approved his application! He's going to be in the Party!"

"That's wonderful," I told her. "I'm really happy for both of you. Now you can go ahead and make your plans for the wedding."

"Oh, that," she said, and calmed down a little. "That will have to wait until I graduate, I guess. And of course we'll both have to get permission from the Party."

I felt happy for her, but I still couldn't understand her viewpoint. In her mind, and perhaps in the minds of all other Communist girls, was the fixed idea that she could rightly love only a political comrade. Her idea came from honest political faith, I hope. But ambitious girls outside the Party who wanted to make sure that they snared a husband with future prospects also began to tell themselves, "I will only marry a Party comrade," or, "I will only love a Youth League member." It was a curious change in the thinking of ambitious college girls. In the earlier years of the Chinese Republic —perhaps until the war against Japan—most intellectual young women clung to the fixed thought, "I can only marry a returned student." That thought was bourgeois through and through, and snobbish, faddish, and vain. The idea, "I can only marry a Party member," was proletarian. But it struck me as just as faddish, and perhaps just as snobbish and calculating.

Problems of love and marriage were discussed not only in the Party and the Youth League but also in the regular classes and departments. The conclusion of these lectures was always the same: selfish romantic love had to give way to more important matters of basic political faith and duty. Our concept of love had to agree with the "proletarian" or Marxist idea of life and the world. After all, love and marriage were concerned with personal happiness; and there could be no personal happiness without the Party. If the party of the proletariat was defeated, personal happiness would be at the best ephemeral.

So all citizens of New China, and especially the young intellectuals lucky enough to enjoy a higher education at the expense of the people, should put work ahead of personal feelings. Indulgent romantic love was backward and bourgeois. Promiscuity was even worse. If relations between men and women were loose and abandoned, such sexual indulgence would divert energies and emotions which should be employed in work and would bring about confusion and rivalries in the ranks of the Party. For students who listened to their political mentors, the formula for their amours was simple: to spend what few idle moments they could find in the pursuit of love, and when the time came along, to get married. Reduced to a few words this rule of conduct was: "If your mind has been remolded and set right, your love should not affect either your *hsueh-hsi* or your work."

Students who still managed to remain aloof from politics and "service to the people" were not as conscious of duty, and lived under fewer restrictions. Thus they had more freedom and were almost their own masters in their personal relations with the boys or girls they were interested in. "Almost" is an important word, however. These students still lived under the eyes of their more politically active schoolmates and could not avoid regular public criticism of their conduct. If a boy spent too much time out walking with a particular girl, or spent too much money on her, he would be labeled "sentimental" or, even worse, "a believer in the love-above-all idea of the bourgeoisie." He could not, for instance, take his girl friend to see an affecting love story at the cinema; after a while the only films they could buy tickets for were of wars or revolution, and reeked with gunpowder. Boating was not as much of a pleasure as it had been, either. There were still as many boats on the lake, but the people who rowed in them were all in gray uniforms, and took their pleasures with a certain sternness. Besides, everybody's personal finances were pretty much under official supervision now, and pocket money was at least as scarce as it had ever been before. Finally, if the custodians of our morals decided that someone was wandering too far afield, they could always find more duties and assignments to take up some of the idle time they thought he was spending in harmful pursuits.

Contrary to sensational reports I've heard in Hong Kong, the Party also encouraged marriage. After all, marriage with its aim of quiet domesticity was a logical and natural part of the theory that the emotional relationship between a man and a woman shouldn't interfere with more important things. Starting a "small family" was all right, of course, as long as it didn't meddle with your participation in the "big family" of the Party.

Weddings did become simpler, in keeping with the new austerity. Most students staged one of three types, depending upon their political status. First was a simplified version of the old civil wedding. (Remember that most students did not practice any religious faith.) However, the elaborate trousseau and the traditional wedding feast were dismissed as "stuck-up bourgeois trimmings." Instead, the bride put on the best dress she had, added more make-up than usual, and sometimes held a bouquet in her hand With the groom, who wore his uniform or a Western-style business suit, she marched into the hall to the sound of music, usually from a piano. The parents and the witness watched the reading of the ceremony. Then the wedding party would go to a restaurant for dinner. After dinner the newly married couple would go off alone to their room by pedicab. No friends came along for the traditional teasing of the bride. This was undoubtedly an improvement; in the old days, with hot wine on the table, the teasing of boisterous guests might become extremely vulgar.

The so-called "democratic" wedding was staged for couples who wanted their ceremony to have Party blessing. Though bride and groom wore the sort of clothes they would have worn for the civil ceremony, before the "democratic" wedding they attended a simple banquet given in an antechamber and arranged and paid for by the guests. The marriage hall itself was decorated with streamers of colored paper hanging down from the ceiling, while the gifts from teachers and fellow students were on display: tea sets, pictures, vertical scrolls with couplets declaiming appropriate sentiments. Out in the center of the room five chairs waited for the wedding party: bride, groom, two of their parents, and the official witness. From the benches they sat on, the guests rose to cheer the bride and groom when they entered. When everybody was seated again, the witness read the marriage certificate. Then teachers and fellow students stood up to make speeches in praise of the couple. After the groom expressed his thanks for the best wishes of his friends, everybody rose again to sing popular songs like "Unity Is Strength" and "The Favors of the Party Are Too Many to Be Told." Following the old custom, the bride, groom, and their parents stood at the door to shake hands with their teachers and schoolmates as they took their leave.

If the man who was getting married was a member of a cadre who received his lodging, board, clothes, and other daily necessities free of charge, but had little pocket money of his own, the government paid for a "Party-sponsored wedding." The hall was decorated in a simple, natural way with a portrait of Chairman Mao flanked by a Party flag and the new five-star banner of the Chinese People's Republic. There wasn't a lavish banquet, but the tables provided snacks for the guests, such as fancy candies, peanuts, and watermelon seeds. At the signal for the ceremony to start, the groom and his bride, dressed in their uniforms, entered amid cheers and loud applause. First, the senior Party members present made short speeches welcoming the bride into the "big family." A close friend or two extended more personal greetings, and finally the bride and groom made appropriate replies. Unpretentious as it was, the Party-sponsored celebration was more impressive than the civil ceremony ordinary students contented themselves with.

After the speechmaking the principal guests presented the nuptial couple with scrolls bearing congratulatory couplets written especially for the occasion. Though these verses might sometimes be unpolished in language, they were never vulgar. Instead, they could sometimes be very witty and appropriate. For instance, instead of being addressed to the couple by their full names, the scrolls might instead be headed by such clever greetings as "Congratulations for the Opening of the Wang-Lee Production Cooperative Society." Finally, amid warm cheers and clapping, the bride and groom marched directly off to their bridal chamber, which was also supplied by the government.

A member of a cadre from any institution could live in the bridal room from three days to a week after his wedding. The chamber was decently furnished, crammed with dazzlingly red things, like a bridal chamber out in the country, where red was the traditional color of joy and happiness. When the bride stepped inside the room, she saw a profusion of cotton-padded quilts with embroidered covers of red brocade, pillows wrapped in embroidered red cases piled high on a real spring bed, tables covered with red cloth, several chairs, and a bureau covered with a red scarf. In winter a cheerful fire would give the whole room a special warmth. All these comforts were installed, I suppose, to impress the cadre member and his new wife with the fact that the "big family of revolutionaries" could give them the same care and affection that the small family could.

These were the three main types of weddings, but some independently minded students practiced even simpler ceremonies. You might be invited by a couple to drop in for refreshments, and arrive just in time to hear an announcement that they were going to be married. It wouldn't look like a wedding at all; except for two big, flaming candles framing the wedding certificate put out on the table for guests to inspect the room had no other decorations. Some of my schoolmates were married without even this ceremony. Their method was to invite some of their friends along on an expedition to Lake Kunming, at the Summer Palace. There, aboard a large barge, to the tune of singing and laughing, the bride and groom would announce the fact of their marriage by word of mouth. After this, the whole group disembarked and picnicked together. To symbolize her status, the bride would pin a flower on her bosom.

Newlyweds quickly settled down to the jobs assigned them. Each of them had his or her own duties; after a few weeks freshly married couples would reply to inquiries about their new state with:

"We're just fine. Of course, we've been very busy." This was especially true of couples engaged in government or Party work. Their jobs sometimes took them away from each other, but if they were in neighboring cities like Peking and Tientsin they still could meet once a week. After the honeymoon they rapidly returned to the old schedule: eight hours of work a day, with meetings and *hsueh-hsi* classes after work. The Party had planned correctly; bourgeois romantic love didn't have a chance to last very long when husband and wife had more serious duties to perform.

Chapter XV

The List of Gold

"Are you finished?"

I hadn't heard the teacher walk up beside me. He must have known that I was finished, though; he surely had seen me put my pen down and start to assemble my papers. I came back to myself and looked around me. Most of my classmates had already handed in their essays and were gone, glad to escape outdoors from the last examination.

"Yes, I am. But I just want to look it over again and see if there isn't some way I can make it better."

He retreated and left me alone to read over my examination essay. Careful and neat, the words I had just written didn't look like mine any more now that they were down on paper. But I began to read, as conscientiously as I could make myself do so. This was the final examination, wasn't it? But what difference did it make to me or to anyone else? I knew that we had already had the final examination that really counted.

Preparations for the real final examination had started almost two months ago, about the time when people who didn't already have definite plans for a career began to talk seriously about what they should do when their schooling was finished. It began with the cheerful official announcement that unemployment for intellectuals was now a thing of the past. In the old days, the statement recalled, college graduates often entered a world where there weren't enough jobs. But now it was going to be different; the government was going to help all graduating students to find appropriate work.

The news wasn't as pleasing to us as it might have been. Seniors who wanted to go on into postgraduate studies or into medical or scientific training were the most worried. Because the government was growing so fast that it was short of administrative help, of people who could read and write, we could see ourselves ending up writing letters and copying reports in government offices. In addition, the government was trying to recruit intellectuals to join land-reform teams to work among the peasants, and the rumors were that the number of applications had been disappointing.

With the threat of compulsory assignment to government work facing us, some seniors began to scurry around trying to line up jobs in the bureau or office they thought it would be most congenial to work in. Young people engaged to be married were especially frightened; both partners wanted to make sure that they stayed in the city. But these foresighted students found their prospective employers even more foresighted; the latter were extremely reluctant to take such seniors on despite the fact that they obviously were in desperate need of help. "It's very difficult now," one petty official explained. "You seem to have all the qualifications, and we'd like to take you on. And we're short-handed—no argument about that. In fact, I can even route a request through my superiors; but they won't be able to take any action until after the assignment move begins."

Back on the campus Communist students began to make little speeches to the rest of us about the importance of putting aside our selfish personal hopes and plans in favor of giving our talents to "serve the people."

"Comrades, we have eaten the millet of the people. The people have invested their sweat and labor in educating us—you, me, every single student at Peita. Most good comrades recognize that, and are grateful. It is only just and right that we who are going to graduate now should go out from Peita, out from our beloved university, to work for the people. Comrades, it is glorious work!

"All of us who know the joy of standing in the vanguard of the revolution stand ready now to pick up our tools and join our comrades where we are needed. There are still a few classmates, however, who have not given up the dreams they dreamed in the old days of using the education the people have given them just to look for posts where they can gain personal glory, where they can impress the worker or the simple peasant with their education and their rank. Our word to these comrades is: Forget those plans! They are not for today, comrades, not for our new life. To you who hold back, I say: Join us, comrades. Join us to build our New China. You will find a ready welcome and a helping hand."

Later they explained the "helping hand." It meant that students who were "confused" about their life plans were to be "psychologically prepared" to make the "correct" decision by the leaders who had watched us for eighteen months. At first we had trouble understanding the imported term "psychological preparation." But by now we could guess in advance the importance of "discussion" as a link in the process. To non-Communists, "discussing the problem of employment after graduation" was to mean examining their own wrong ideas, listening quietly to the comments and recommendations of Party and Youth League leaders, and sitting tight until their jobs were arranged for them. The discussions gave us many valuable by-products, too, such as learning how to take hints, how to interpret facial expressions, and how to develop patience in the face of growing irritation. But the most valuable lesson to be learned again from this discussion was one we had already learned before. "If you can remain silent, stay silent. If you cannot, say a little. If you must say more, then do so. Better to tell less truth than more truth, or no truth at all than even a little truth."

After a month or so our leaders apparently thought that we were sufficiently "prepared" to fill out the new employment forms. Each student was asked to fill in four copies. One was for the university and two were for the government. The fourth and last copy would accompany the applicant forever; after his superiors had added their remarks about him, he would hand the form in a sealed envelope to the institution he was to work in. If he left that job, the form would accompany him while he looked for another one, to tell prospective employers facts about him which he could never read himself.

Some students were taken aback by the length and complexity of the form. First, of course, were the obvious questions:

Name?

Age?

Sex?

Birthplace?

General health?

Health, of course, was important, if our superiors were to select young cadre members who could work a full eight or ten hours and then go on to *hsueh-hsi* two to four hours more. Apparently there was so much work to be done, it was not a cause for surprise that the daily schedule for a Party or government worker was so demanding. If a member of a cadre came down with tuberculosis, of course, he could expect a special allowance. For any other disease he could expect at most extra monthly compensation of a little more than JMP$10,000 * in the way of "health preservation fees." You could read one strong hint of the situation in the form itself: the space in which your "health" was to be recorded was indeed very small. You were evidently expected to write in "normal" or "T.B." If you had unfortunately caught pleurisy, there would not be enough space for the word.

Hobbies and specialties did not get much space, either. Was this perhaps a hint that they should coincide with the needs of the people? Next was a question on your knowledge of foreign languages and the different Chinese dialects. These were more pertinent. No one who knew Russian or English or the Hunan dialect was likely to be left unheeded.

Then the questions became more personal. You could declare yourself married or single; but whichever it was, you were asked the name of your *ai-jen*, your "lover" or "beloved." This person

---

* JMP: *Jen Min Piao* (People's Bank Notes). The approximate exchange rate in 1950 was JMP$22,700 to US$1.00.

would be your husband or wife if you were married, and your sweetheart if you were single. Space was also provided to report your lover's political attitude, his profession, his address. This question was just as essential as the one on your parents. The Communists knew that many young people might forsake their relatives, but that few would abandon their *ai-jen*. Besides, anyone who loved a Communist was apt at the least to be a dependable progressive.

After your *ai-jen* was taken care of, there were questions about the names, professions, and political attitudes of your family members. None of the graduating students had proletarian parents. Many, if the truth must be told, had parents who were actually quite old-fashioned and conservative. No student, however, wanted to admit that on the form. They could not call them progressive, either; many of our parents—especially our mothers—had no clear political opinions at all, but would support anybody who might improve their economic situation. The most accurate description you could put down would be "political attitude not clear"—but that would suggest that your parents might be secret agents. The political views of one's brothers and sisters were even harder to define. It would be a very easy job, of course, if they were all members of the Party—or perhaps it would be even more difficult.

Next came a section on the employment form devoted to "social relations." Our leaders turned out to be most particular about personal connections. If you had eminent relatives or distinguished friends, you had better tell all about them. Who knows, it might help you. If you were unlucky enough to have reactionary relatives or friends, however, you had better not mention them. Later, if anybody happened to ask, simply tell him you had severed connections with them over politics. The inquirer might or might not believe it, but it was always safer not to fill in that column.

When you turned the employment questionnaire over, there was room on the other side for your own personal history. What organizations did you belong to before the Liberation? What middle schools have you studied in? What executive positions have you held in student organizations? We went through these questions quickly. We were only surprised that they were asked again, because they had been asked so often before.

At last: the personal-preference column. What profession are you most interested in entering? In what part of the country? In what institution or organization? Here most of us weighed our answers with great care.

Down at the bottom was the "class judgment column," with its promise of what was to come. Yes, this was the most important decision any student could face; his class would have to help him make it by discussing his qualifications and plans with him. Under this space was room for "views of the Department." But certainly any nitwit could see that the Department would undoubtedly respect the "democratic sentences" passed on the students by their classes.

And down underneath all this was a column for future use by our leaders. It was simply headed "Remarks."

We filled out the forms to the best of our ability, handed them in, and waited for the summons to appear before the tribunal of our classmates for judgment on our hopes. In collective activities such as class judging, it seems that there must always be some deviation, leftist or rightist. This time the deviation was leftist: in some of the classes the questions we were egged on by our leaders to ask were too harsh and brutal. Some students were cross-examined so aggressively that some of their more outspoken classmates protested on their behalf. Our leaders got the idea; the meetings were adjourned without notice, and the stiff judgments handed down on the first victims were revised.

After the class-criticism meetings were resumed, the "democratic sentences" passed on graduating students were on the whole really quite "democratic." After passionate debating the leftist extremists usually gave way, and the group verdict of the class was mild. "A hard worker in *hsueh-hsi*." "Very good, too, in her academic work." "On good terms with the masses." Why shouldn't we be moderate? When we handed down our verdicts, we remembered that we were soon to be judged ourselves by the classmates whose future we were now debating. Very rarely were serious defects mentioned, although there might be a few mild comments. "We hope you will step up your *hsueh-hsi*." "Your comrades hope you will mix more with the masses." "Your comrades hope you will pick up more Communist theories." "Your comrades fervently hope you will work hard to rid yourself of your slack and free style of living."

Despite the general mildness of the verdicts, many students were compelled to recant their first preferences for employment and accept the choices thrust upon them by the class leaders. We began to appreciate how desperately the new government needed educated young people to train as cadres for the mushrooming government bureaus and offices. Students who wanted to go into private employment, even as teachers, or who wanted to proceed with advanced study, even in medicine, were criticized by the Party as "selfish" and "individualistic," unwilling to return to the people what belonged to the people. Of course, stubborn applicants could always insist on their own choice, but face was, after all, important. So, after bearing attacks from all sides, even stubborn classmates were usually pushed into accepting the suggestions of their comrades. The few who held out, and insisted on their own choices, eventually triumphed and felt quite proud of themselves.

After such a demonstration of the "democratic spirit" advocated by our leaders, we felt that the "democratic sentences" handed down by the various classes would be treated with respect. Since, as I have said, most of these sentences were quite favorable, the more naïve among us felt immensely pleased, and slept soundly after their "trial" before their peers.

What about me? Could I sleep soundly too? I sat in the classroom now, looking at the examination paper I had just written, remembering how the class had tried to argue me into giving up my ambition to teach, and perhaps to write, and to enter government service instead. "Your comrades hope, Miss Yen, that you will examine again this notion of yours, which we are afraid shows you think more of your own personal ambitions than you do of the people. This is a time to abandon such individualistic dreams, and to take your proper place side by side with your comrades. The people need you, just as they need all of us!"

Who needs me? I wondered, sitting in the silent classroom—the government, the Military Control Commission, or the people? Is this the revolution of the proletariat we had been promised, the new road to freedom and peace we had been told about before the Liberation? We had tried so hard to believe. Could I come to believe if I kept trying, if I kept listening to the encouragement and exhortations of our leaders? In my heart I knew the answer. But did I have the courage to act on the answer?

Because the answer was that I couldn't believe. The reality had destroyed my faith. Or rather, I had never had the faith, just a hope that the promises would turn out to be true. Perhaps the person who has been promised heaven should not have it delivered to him, at least in this world. I know now that the reality will never be as bright as the expectation. My classmates and I were at exactly the wrong age to come to terms. If we were older, with families of our own and a position to keep, self-interest might help us convince ourselves that we did believe. If we were younger, in middle school instead of at Peita, and had never bumped up against some of the books and ideas we had been exposed to at Peita, we might believe too. Because now our younger brothers and sisters would never know anything else except what our leaders wanted them to know. They might come to believe that the promises really had come true. They might even be happier for so believing.

But our hope that the Communists would bring us freedom and plenty and peace—the things they promised us—was grafted on ideas about these things which we didn't get from the Communists. And we were finding out that our leaders carried their own original definitions of these things with them. We could be useful to the new leaders—but we could also be dangerous, unless we were made over to be the people that they wanted us to be.

Perhaps it was just self-pity, but I was sure now that some of my generation could never find the security or happiness we had thought a year ago was almost within our reach. We could be trained, yes; we were already being trained to fit in. And we could compromise with what we had been so unfortunate as to learn before the Liberation. We had already compromised—every time we wrote an essay, every time we went to a meeting, every time we parroted the things we were being told, every time we confessed our own sins or attacked the thoughts of our friends.

Had I compromised too much already? Perhaps it was too late for me to do anything else but give in and find the place where I could get by with the least loss in self-respect, the place where the self-loathing wouldn't be too hard to bear. Sometimes I thought it was too late. But that was what they wanted me to think. Had they really calculated me and my classmates so well?

Suppose they were wrong? They were so sure of themselves, so confident—some of it was sure to rub off on us. Suppose I still had enough stubbornness left not to join them. It wouldn't make much difference; it couldn't hurt them very much. But it would mean to me, at least, and to a few friends, that their belief in themselves and their triumph wasn't 100 per cent sure. But it would also mean far more than that for me. I am selfish enough to want to live in some place where the conspiracy against truth isn't as well organized as they had succeeded in making it. My self-respect is important to me, if to no one else. Suppose I really did have the courage to run. It would be running—I might as well admit that. And would I get the chance? It was getting more difficult. But all my heart told me now that I must wait and watch for that chance. I wouldn't know until I tried whether I had the courage to break away. But I knew that I couldn't reconcile myself to the life I was living now until I had taken the test.

The last page of my essay lay on the desk in front of me. I had tried to put as much of myself in the essay as I could, but I had finished it off with the expected tribute to the wise leadership of the Party under the guidance of Chairman Mao Tse-tung. I didn't want to read the last page again. I pinned it to the other pages and stood up.

"I think I'm finished now," I told the instructor. He accepted the paper and I smiled at him. He had been a good teacher, I told myself.

I came out of the classroom feeling somewhat lost, now that everything was over. I got my school things together, packed them noiselessly, hailed a pedicab at the gate, and returned home.

In the next week friends stopped by to ask me to attend the commencement ceremonies. I managed to find excuses not to go; the fact was that I honestly wasn't feeling very well, and my excuses were convincing when my friends took a good look at me. Then other schoolmates came by to invite me to take part in the summer work and study activities before we went off to take the posts we were still waiting to be assigned. I told them again that my health wasn't good after the last year of work. My friend Chang saw that

I seemed to be worried about something, and with the best intentions in the world he asked me over to visit him.

"You seem to be out of sorts, comrade. I hope you're not afraid that the work to be assigned to you won't suit you," he asked, while he poured my tea.

"No, not that. I already expect that."

"Well—I hope you're not saying the government will not assign suitable work for us. You mustn't be so distrustful," he said seriously but kindly. "In two weeks or so our jobs are going to be announced. I'm sure you'll be satisfied with what you get. And you won't want to give it up."

"Huh," I replied listlessly. "Six months ago, when your friend Wang tried to talk me into applying for the Youth League, do you know what he told me? He told me: 'You're looking forward to graduating, aren't you? And after your graduation, don't you want to work for us? You certainly want to work instead of sitting around at home like an old-fashioned bourgeois woman waiting for somebody to come along and marry you! If you want me to be frank about it, if you don't join the organization how can the government give you the right kind of work? How can the government trust you if you stay on the outside like this?' You know, I almost made up my mind right there."

Although the boy I was talking to was a "progressive element," I knew that he was less blindly obedient than most Party and Youth League members, and still was guilty sometimes of thinking for himself. I didn't have to speak too guardedly with him, but I had just said something about making up my mind. I wondered briefly if what I had said wasn't perhaps a bit too revealing.

"Making up your mind about what?" he asked after waiting for me to go on.

I didn't dare tell him I'd made up my mind to try to resist, so I fibbed: "Oh, I've just decided not to rely on the government entirely. Maybe I'd better get out and look for work myself if I want to serve the people."

"You're just too proud," he said with a laugh, so I laughed too. Then he became serious. "No, you didn't seem to be so set in your ways before. You'd better look at your ideas again, very carefully. If you don't, people will say that you are being smothered by the egotism of the bourgeoisie. You know, they'll say that you cling to the idea of individual heroism, that you don't want to follow the government policy of assigning work centrally, and that you don't care about the over-all needs of the government. But I don't want to say so. I feel you are basically . . ." He stopped, embarrassed. "Anyhow, I believe you do want to serve the people. If I didn't believe that, I wouldn't be here talking to you. But you don't trust the government. And if you want my honest opinion, you're just too stubborn."

Well, if he wanted an argument I was prepared to give him one. But we were interrupted by Ho Li-ling, his sweetheart, who found us both bristling, and started talking about an expedition to the Summer Palace. The talk stayed on lighter things, and about sundown I said goodbye. They saw me to the door, and his parting words were: "Trust the Party not to deceive us. The Party, you should know by now, cherishes youth. The best thing you can do for yourself is to build up your confidence and obey the policy of letting the people who know best assign the right jobs for us."

If I remember the date, the first group of students heard about their fate on July 12th, when a list made up of the names of a small group of Party and Youth League members from the College of Arts and Sciences was posted. It was good news for them; they were assigned to the Cultural and Educational Committee for unspecified duties. Then it was announced that they would be sent to the People's Democracies in East Europe for special schooling.

Since the first contingent was handed first-rate jobs, perhaps the second group might receive second-rate jobs. Some worried students whose trust in the government was not so great as it was supposed to be set up a murmur which reached the ears of the Party. Because the Party apparently realized that it was handling the announcements in an unnecessarily provocative manner, it changed its original plans of announcing the jobs in batches and told us it would make everybody's assignments public at one stroke.

Called together in the assembly hall of the North Mansion on the morning of July 29th, we heard an official representative read off the posts we graduates were asked to take. We leaned forward, tense and excited, to hear what our leaders had decided.

"Chen Liang-kuo—Financial and Economic Committee!"
"Chen Ma-kwei—State Administrative Council!"
"Chen Ying-te—Political and Law Committee!"
"Feng Ta-wei—Ministry of Foreign Affairs!"
"Feng Yang-hsi—Ping-yuan Provincial Government."
My name would be near the end of the list. While I waited, I looked around me. The hardest-hit of my classmates were those who had slept the most soundly. Indeed, they did not begin to wake up until now. But classmates who had revised their references in accord with the suggestions of our leaders showed no surprise or disappointment whatever.

Most of us, I saw, were being commissioned to work in the various offices of the Central People's Government in Peking and Tientsin. Less fortunate comrades were getting assignments to work in undisclosed institutions in Inner Mongolia, Ping-yuan Province, and so on. Then the man at the speaker's stand came to my name.

"Maria Yen—the Political and Law Committee!"

What should I have expected—a miraculous reprieve? I sat without much feeling, with only a certain sad joy that I had decided to resist before my assignment fixed my conviction. The police and the People's Court—they must trust me more than I thought. But they needed people with at least a reading knowledge of foreign languages, and I fit that category.

After the speaker had finished reading our assignments, students who were going to work in the same organizations were ordered to assemble on the spot and elect representatives to keep in touch with their organizations so that they would learn the exact offices in which they were to work and the precise dates on which to report. Except for a few privileged student Party members, graduates knew only what Ministry they were going to work in and the names of the classmates who would go along with them.

It was already too late to regret; there was no choice for anyone who wanted to conform except to go along and report for service. Now students who had not received jobs they thought they were qualified for baited themselves with inevitable questions. "Why didn't I join the organization?" "Why didn't I make the right psychological preparation?" "Why didn't I swallow my pride and accept the suggestions at the criticism meeting?" Why, indeed? From where I sat, I saw that in the distribution of jobs the Communist students, whether they had done well in the regular academic courses or not, had been given the choice places. Next came the Youth League members. Students with the wrong political attitudes, or students indifferent to politics, had in most cases been given "rough" assignments which had little or nothing to do with their talents or interests. Since these students included some of our best scholars and ablest workers, it seemed to me that our leaders had decided to condemn these "silly bookworms" to hard labor like stupid donkeys. Perhaps the Communists were thinking, "Let's give these stubborn cases a lesson and see whether they still turn up their noses at our organization."

The third day after the list of jobs had been announced, Chang came back to see me again. Sure that he was going to try to persuade me to take the job assigned me, I didn't wait for him to begin talking, but told him right off that I had got another job on my own. And since the job wasn't in Peking, I must leave Peking.

"I didn't think that you had really made up your mind." He sounded disappointed. "Taking the job the government offered you is voluntary, of course. But the job you got on your own hook—do you think it's wise to take it unless you get the approval of the State Administrative Council?"

"I know all that." I looked down because I didn't want to look at his face. "But, as a matter of fact, I have my choice of two jobs, all through a friend in the South. One of the jobs is teaching in a private middle school, and I believe that for a job with a private organization you don't have to get government approval here. After all, the school is willing to hire me."

Fearful that he might go on to question me about the non-existent school, I hastily changed the subject. "And what about you? Aren't you about due to report to your working station? Do you know when yet?"

"I don't know the exact date, but I hope pretty soon. Maria, I do hope you'll make the right final decision and trust the Party. Trust the government not to deceive its young people. Trust that the jobs assigned us will suit our individual interests and meet the people's needs. . . ."

He said more, but I didn't want to listen any longer.

At last he went away, half angry and half disappointed. I had repeated my statement: "I have made up my mind. Do you think I change my mind all the time?"

My mind *was* made up, too. I wasn't quite sure what I was going to do, but I was very sure that I wasn't going to work for the Party or for the government, for the Public Security police or the People's Courts, not in any other Ministry or Bureau in any sort of job, high or low. I stayed at home for almost three weeks trying to decide what to do. By this time my parents were becoming concerned about me, and tried to urge me to go out. I thought about Chang. Although our goodbyes had been chilly, he was still a friend of mine after all. I decided to run over to ask his mother how he was coming along on his new job.

But when the servant opened the door, it was not Chang's mother, but his sweetheart, Ho Li-ling, who greeted me. She looked tired and troubled. She was thinking too much about Chang, so I tapped her on the shoulder. "What are you looking so down in the mouth about? Don't worry about him; he can come back home every week to see you. Isn't he still in Peking?"

"He's right here," she smiled wryly. "Wait and I'll call him in."

Out came Chang, looking disheveled and sporting several days' growth of beard. He tried to smile when he saw me standing there, but it wasn't convincing.

After a silence he asked, "Well, Maria, when do you plan to leave Peking?"

Because I was not in a mood to invent details about my non-existent job, and was anxious to find out what had happened to him, I shrugged his question aside and asked: "You've certainly been busy, haven't you? But how come you're back here in a state like this?"

His sweetheart was more straightforward than he was, and answered for him. "He's quit and has come back home. I don't want him to go back again."

"What in the world happened?"

Chang still kept silent, as if debating with himself. Finally he spoke up in a self-mocking tone: "You know, I must have cut a comical figure a few weeks ago, telling you that you should trust everybody. Well, I should have been smart enough not to take my own advice. We really must have looked like a herd of innocent sheep when we marched off to our jobs. But—well, maybe it's good to learn even if you learn the way I did."

I looked at Li-ling. She was obviously of two minds. She had heard the story before and didn't want to hear it again, but she wanted to stay with him.

"I finally got word to report for duty about two weeks ago," he went on. "The day before we set out, the cadre members asked us to pack our things and assemble the next morning on the campus. We were supposed to catch a truck there to take us to a big building on a certain street where they told us we were going to work. Because we were excited about going to work at last, we went off and packed our stuff and showed up on time at Peita. The send-off team was there waiting for us, and we all felt like real heroes when they cheered us and shouted slogans."

He rubbed at the stubble of his beard. "Who would have guessed, after our things had been tossed on the truck and we had climbed on behind them, that the cadre members would tell us that there had been a change in orders and we were not going to the big building. Instead, we were headed for a place outside the city."

"Did you all agree?" I would be angry if they had.

"With the gongs beating and all the cheers of the send-off team, do you think anybody was going to jump down off the truck?"

"What happened then? Where did you go?"

"Who knew what place?" Chang seemed irritated. "We knew only that we passed a lot of trees, farmhouses, fields, gravemounds— we don't know the country that well. Finally we ended up in front of a long building. Everybody inside was in uniform."

"What was it?" I interrupted him, surprised. "You weren't supposed to be assigned to the Military Council. How come there were soldiers in the building?"

"Ask yourself!" He was angry enough now to shout.

"Ask myself! Weren't you the one who told me how much the Party loves youth, how they'd never, never cheat us." As soon as I had spoken, I was sorry that I had mocked him. He stopped, we smiled at each other, and then he went on, more quickly. "The cadre members saw that we didn't like the business—some hotheads were already mumbling things about being kidnaped. So the head of the cadre told us that somebody had made a mistake, that we should have been informed yesterday of the sudden shift in orders. The other cadre members laughed and joked and persuaded us to eat first while they tried to find out what had happened. Well, I ask you, who could eat? Several students even cursed the cadre members right to their faces."

"You mean even Youth League comrades cursed?" I couldn't believe it. If Youth League members, who had expected the better jobs, were in such a pickle, what could we think? I went on. "Naturally, if you're not in the organization, you might expect your assignment to be changed like that, overnight. But imagine comrades from the Youth League being treated so!" I made the remark sound as innocent as I could.

"Maria, let me finish. Several comrades from the Youth League surrounded the Number One cadre member and shouted that they wanted to go back to Peita to get all the facts and get the whole business cleared up. He told them that they were too young and excitable and that they had better calm down and think about the consequences. That didn't scare some of us, and we tried to negotiate with them for our freedom to go back."

"Why bother to negotiate? Why not just simply walk out?"

"Easier said than done. We'd come to the place by truck, and it had taken three hours to reach it. Even if we had known the way back—which we didn't—we couldn't have walked back before the city gates were closed. But we didn't want to wait, either. If we waited until the next day, maybe they'd truck us to a place even farther away from the city. And what about our stuff? Our luggage was still on the truck, and nobody could get his things without a leave slip."

"You should have sacrificed your luggage. After all, more than that was at stake."

"How stupid do you think I am? I could have walked off and left my stuff without flicking an eyelid. But how did you think I was going to find my way back to the city? By my nose?"

I wanted to stop him before he got more angry than he was already. "All right, the important thing is that you got away. Now what are you planning to do?"

"I don't know." He looked sheepish. "I suppose I'm planning to ask the government to reassign me to other work."

"You think you won't get cheated again?" I asked in a low voice. "Aren't you satisfied when they cheat you once?"

Another wry smile. "Once—more than once. After the Youth League members set up a hubbub, the cadre member promised us that we would be hauled back to the city as soon as the truck came back. Meanwhile he asked us to listen to a talk. The talk lasted three hours. Three hours—and mostly illogical, nothing but mixed-up threats and cajoling. He said if we would quiet down and take the new work that had been assigned to us, we would have a bright future ahead of us and would soon be promoted to better jobs. We heard the truck coming, but the cadre member kept right on talking. The more we heard, the more anxious we were to get out. Finally, after he finished, we demanded again to be sent back to Peking. The cadre member went out to see if the truck had come. When he came back to the room, he told us: 'My goodness, comrades, I really am sorry! The truck has come and gone. The driver was all mixed up, I guess. Please go by the next truck tomorrow.'

"Our anger really boiled up. We shouted in chorus to go back. Only one candidate for Party membership asked the rest of us to calm down and consider the facts. We shouted back that the only fact was that we wanted to go back. Well, the next morning they let us go—after another three-hour speech in which the Number One cadre member told us how much they were disappointed in us."

"Do you honestly believe the government will reassign you to a better job?" I asked him.

"Maybe not a better job. But I don't want you to think I've lost all confidence in our leaders. I can't believe that all the things we've heard are lies. I don't see how a new proletarian regime based on the people like this can slide downhill so easily. Anyway, I want to wait and watch before I decide. Maybe we have formed mistaken ideas of our own which keep us from understanding things clearly. If you are not a revolutionary, you are counter-revolutionary. I want to stay on the side of the oppressed workers and toilers. You can't expect me to surrender to the running dogs and imperialists!"

Five minutes earlier I would have tried my best to persuade him to be on our side, but I gave up the idea after hearing him through. "What you just said might as well have been taken straight out of the cadre member's speech. And you saw how he cheated you!"

"I hope that was just a small slice of the whole picture. You know—a partial deviation."

"A partial deviation!" I mocked him. "What nonsense that is! You must have forgotten. Why do you hate the cadre member? Or why do you blame him? I don't hate this single cadre member at all!" I was so annoyed that I slammed my clenched fist down on the table. "I'll tell you what I believe. I believe the government has assigned work to us so that we will become cadre members ourselves to cheat other young people, just as this cadre member has cheated—"

"What's got into you?" he broke in. "What are you so excited for? Come, try to collect yourself."

"Is that what the cadre member told you?"

"Listen! You don't—" He stopped himself with an effort. "Well, that's enough. I don't want to talk about it any more."

I was truly sorry that I had lost my temper. He wanted to believe so badly after hoping and trusting for so long. And was there a chance that he was right? Down deep in my heart I knew that there wasn't. I thought back over the past eighteen months and the things we had learned: how to conform, how to give lip service, how to cheer. But I couldn't convince him otherwise; he would have to convince himself, and perhaps he could continue to hang on to the illusions he had if he could only hear the speeches often enough. He would have to go his way, and I would have to go mine. Had I hurt him so badly that he would inform on me? I didn't think so: Chang hadn't learned to do that yet.

As soon as I could I took leave. We shook hands warmly to show that our anger had vanished. I apologized. "I'm sorry that

I've offended you. You must be tired and discouraged. You'd better relax and get some rest. I'll come back to see how you're coming along one of these days."

I took his hand again because I knew that I would not come back again. The chances were that this was the last time we would ever meet as friends.

CHAPTER XVI

Decision

In the early winter of 1949, half a year before we were scheduled to graduate, when the new government was riding on the crest of its military conquests in the South, something strange happened on the campus. Two of our schoolmates packed up a few belongings, tricked the school authorities into giving them papers, got on a train to Tientsin without being detected, and then slipped on board a ship to Hong Kong. Their escape had been so well planned that not even their best friends had suspected; they had attended classes and a political meeting the day before they disappeared.

One of the fugitives—call him Hsiao—had been a student in the Philosophy Department. He had made a promising record; for several years he had scored average marks of 85 or 90 in most of the courses he had taken. That was phenomenal at Peita, where grading was strict and where 75 was considered the mark of a good student. In fact, in the previous year Hsiao had ranked first among students in the College of Arts. True, he had not been a very social person; but practically everyone on the campus knew who he was, and respected his ability.

His companion, Hsu, had been a student in Western literature. Like Hsiao, he had been regarded as one of the best students in his department. While he hadn't bothered too much with dates and names, and hence hadn't scored quite as well in exams as Hsiao, he had an original turn of mind which gave the promise of genuine literary talent. His professors thought highly of him, and several were enthusiastic enough to tutor him in private.

The flight of the two classmates, who only had six months to wait for their degrees, created a disturbing undercurrent at Peita. Youth League leaders announced that they had always suspected them of being reactionaries. We heard one leader remark with bitter confidence: "Maybe they're safe for now. But where can they go where the Liberation won't catch up with them?" We all joined in the chorus of contempt and abuse when our leaders wanted us to, but secretly I wondered how many of us weren't privately glad that our two friends had managed to get away.

You see, I remembered that day back in 1948 when Peita students were fleeing into the liberated area, and a professor had told a friend that this was an omen of the collapse of the old government. "Look at those young people fleeing across to the other side. In the past forty years our students have always acted as a vanguard of the times. An exodus like this certainly means the old government is doomed." Now the trend was reversed; but if the professor wanted to draw a parallel he was prudent enough to draw it to himself. All he would say was a cryptic, "Yes . . . well, it seems to be something of a surprise, doesn't it?"

I am not suggesting, when I tell you about my friends and myself, that the decampment of a handful of students from Peita means the downfall tomorrow of the Communist Government with its armies, its police powers, its millions of loyal and disciplined Party members. The flight of a few is the only witness I can give you for the fact that they left behind them other young people who were disappointed that the promises weren't coming true, but who lacked the courage or the opportunity to join them.

I didn't make up my mind to go for another six months after the flight of the two students—perhaps I had not mustered the courage and determination then to follow their example, to leave my family and my friends for a life outside of China, a life that appeared as unattractive as it was uncertain. Besides, I was selfish enough to want to graduate. And, of course, I was buoyed up by the illogical hope (which is one of the best allies I think the Communists have) that somehow things were bound to improve. That is what many of us told ourselves in the eighteen months after the Liberation. Though things had turned out to be not quite what we'd been promised, we had to admit that the new government had immense problems. And if it was sometimes arbitrary or peremptory, why it had too many things to do, and too little time, to do them in any more "democratic" way. Wouldn't the democracy come later, when the debris was cleared out of the way and the building was started?

Each one of us at Peita had to work out his own secret answer to that question, and I'm afraid that for most of us the wrestling with our thoughts was not dramatic or easy. Too many things had to go into the answer—our hopes for ourselves as well as for China, our family ties, the work we had put in during the four years at Peita to prepare ourselves for the task of building a new China. Yes, we were ready now to leave the classroom, ready to pick up our tools. But what sort of new China was it that our leaders were training us to build?

Oh, we would do all right personally. After all, we were going to be the élite; and, by trying hard, I could find an excuse for almost everything that had happened, for almost everything the new government had done. When I couldn't find an excuse, my friends were always ready to find one for me. But somehow all of the individual excuses could not add up to the one big excuse I needed to surrender to the thing that the "rule of the people" had turned out to be. Some day, I knew, I would come to the end of all excuses. Ahead of us, if I wanted to be honest with myself, I could see nothing but a tyranny more thorough and efficient than any we had ever known.

We had wanted so badly to believe. We had wanted so much to have something to work for and to fight for. By an act of faith, we did get ourselves to believe for a long time. Many of my friends believe yet. The day will come, I know, when some of them will confess to themselves, with the doors and windows shut, that they no longer trust and hope. With a little imagination I can guess what courage it will take to stay and resist when that happens—it is too late for most of them to flee now—to hold on to as much integrity as you can, to swallow your pride in public and struggle with your dissent in private. In exile you are lonely, even when thousands are in exile with you. But in the midst of the flags, the beating on the drums, the disciplined cheers, I know you can be just as lonely in Peking.

Was it one single thing that made me go, or a heaping up of things? It was possible to wait too long to make up your mind, to make too many small compromises, to come to terms too often with the petty humiliations and defeats that were intended to teach you discipline. Already I knew how easy it might be to keep your mouth shut and take the job that had been offered you by the government. Perhaps I'd better go now, or I might never summon up the courage to leave.

Right now, if you used your head and had your share of luck, it was still possible to get out. Later on it might not be. Already the police were much more curious about travelers than they had been a year before. Foreigners needed travel passes even to move outside the city gates. Before too long perhaps Chinese might need passes too.

All of these things told me it was time to go. But once I had made up my mind to try, it took me almost a week to think of a plan that might work. If I succeeded in leaving Peking without too much fuss, I might be able to travel to Canton, on the excuse of having taken a job as teacher in a middle school there. Canton was only eighty miles or so from the British colony of Hong Kong. Only— would my excuse take me all the way? Wouldn't I be more and more likely to run into people who could see through it the closer I got to Canton? I didn't really know enough about the place to concoct a very plausible story. I would have to take the chance, I decided; and once in Canton I would have to take the chance of finding some way to cross the border into Hong Kong.

After talking my supposed job over with a friend whom I'll call Mr. Niu, I got him to write a letter of recommendation to a Mrs. Loh in Canton. I did my best to hint to Mr. Niu what kind of help I wanted from Mrs. Loh; I didn't dare tell him in so many words that I was not going to stay in Canton and look for a job. Then, with my letter in hand, I went home to face the job of breaking the news to my family that I wanted to leave Peking.

My father did not like the idea of my going to Canton. I didn't tell my family that I intended Canton to be only a stop on my way. They didn't dream that I would think of going to a foreign place like Hong Kong, I was sure. Because I couldn't tell them, because I knew the sort of debate my decision would bring, I produced all the arguments I could think of to defend my plan to "take the teaching job in Canton." Against their opposition I stood firm, and my mother softened first.

"I suppose it wouldn't do any great harm to let Maria try it." She moved over to my side, and finally my father gave in, with great reluctance.

With this great obstacle removed, I went to the district police station to apply for permission to cancel my residential registration and transfer it to Canton. I was still lucky; the man I talked to at the station seemed to be out of sorts with his job that morning. Making no effort to hide his boredom, he shuffled through the census books until he found my name, and then, without too many questions, after he had looked at my student credentials, granted my request. I stepped outside the police station with a lighter heart and went straight to the Chien Men station to book my ticket.

I went around to say my goodbyes. First, I stopped at the faculty house shared by Professor Chi and Professor Peng, who, I knew, were advanced "progressives," but who had been quite good to me. After ten minutes of chitchat I stood up and remarked as calmly as I could, "I do want to thank you for the help you have given me all these years, because this may be the last time I'll come to see you." I started to open the door myself.

"What do you mean? Wait a minute. You're assigned to work in Peking, aren't you? You don't have to go yet. Come on back and let's have a talk about this."

I didn't want to deceive men I liked and respected, but I couldn't tell them the truth. I had to reply, "Well, perhaps I might come back once more. Anyway, I shouldn't take up your time talking about it today."

"Don't tell me you've been assigned to some other place?" Professor Chi pressed for an answer.

Professor Peng was on his feet too. "At least you can stay long enough to tell us what's wrong."

I had to let go of the door handle and sit down again. All I wanted to do was to say goodbye as soon as I could. So I told them in one breath what they wanted to know. "I know you're going to be disappointed in me. But I'm more disappointed than you are— so I have to do what I'm doing now. I just can't take the work the government has assigned me." My memory darted back to the end of 1948, when the teachers called roll and found so many classmates missing. "Now, please understand me, I still want to serve the people. I honestly mean that. But I want to go away from here—I want to find some work I really think I'm fit for. I believe I understand myself better than the government does. You probably think I'm selfish. But I can't stay here any more."

Professor Chi was silent, but Professor Peng said: "We haven't heard. What job has the government assigned you?"

I told them. "The Political and Law Committee."

I waited for them to say something. Finally I broke the silence. "Well, now I've told you. I don't want to take up any more of your time—I hope you're not too disappointed in me."

Professor Peng finally had something to say. "I suppose we have to admit that this isn't the sort of post you'd expect a student to be assigned to who has taken her major in the College of Arts. You should realize that it's not just a job with the police, but a real chance to serve your country. . . . Tell me, are you a member of the Youth League?"

"No, I'm not."

"You're not? Why haven't you joined it earlier?"

I knew they were both sincere in their concern for me, but I couldn't let myself forget that they were "progressives." I spoke up: "Honestly, I don't have the slightest idea of blaming the government. The government has been good to me. Hasn't my education come from the people? I don't think they've discriminated against me by asking me to take this job. Some Youth League comrades in our class have been assigned with me, and they say they're proud to be called for such an important task. Just as I said, I'm disappointed only because the government doesn't understand what I can and can not do."

It was Professor Chi's cue to look disappointed, too. "I should have—uh—advised you before this to obey the government's leadership and follow its policy of unified assignment. But I won't talk about that today." He raised his head and tried to catch my eye. "I can only tell you today not to give up your hope and your enthusiasm just because your assignment has not turned out to be what you expected. Not that I want to suggest that the government has not done its best to put you in a job for which you are well qualified, but it may not be too late to do something about it. It would be a shame if you gave up all hope of going on with more study—I know you are interested in that. Nobody who wants to join in the most glorious task we have, the glorious task of building up a new China, can afford to give up the study of Marxism-Leninism and the New Democracy. But you'll have time to follow your own first love, too." He stopped for breath.

"If"—Professor Peng looked fatherly— "If the staff system at the university hadn't been changed this year, I think we would have liked to keep you on as an assistant. Do you think you could manage to stay here a little longer? I can't make you any guarantees, understand. But I believe I can find you a suitable job here if you let me try."

What he said might be true; Professor Peng had been given considerable responsibility in the administration of the university and had good contacts among cultural circles. But I had already decided; the decision had been reached after too much thinking and worrying to change it now.

Though I thanked them for their kindness, I said that because a friend had promised to get the job for me in Canton they shouldn't take so much trouble on my account. Then I got up again to say goodbye. Goodbye was easier to say than I ever dreamed it would be.

Then I walked over to call on another one of my favorite professors. Because he had not gone to much trouble to hide his restiveness about what had happened to Peita during the past year, I told him the truth. He was silent for a long time while I sat waiting for his advice not to go.

At last he said, with the utmost calmness, "I think you are

doing what is best for you." He stopped. "I wish I could go. But that's impossible, really impossible." I looked across at his face, weary and old and regretful. "But send me a letter when you get wherever you're going. Good luck." Then he added, "We don't have to say anything else about it." Inside the door I offered to shake hands, and he took my hand in a tight grip. "Good luck again." He didn't look up. I left him standing inside and closed the door softly behind me.

Then came the day when I climbed on the train at last and found my seat alone. When I saw my suitcase on the baggage rack over my head, my canvas roll beside me on the train seat, and through the window the people on the platform down to say fare-well to their friends, I gave up and started to cry. Until now worry about getting through the search at the platform gate had kept other emotions out of my mind; but the soldiers had pawed through my belongings with only casual interest, in a hurry to get to the middle-aged merchant in line behind me. So there I was, with a three days' ride ahead of me, and nothing to do but sit and think how shabby and full of holes the story was I had invented to get me through.

The engine up ahead gave a thin, satirical hoot, and under me the wheels began to roll. This was goodbye to everything I knew. I couldn't afford to keep on crying; people around me were be-ginning to look at me with curiosity. Perhaps if I held a book up in front of my eyes it would help. I fished around in my canvas bundle until I found the book of Tang poetry I had brought along. I turned to a poem I knew almost by heart; I didn't expect the close-set characters to squirm like wavering lines of black insects through my tears. I wished that I'd brought along an English book to read. At least the English type wouldn't thrust out wriggling arms and legs. But, no, it wouldn't have been wise. The guards who searched my baggage might have commented on it.

I told myself that I had better stop crying, that it was a luxury I should postpone enjoying. But there would have been something wrong with me if I hadn't cried then. Wasn't I leaving home? The train had already followed the curve in the track and had come out again from the tunnel through the city wall. My parents had said they were old and did not wish their children to go too far away.

I had clenched my teeth and said for the tenth time that I had already decided, that I had to go. They finally gave in. Though they had let me go, they had asked me to study or take a quiet job somewhere that would keep me out of political activities. I had bit my lower lip and pretended to agree.

Why had I deceived the two people who loved me best in the world? How could I be so hardhearted as to desert my father and my mother and run away like this? My flight could only do them harm. My promise was false. Wherever I was going, I was quite sure that I'd want to fight back. I was going farther than my parents knew. But that was the wrong thing to think about now. Yet I did think about it—to live alone in a strange place, maybe to die there, too; not to see those who loved me most, not to know whether I'd come back again to Peking. I knew all about exiles. Hadn't I seen the White Russians, thirty years without a country, living where they could find room for a while, despised by Chinese and foreigners alike? Their sons taking the jobs no one else wanted, their daughters lucky if they looked pretty enough for the foreign soldiers and sailors. Now the papers were beginning to mock at White Chinese, too, the wealthy merchants, the corrupt officials, the go-betweens for the white men, who had fled to Hong Kong ahead of me.

I told myself to put my head back, and it would be better; it's harder to cry with your head tilted back against the edge of the seat. I told myself to close my eyes, too, and pretend I was dozing; pretend I was sleeping, until the jolting and swaying and the shuffle of noise under my feet really put me to sleep.

It was already deep in the night when I woke up, feeling dirty and cramped. Under the one dim light that burned in the center of the coach, everything was quiet as death except for the wheels, the rattle of the window, loose in its frame, and an occasional sigh or snort from the sleepers around me. Outside the window everything was dark. I rubbed my eyes, which were sore and gritty and swollen. I felt hungry now, but I was the only one awake in the car. I looked around at my fellow travelers and remembered some dim fragment of something I had read about the sleepers, their bodies bent this way or that, sleeping like corpses on an abandoned battlefield, corpses with no feeling left but the love of absolute silence.

For the first time in my life I felt the taste of stark loneliness.

In my clenched hand I could feel the salt-stiff, dry wad of the handkerchief I had held on to in my sleep. It felt nasty; I pushed it back in my bundle and groped around for a clean one. But no more tears were coming. I held on to the handkerchief while I listened to the click of the wheels and gave myself to the sway of the coach and fell asleep again.

The early sun through the windows woke me up. I looked out at China going by me, the northern plain stretching away yellow and green as far as I could see. My eyes weren't so sore now. I thought about breakfast; but I'd better forget it for a while and start concentrating on the best way to tell my invented story. Someone was bound to ask me soon.

When the train stopped later in the morning, two soldiers with rifles strapped on their backs climbed on to inspect our baggage. I dragged my suitcase down from overhead and opened it for them. They turned over my clothes cursorily and looked at my books with more interest. I was sure they couldn't read, but they flipped through the pages anyway. The man in front looked at me from head to foot and asked me in my own Northern dialect:

"Are you a student?"

"Yes, comrades. From the capital."

"Where are you going?"

It was clearly written on my ticket, which he held in his hand. But I made my reply polite.

"To Canton, comrade."

"What for?" He was still curious. "You speak the Northern dialect. Your home isn't in Canton, is it?"

I got ready to give him the answer I had been rehearsing, but the other soldier clapped him on the shoulder. "Let's go. We've got more important things to do. Our duty is to look for smugglers and prohibited goods. You don't think this student comrade is carrying Chiang Kai-shek around in her pocket, do you?"

They left me and moved on down the car. I started breathing again; I swung my suitcase up on the rack, dug out my book of poetry, and sat down to read it while they searched other passengers. I opened the book at random and my eyes landed on the old line, "The journey is hard; I will turn my steps back home." Hurriedly I turned the page.

"Miss?"

It was a man's voice. He stood in the aisle beside my seat, but I was afraid to turn my head.

"Miss?"

What sort of impertinent, forward man was this? I'd better not pay any attention to him. I'd better not even look up at him.

"Miss, could I have just a word with you?"

I kept on reading my book, but I didn't see very much of what was on the page before me.

His voice was gentle but insistent. "Can I have a word with you, Miss? I think we know each other."

The last sentence startled me into looking up. Yes, indeed, we knew each other. I saw a familiar face looking down at me. Even the coffee-colored jacket and the yellow khaki trousers were not strange. But try as I might, I could not remember where I had met him.

He smiled at me politely and sat down opposite me. Who was he? I ransacked my memory desperately.

"You just graduated three weeks ago, didn't you? I remember you. I often saw you going to class. Your face, your dress. Even"— he pointed at the embroidered cloth bag stuffed in the seat beside me— "Even this bag of yours I recognize. Please don't blame me too much for being so abrupt, but it's really a coincidence that we meet so unexpectedly like this on a train. You don't mind my sitting down and talking with you, do you?"

Another Peita student. What could I do if he was going to Canton, too, and insisted on getting off the train with me? I congratulated myself that he hadn't been sitting there a few minutes ago when the soldiers came through to inspect us. Suppose the search party had pressed me for a definite answer. My story—"I just graduated from a middle school. I have a job in Canton—" would have been a disaster if it had been heard by my fellow student.

He took my silence for consent and began reeling off stories about himself, how happy he was to be on his way to his job assignment. I didn't listen very well. I was too busy trying to invent a new story to satisfy him and anyone else who might question me.

"Look, why don't we keep together the rest of the way down to Canton, comrade?" He used the word "comrade" after some hesitation. "It's still a long way. I'm quite worried about your taking care of yourself and your luggage. If you can trust an old Peita schoolmate, why can't I be your bodyguard?" Through his air of genial sincerity I caught a glimpse of something else. He preened himself. Did he think he was a gallant medieval courtier? "Well, what about it, comrade? Really, it's all for your own good—a young girl, with no companion. Aren't you afraid of meeting—"

"Afraid of meeting people like you, you mean?" I repented of the words as soon as I had spoken them. If he got angry, it wouldn't be good to have a public scene on the train. I hastily changed my tone. "No, I didn't mean that. I'm sorry; I apologize for being rude. I really appreciate your offer, but I'm used to traveling alone. I can take care of my things. Anyhow, thanks for your kindness."

Perhaps I had made my reply too soft. He bent over the table between our seats as if I had given him a hint to do so. "Oh, come on, comrade, stop telling lies. Look at your own eyes. Come on, let your fellow student take care of you."

I didn't know whether to laugh or to get angry, but I had to drive him away. "But, comrade, the railway now belongs to the people. It's controlled by the people, and everything is well run and completely safe. I don't think I'll run into any trouble." I bent down my head modestly. "Besides, when I arrive in Canton"—I patted at my lips with my handkerchief—"my lover will be waiting there at the station to meet me."

He withdrew the hand he had placed on the table. "Well, that's fine—that's very good, miss." He sat back against the seat. "In that case I certainly don't have to worry. Yes, I—I am very happy for you."

He mustered the nearest thing he could to a brotherly smile and took his leave.

I had discovered that reading a book wouldn't prevent people from bothering me. I turned my head to the window for a while, then leaned back and pretended to be asleep. Surely people wouldn't wake me up just to have someone to talk to. I closed my eyes and thought of the fields and towns that already lay between me and Peking and my family. It was better to open my eyes again and look at the country flicking past.

The seat opposite had been empty. Now there was a man in a Lenin uniform sitting there; he looked about forty and had a broad face with a flattened nose and wide-set eyes. He smiled briefly. "Well, comrade, you're awake. You're lucky to be able to sleep. It's a long trip, isn't it? And I don't think you've taken such a long journey alone ever before, have you? At least, you didn't look very happy about it yesterday. When I walked by then, I noticed you crying. But you're feeling better today, aren't you?"

There wasn't anything for me to do but smile back. "Thank you, comrade. As a matter of fact I've traveled alone before. I'm all right. I was only thinking of—" I didn't dare say my parents. That would be "feudalistic clannish ideology" or "petty bourgeois sentimentalism." "Thinking of the comrades who used to work with me."

"You look like a student. From your accent, you are not a Southerner. What are you doing, going to the South all by yourself? Where are you headed for?"

"Canton."

"Canton? *Hen hau*—very good! I'm headed for Canton too. I thought maybe you were going to study at some place near Wu-han. To Canton, eh? Can you understand Cantonese?"

"Well, I'm not going to study there, you see. It doesn't matter very much if I don't understand the dialect."

"Then what are you going there for?"

I waited a few seconds. At last I said, "To see my lover."

"Oh—where's he working?"

"In a school."

"Which school?" He had a loud voice that was probably very good for shouting orders.

I thought that if I named a school, he would certainly ask me if my lover was a teacher or student, what he was teaching, in what department, what his given name was, his surname. If I picked a school that didn't exist, and if this man knew Canton very well, I might as well give up.

"He used to work in Sun Yat-sen University, but because he got sick he has to stay at home. He just wrote that his sickness is getting worse—I certainly hope it's not tuberculosis—and he wants me to come and see him."

"I see." He laughed and rubbed the perspiration off his nose with the palm of his hand. "You wept so long yesterday, I thought there must be some reason for it. You said you were thinking about your comrades." The coy look on his flat face was almost comical. "I think instead you're just lonesome for your lover."

To push aside more questions I began to fire questions about him. Where was he from? What did he do? He was in high spirits, and could talk at least ten minutes on any subject I brought up. Finally he looked at his watch and interrupted himself. He stood up over me. "Comrade, I'm sorry, but I have to eat with my group. But we'll have a chance to see each other again later."

More talk with him? It was too dangerous. But even if I could avoid him, there were so many people on the train that somebody else would be sure to come and ask me more questions. Whether my questioners were well intentioned or not, I was now an "escaped prisoner," and the more people I came into contact with, and the more questions I was asked, the greater became the risk that I would be found out and sent back. While I was eating in the dining car, I looked fixedly out the window: farmhouses, trees, the clump of a village over there, a small bridge over a stream—all seemed to be as lonely as I was, under the summer light. I made myself finish a dish of fried rice with shredded pork and drink a bowl of soup. Back through the swaying cars I walked unsteadily from the dining car to my seat, my mind still full of worry and suspicion.

Then from somewhere I got an inspiration. I took my money with me and walked back to see the conductor in charge of the train. I told him I wasn't feeling well, and asked him if he could possibly give me a berth. He was very polite. "I only have one empty place left. Unfortunately, it's in a compartment of four. The other three are male passengers. I don't think that would be so convenient for you, would it?"

I put the pile of folded banknotes on his table. "Thank you, comrade. I'm really moved by your spirit to serve us travelers. But I don't think I should take this vacancy. But would you please be on the lookout for me if another place becomes empty? I think it would be better for me to share a compartment with some other woman, or at least a married couple or somebody like that."

He pushed the money back at me. "Comrade, I'll be glad to

try. I imagine some of our sleeper passengers will be getting off the train after a few more stops. Come back with your money then. If you leave it here now in public like this, people will think I am taking bribes."

From then on, whenever the train stopped at a station, I hurried back to ask the conductor to keep anybody else from getting a berth ahead of me. Finally, just before supper, he gave me a lower berth. The other lower berth in the compartment was vacant. The two upper berths were occupied by a married couple speaking the Shanghai dialect. Although they were middle-aged, they seemed to be more devoted to each other than newlyweds, and lay up there until late chatting and joking at each other's expense. I congratulated myself on their company; they were so occupied with each other they wouldn't pay any attention to me. I closed the door to the outside, lay down on my berth, and started reading the books I had. Except for hasty trips to the diner and the lavatory, I did not dare take one step outside my shelter.

Hiding thus, I waited two more days and nights. Then the train pulled into the Canton railway station.

Outside the window I could hear the unfamiliar, angry-sounding Southern dialect as peddlers cried their wares and the baggage porters shouted for the attention of the passengers. It was noisy and frightening and strange, and I didn't want to leave the familiar safety of the train. Then a husky, sweating porter in a thin shirt and shorts pushed his way into the compartment and seized my bag. He shouldered his way through the crowd in the passageway so roughly that I was half afraid he would steal my bag, so I hustled after him as fast as I could make headway. Perspiring in the muggy Southern heat, I had scarcely caught up with him outside the train when he set the bag down and asked me for a tip. Because the soldiers were waiting to search us, I thrust twice as much money at him as I knew I should pay, but he still yelled as if I'd robbed him. I peeled two more bills from my small stack of money, and he snatched them without any formalities of thanks before he ran off to find another victim.

Out past the inspectors and safe in the street, I looked into my handbag to make sure that my letter of introduction to Mrs. Loh was still inside. I hailed a pedicab and showed the driver the address on the envelope—I couldn't speak Cantonese and he wouldn't understand my Northern dialect. He proposed a price. I shook my head to show him I didn't understand. He showed me two fingers and waved them wildly while he jabbered at me. Did he want two thousand *jen min* dollars or twenty thousand? Suddenly I remembered that I was close now to being a fugitive. How could an escaped convict stop to bargain? I motioned him to put my bag up in the pedicab. He took it for granted that I had agreed to pay him whatever it was he had asked, hopped on, and pedaled me off. I climbed down when he stopped and took out several banknotes of big denomination and politely asked for change, any change he could give me. He jabbered at me again, shook his head, and rode off. I gave up and walked up to the house.

A young girl dressed in the uniform of a middle-school student opened the door at my ring. I asked her if Mrs. Loh was at home. She looked me over and replied in limping Mandarin: "Mama is out. Please come back again tonight."

"I've come from Peking," I said desperately. "I don't know anybody else in Canton—I've never been here before. I have a letter from your mother's friend asking her to let me stay here a few days. Can't I come in and rest here for a while?"

She nodded her head in reluctant consent, helped me carry in the suitcase, offered me a cup of tea, and then went back to her own room without any more words. Her young sister, six or seven, stayed behind and giggled at my accent when I tried to speak with her.

I waited anxiously in the sitting room. At last, toward evening, Mrs. Loh came back. She was in her forties, her face long and expressionless. She wore a Cantonese-style jacket and trousers made of printed linen. Handing her package to her eldest daughter, she asked me in careful Mandarin: "What is your honorable name? Who told you you should come here?"

I told her who I was and handed her the letter. She read it over carefully and smiled for the first time. "So Professor Niu recommends you. That's good. He's been an old friend—more than ten years. How is he with all these new things going on?"

I told her that he was well and still teaching. She listened attentively, as if very much interested. When I had finished, she said: "Mr. Niu's friend is also my friend. If you have some trouble, I'll do my best to try to help you. In the letter here he only asks me to help you out. But he doesn't mention what help I can give you. Old friend Niu must be getting very careless and absentminded."

Didn't she realize this really showed how careful and prudent he had been? I'm sure she did. If he had asked her in black and white to help me get across the border into Hong Kong, and if one of the people who had searched my baggage along the way had found the letter, I would be sent back to Peking and both she and Mr. Niu would have been called upon by the police. I had to trust her, so I was blunt.

"I have two big favors to ask: first, let me stay here a few days; second, please help me to get into Hong Kong."

I was surprised that she wasn't surprised. Calmly she said: "Of course, it wouldn't be very nice for a young girl like you to live alone in a hotel. This house isn't very comfortable, but at least you'll feel more at home here. As for going to Hong Kong—well, that's not so hard right now if you're careful."

"What! You mean it's really not very hard?" I interrupted her. Back in Peking friends had told me how difficult it was to get out. First, you had to talk your way by the Communist sentries; then you had to have an entry permit from the British before the British police at the border admitted you; and if you were turned back by the British police you were likely to rouse the suspicion of the Communist guards and end up in a police station.

"Not so hard right now. It seems to run in spells. Right now, if you look like an ordinary trader, the guards usually won't give you much trouble."

"How about the Hong Kong police?"

"Not much trouble there right now, either. We Cantonese don't need entry permits to get past the Hong Kong police. We can come and go at will if we don't look suspicious."

"But I'm not Cantonese, and I don't speak the Cantonese dialect. How can you pass a fish eye off as a pearl?"

"I think we can fix that. You'll have to dress up as a Cantonese traveling trader and learn some Cantonese. If you are lucky, everything will be all right."

I still couldn't believe that it would be so easy. "If I use up the few words I can learn and they ask me more questions I don't understand, what can I do? And if the Hong Kong police discover me once and send me back and I get a second chance, I'll be so nervous I'm afraid I'll burst out laughing before they ask me a thing."

"The questions they ask are always the same questions, nothing unusual. We'll have the answers practiced before we try it. But we'd better not miss the first time. If you do, it will cut down your chance. You'll have to wait at least a month, until people have forgotten about you and you get another chance to squeeze through.

"But don't worry too much about it right now. Even if they discover you're not a Cantonese and turn you back, there are other ways of getting across. We may have to look for a yellow ox * to take you on through. Of course that will cost you a lot of money; and you'll have to follow a rough path, climb the hills, and sometimes even wade across streams. You're a young girl. It would be much better if you can get across on the main route."

I asked her why the government of Hong Kong should treat Cantonese with special favor and let them come and go at will. She told me that it was probably because Hong Kong was afraid that more refugees from the interior of China would add to its burden. They didn't stop traveling traders, because such people helped feed the colony and traveled back and forth without settling down in Hong Kong.

"Another thing worries me: What do I have to do about registering with the police station in your street?"

"That's simple. Wait just a minute. I'll write a note and ask my daughter to send it there." She looked into my eyes. "What's your name? What's your native town? Wait—you'd better write everything down yourself. I don't want to make a mistake."

Without hesitation I wrote down a false name and particulars about myself. I didn't blame her for wanting it in my handwriting. If it was discovered to be false, she could always claim ignorance.

She sipped her tea while she watched me write. Then she asked

---

* The Yellow Ox gang on the China-Hong Kong border undertakes to smuggle people as well as goods either way across the border.

me a question I did not want to answer. "What are you going to Hong Kong for? Looking for people or looking for a job?"

"First, to look for people, then to try to find a job." Since I could not avoid her eyes anyway, I looked straight back at her. "My lover is in Hong Kong. He's doing very well, too—working in a foreign import-export firm. I hope he can find me a job I like."

"I suppose you know enough English. But do you know typing and shorthand? There are thousands of girls there now, and it's hard to get a job. But if you know those things," she glanced at my student uniform and my travel-stained shoes, "and if you change your dress and your shoes, make them brighter and in the fashion, you might do all right. And you'd better get somebody to show you how to use make-up, too."

"What difference does that make? If I can type fast, and am a good stenographer, can't I find a job somewhere?"

"What's wrong with dressing up? You sound very progressive indeed! Can you blame an office for wanting to hire young and attractive people?"

"Well, suppose a girl is young and pretty but doesn't know much English and doesn't know how to type. Does she stand much chance of finding a job there?" Hong Kong, a semi-tropical city, must be very vain and romantic, I thought.

"That's not so good, either. You see, there are so many pretty girls without anything to do in Hong Kong." I began to see the situation I was going to find myself in.

At that moment the little girl who had giggled at my accent came running in to greet her mother and take another look at me. Mrs. Loh kissed her and asked, "Li-li, have you finished your homework?"

Li-li answered in Cantonese. From the word or two I caught, she was asking for something from her mother. Mrs. Loh replied in Cantonese—still over my head. Then Li-li romped off, humming one of the new "Liberation songs" she had been taught in school.

Mrs. Loh saw that I was feeling downhearted, and changed her tune. "But you probably won't have any trouble, I hope. Besides, you have your lover in Hong Kong. What do you have to worry about! You see how thoughtless I am. You've been on a train all those days and here I am, chattering away without giving you a chance to rest. After supper I think the best thing for you to do is to take a bath and go right to bed. We can talk all about your problems tomorrow."

Alone I felt like giving in to tears again, this time of relief. At least I was this far, and I had a good chance of getting the rest of the way. How far I was I didn't realize until I walked from my bedroom out on the veranda and looked up at the stars in the Southern sky.

The next morning Mrs. Loh took me along with her and tried to show me a few points of interest in Canton, to try to cheer me up, I suppose. Now, however, because I was eager to keep going, I pestered her to teach me the words I would need to know in Cantonese to get by the police, and how to dress like a Cantonese woman trader. At last she yielded to my insistence and took me to a shop to have a suit of Cantonese clothes made out of black lacquered silk. "Better wear them every day and wash them every night. It might look suspicious if they're too new," Mrs. Loh told me when we came back out of the store. Then we went across the street to buy a pair of black, flat-heeled, fancy Cantonese shoes for me.

When we got home Mrs. Loh told me that after we crossed the bridge at Shumchun into British-held territory, somebody on the Hong Kong side would ask me where I was going. I should say: Hong Kong. Then he would ask about my address. I should tell him: Number 6 Woosung Street, first floor, Kowloon. Mrs. Loh drilled these answers into me again and again, correcting my accent whenever I made a mistake. Eating, reading, or even talking with people, I always practiced the sound of the Cantonese in my head: Hong Kong, Kowloon, first floor, Number 6 Woosung Street.

On the third day, just when it was beginning to get light, Mrs. Loh called me. I jumped out of bed and washed my face in a hurry. Then I dumped some oil on my head and pleated my hair into a long, solid queue. After that I put on the Cantonese clothes and the flat-heeled shoes. When I looked at my reflection in the mirror under the weak, unshaded bulb in the bathroom, I thought I looked very much like a real Cantonese. My reflection smiled back at me, the first smile since I had arrived in Canton.

Mrs. Loh was going with me. Each of us took two baskets

of fresh cabbages and a bundle of clothes. Not my own clothes—I would have to leave them behind. Without waking anybody else in the house, we left the house, got a pedicab, and arrived at the station before sunrise. There was half an hour's wait in line before we got tickets—third class, of course. Traveling women traders couldn't afford first or second. We stood in line again and walked by the soldiers standing with their rifles studying the crowd. But they didn't single us out for a search; after all, there was another set of guards at the border.

After I found seats in the coach, I looked around me and almost burst into a laugh. Perhaps everyone in the car really was a traveling trader. At least each of them carried two baskets, crammed with eggs, cabbages, fruit, any foodstuff which would fetch a higher price in Hong Kong than in Canton. Everybody had on Cantonese clothes and flat-heeled shoes. Everybody who was speaking any language was speaking fluent Cantonese. Everybody looked unbelievably like everybody else. I knew that if I had still been in student uniform, I would probably already be inside the police booth answering questions.

We had missed breakfast. I told Mrs. Loh I wasn't hungry, but she thought I was being polite, and she bought two bowls of rice with sausage. By forcing myself, I got two pieces of sausage down, but I couldn't touch the rice. I was getting nervous, and the familiar shuffle and jolt of the train had brought back all the fears and regrets of the ride down from Peking.

Two hours later the train stopped near the border. This was as far as it went; the rails had been taken up across the bridge, and passengers going on to Hong Kong had to get down and walk across the footbridge to catch another train waiting there with a crew from Hong Kong. We battled our way toward the door; everyone in the car was struggling to jump down ahead of everyone else. Under the sun, which was just becoming hot, we joined the hurrying stream of traders toward the barbed-wire barricade. There were so many people, the soldiers couldn't keep order. With the jostling and the shoving and pushing, we advanced only a few steps in as many minutes.

For more than a week I had not had a single day of quiet rest. Besides, I was hot, hungry now, and thirsty. I began to get dizzy with the clamor, the smell of perspiration, the cries I was sure were curses. My knees, I felt, were sinking under me, and I looked down at them. I struggled hard to breathe; I wished now I'd forced myself to eat something more than the slice of raw-looking sausage. My head began to swim—this would be the wrong place to faint. Suddenly the woman ahead of me bumped against me, turned her head, and started to curse. Her shrill voice roused me from my own faintness. Mrs. Loh pulled me back and apologized for me. I stayed mute, as Mrs. Loh had warned me I must be.

By now the soldiers had pushed us into a rough semblance of a queue, as we shouldered each other for a place close to the open place in the wire. When I saw the bridge, with more barbed wire nailed to X-shaped portable gates in the middle and the British flag flying from a pole just past the bridge on the other side, I forgot my discomfort, pulled myself together, and tried to remember the sentences of Cantonese I needed.

"Comrade, let me search you!" The woman soldier who stopped me spoke a Cantonese so bad that I could understand her—a Northerner like myself. I did not realize until then that I had already arrived at the last search point in the liberated area.

I looked at her stupidly, pretending that I could barely understand her Northern speech. I stood quiet while she searched among my cabbages and then poked through the bundle of old clothes. "You're quite honest," she said with a smile. She patted me around the body and then said, "All right. Go."

This time I was really liberated.

I walked out on the bridge with Mrs. Loh. The nervousness had left me. At the barrier in the middle a Chinese policeman in shorts and a khaki shirt with British insignia on his shoulders asked me in Cantonese where I was going. In Cantonese I told him I was going to Hong Kong. At the end of the bridge a second inspector asked me again where I was going to live in Hong Kong. I recited the address, No. 6, Woosung Street, first floor.

A third Hong Kong policeman made us stand in a line to be vaccinated for smallpox. Scarcely had we received our certificates and walked over to buy our railroad tickets for Kowloon, when we heard a burst of shouting and then crying. What had happened? I asked Mrs. Loh. Had the British police discovered some Northerners pretending to be Cantonese, and were they forcing them back across?

"Let's not get involved." Mrs. Loh tugged at me. "It's not our business. Come on, it happens all the time. Let's move along and get away from here." She was speaking Mandarin as softly as she could and still be heard. "Come on. Such crying is quite common on this route. Everyone has his own reasons. Don't let it bother you. Come over here and let's get our tickets for the Kowloon station."

We boarded a train, one that didn't belong to the "people." I asked Mrs. Loh how long we would have to ride before we reached Kowloon. "Not so loud," she cautioned me. "We're not over the dangerous stretch yet. Last time I saw the police send two young Northerners, students, I suppose, back to Shumchun. They were very stupid. They were so happy about getting across that they started shouting and joking with each other in the Northern dialect as soon as they got on the Kowloon train. Really—fifteen minutes more and they would have been safe!"

We got off the train at the Kowloon station. The station is close to the ferry across the narrow harbor to the island that gives the colony its name. We came out of the big dark station into a medley of foreign sights and sounds: big red two-story busses, the small darting taxis, British soldiers, sunburned and hairy in their shorts; European women, dark-faced Indian inspectors at the ferry turnstiles. One waved us and our baskets of cabbages to the third-class gate. Down on the lower deck Mrs. Loh smiled at me. "So, here you are at last. And I can imagine how excited and happy your lover is going to be. What about it? Do I get an invitation to the wedding feast?"

I could tell her the truth now. "My lover isn't a man," I said. "I'm not sure what he is—something I can't tell you in so many words right now. And he isn't running after me. I'm running after him."

Mrs. Loh didn't understand and I couldn't explain; I would have to find the words for myself first. Her goodbye, and the other farewells, "Good luck—send us a letter," are still sounding in my ears.

Have I really arrived? Have I really arrived in Hong Kong? Two years, and the blue sky over the wool-green hills, the green sea, the big ships riding at anchor, the white sailboats and the fishing junks still look like the scenery in a stage play or a film. I'm still just somebody in the audience who has bought a ticket—or rather, who has crept in without a ticket—to sit and watch the film. The peaks, the gentler hills below them, the white buildings scattered around the waist and huddled at the foot of the mountain island are still unreal to me. I am sitting as quietly as I can, watching the play. I can't get excited about it. I don't feel happy. But I'm not sad or angry or afraid any more.

You might think that I have given up feeling and hoping any more.

My old hopes, already tired out, have withered in the too bright sun of this place. But reason is beginning to stir and raise its head. It is telling me that hope has not grown numb. It is seeking quietly and secretly, seeking for the object of my love.

Epilogue

My desk was jammed up against a small window. Out of the window I could see a row of huts straggling up a small slope where the green had been torn from the hillside. Other refugees lived there; all day long I heard loud arguments, quarrels, children bawling, the cries of men trying to hawk food or secondhand clothes to one another. Though at night these voices were quiet, through my window sifted smells from the camp which made a person feel like vomiting—smells from the night soil spread on the vegetable patches gouged out of the hill, nearer smells from the fresh excrement left by passers-by. It was a long way from Peita and the smell of books. It was the real world, the world of dirt and filth and squalor, which nothing in my life had prepared me for.

At night I lit a kerosene lamp. Under its dim light the book I was reading or the paper I was writing on seemed to turn yellow. The flame smoked and wavered. But the smell of burning kerosene was better than the odors the night breeze brought through my window. When I turned away from the lamp and looked at the shadows around me, I wanted to write gloomy little poems full of sadness and philosophy. But the work I had started on required that I write very rational, sparkling things, so I made the fountain pen scrape along faster.

When I had spent enough ink for one evening, I'd turn out the light, undress, and crawl into bed. The bed was wedged in beside the desk. It was a hard, rickety wooden bunk which creaked alarmingly when I got in and every time I moved.

One more day, I'd think, as I lay there in the dark in the cubicle I'd found after several days of searching for my friends. I should have felt lucky to have it—a bed, a desk to write my book on, friends around who had been through the same experience and who were now in the same boat. But I remembered my own room in my parents' house in Peking. I had had an electric lamp to read by, a soft bed, a cupboard to keep my clothes in. I'll admit that I sometimes felt sorry for myself.

Do you know what it feels like to be a refugee? You go through the honking, clanging traffic of a foreign city to the only address you have, the flat of a distant relative. He's crowded already with his own family, but family obligations make him take you in. So in you move with what you've managed to bring with you, into the dark corner of a room. You dare not talk much when there is a guest. You dare not eat too much from the dishes at meals. You dare reach your chopsticks only into the dishes nearest you. You are afraid to use the desk; you sit on a chair or the edge of your cot to scribble your letter on a sheet of paper laid on a book placed across your knees. Later, when the lights are out, you can breathe more freely; you can't see the glances that people can't help turning at refugees.

But in the morning you are a refugee again. You have to go out and look for a job—not that you hope that your appearance as a refugee student who can't even speak Cantonese will impress any prospective employer, but you have to make the effort. When you come back home at night you're as far away from a job as ever. And how are you going to face those distant relatives of yours?

Better the cubicle and the hard bed and the smells; at least you have a chance there to work among your friends and support yourself. You were lucky twice, first to have the "distant relative," and second, to find friends. But with any imagination at all you could guess about the unlucky ones, without money or friends to look for. They wander the streets looking for shelter, begging for coins enough to buy some coarse bread to chew. Where can they sleep? In the street, perhaps. But there is always the chance that a policeman will wake them up and send them on to some other place. Another place? What about the sign: "Private property. Keep out"?

One boy found temporary quarters on the staircase of an apartment house. It was chilly but it was out of the wind. Like the rest of us, he hadn't realized that winter in Hong Kong was so chilly and damp. Most of the tenants ignored him, but one young dandy who lived on the second floor woke him up one night with a kick when he found him blocking the stairway. At another time an impatient lady who lived on the next floor spat on his arm, which he had used to shield his face. And once an amah who was clumping upstairs with a pot full of filthy slops deliberately waved the stinking vessel over his head. But his plight didn't last forever. In the dark, noisy kennel the boy used his only valuable possession, his fountain pen, to write stories which somehow got published in one of the refugee magazines. Then our group found him and invited him to join us.

Two other boys I know were much more fortunate. They made friends with the night watchman at a school and finally got his permission to sleep in one of the classrooms. Every night they sneaked into the room, moved some work tables together, and made a bed of them. Before dawn the watchman came in to wake them and warn them to get out. They carried the tables back to their old places, washed hastily, and sneaked out on the streets again like a pair of thieves.

Why didn't these healthy young men look for jobs? They did— and a few found them. One former student found himself doing something which a year before he had never dreamed he would do. When old-fashioned families have a marriage or a funeral to celebrate, they hire a band of ragged, tattered musicians to make the proper amount of noise. My friend joined one of these bands, put on a dirty old embroidered robe and a big motley-colored bonnet which hung down almost to his eyebrows and marched in the ceremonial processions blowing a trumpet or beating on a drum. In the hideous din he may have felt like laughing or crying, but he had to keep his lips on the trumpet and tootle away until the corpse had been serenaded into the ground or the happy couple had disappeared into the bridal chamber. Otherwise his job, so hard to find but not quite enough to give him food and clothing, might be taken by another refugee.

What one thing about his job did my friend like best? Although a newcomer, he did know quite a few people in Hong Kong. Some of them were unwilling or unable to help him. Some suspected him of being pro-Communist because he hadn't run on ahead of the

Communist soldiers. The help of others he didn't want because he would have had to do work he thought was dishonest. But suppose any of his acquaintances had seen him in such a comical rig, blowing a trumpet and following a corpse? The thing my friend liked best was the big floppy bonnet that hung down almost to his nose.

Of course, there aren't enough funerals and weddings in Hong Kong to keep everybody busy who would like to have work. A few students found jobs as unskilled help in the cotton factories. Others got odd jobs making match boxes or folding gold and silver ceremonial paper or doing embroidery for shops to sell to tourists. Some lived off the debris of the city, collected cigarette stubs to be remade into cheap smokes, picked up discarded paper and tinfoil wrappings, or repaired the old nylon stockings that had started out on the legs of a well-to-do foreign woman and had passed down from wearer to wearer.

I wonder how many sons and daughters of middle-class merchants and landowners, of teachers and journalists and government officials, have discovered in Hong Kong that one full meal a day can keep life in even if it can't keep hunger out. What you wear isn't so important any more, or the way you look. You may have let your hair grow at school because it singled you out from other men as an artist or a poet; now you let it grow because you couldn't afford to get it cut. You learned how important the necessities were, shelter and heat. If you were lucky, you might share a room in one of the squatter huts with two or three friends; there was room for you to sleep if you got used to sleeping with your legs doubled up. The huts trapped the heat of the summer sun and let the damp breezes of winter through. In the summer the day-long downpours were the nastiest things to endure. Every time the rain poured down outside, it drizzled inside in sympathy with the outdoor weather.

But I don't want to make the picture too dark, and I don't want to spend too much time painting it. Not many people in Hong Kong are free of some self-pity, I suppose. But finally the first feeling of hopelessness and apathy turns into grumbling, and then most people set about finding some way out. Some reconcile themselves to living in squatter huts and settle down to making the best life they can under the circumstances. Others move a step up and become clerks or *fokis* in the new shops and businesses started by older and more provident refugees who managed to bring some money with them. A few find jobs teaching or tutoring. Fewer still manage to climb over the passport and visa barriers that await them and go on to foreign countries to complete their education.

And the rest of us? The ones who feel like us are gradually getting in touch, gradually finding each other. We don't want the title of refugees any longer—not so long as we can come together and get to work on the job of getting back where we belong, the places and the people we left behind. One thing we students think we have learned from the Communists if we learned nothing else— how to organize. However, this time we want to do the organizing ourselves.

Those of us who think along the same lines have joined together in an organized group, a union, which at least is stronger now than it was when we started it. We think we have two jobs. One is to help ourselves and our friends until we can do something to change things on the mainland; but more important, we somehow have to find something effective to do.

So far we have written a number of books, published some pamphlets and periodicals. We've also tried to get in touch with other groups here and elsewhere. What this adds up to, whether it has accomplished much, whether there are many people listening, we don't know. We are sure of one thing, however—at least we are doing the right thing by starting at the bottom.

By that I mean that we look upon it as our job to try to follow what is going on back in the China we left, and to analyze and report as objectively as possible whatever we can find out. We want to study how the Communists managed to convince so many of our friends and to deceive so many more until it was too late. What is the basis of the Communist appeal? Why did they win? How do they maintain and broaden their power? Some of the answers are already apparent. But some take observation and digging. In other words I suppose you might say that our job is to find out what happened and what is happening now before we plan what we can do about it.

This task of research and analysis was already started when I joined the group. When I felt like complaining about the cubicle I had been assigned, all I had to do was to think about the girl in the next room. She had a desk and a bed wedged together too—and less room than I had, for one whole side of the room was filled with rough shelves piled high with back copies of Communist newspapers and magazines from the mainland. This was our first "research center." It's grown now and has expanded to bigger quarters. The people working in this project have now clipped and filed 145,000 items about everything we happen to be interested in, from the crimes committed in the name of land reform to the public renunciations our old teachers have been forced to make of everything they have always believed in and fought for. Members of our group, and other writers too, draw upon this material for the articles and books we write.

And what have we been able to find out? Only what the Communists want us to read, or what they inadvertently let slip. Nevertheless, it is enough for us to see at least a dim shadowing of the great changes that have swept over our country since I left in 1950: the land reform; the great thought reform; the hunting down of "reactionaries" (surely the most trumpeted purge of modern times, for we have articles from Communist newspapers ordering cadres to make it "suppression with fanfare"); the economic attacks on the middle class; the Anti-America, Aid-Korea Campaign; The San Fan-Wu Fan Campaign against the "Three Vices" and "Five Vices," which started in the Party and spread to schools and other official organs and finally reached every shopkeeper in China.

But the story of all that has happened to my family and the rest of my countrymen is beyond my capacity to tell here. Our most intense personal interest naturally is what has happened to our classmates and the younger brothers and sisters we left behind. We try to get in touch with anybody we hear about who has escaped later than we did, but their stories add little to the bits and scraps we pick up from the mainland newspapers we subscribe to and read until we're bleary-eyed trying to find something useful.

We do know a few things, though. Living conditions in universities and middle schools apparently have become more "austere" than they were in 1950, when we felt sorry for ourselves because we were getting 52,000 *jen min piao* worth of millet a month for our food, or somewhat less than ten cents' worth of food a day, in terms of American money. A report in the July 19, 1951, issue of the *Chang Chiang Daily News*, the official Communist organ for Central South China, said that each student at Honan University was only getting 45,000 JMP worth of food a month. Middle-school students apparently don't get as much as that. The Chungking *Ta Kung Pao* reported on December 21, 1951, that pupils of the Loshan Girls' Middle School each got 42,000 JMP worth of food a month. The Peking *Kwang Ming Daily News* complained six months later, on June 17, 1952, that each student in the Fourth Municipal Middle School was surviving on three-year-old Manchurian corn which had turned green and bitter-tasting. To the corn was added nothing but a ration of ten ounces of cabbage and 0.2 ounce of vegetable oil a day.

But it is probably a mistake to make too much of such isolated facts as these. Chinese newspapers have printed other reports which claim that the life of students is constantly improving. The only real letting down of the bars for more than a peep at what was really happening in China's schools came in the summer and fall of 1951, when a campaign started in Central China and spread over the nation to improve what the Communist press called "the state of confusion" in educational work. What we saw in this momentary glimpse made us feel right at home; the new leaders were recognizing a year or eighteen months later some of the abuses we had suffered at Peita.

The campaign I want to describe began quietly enough in early summer when the Chungking *Hsin Hua Jih Pao* admitted that "the number of students in the private and public schools of higher learning (in Southwest China) had dropped by 23 per cent during the past six months." Enrollment in Chungking middle schools, the story added, had fallen off even more—54 per cent. Why? "Party, military, political, and civil organs everywhere have summoned students at will to work as cadres. They have mobilized students and teachers to participate in inappropriate social activities, or have requisitioned and seized the schools for their meeting places, and so on. All this has created great confusion." *

---

* The date of original publication is unknown. The story was quoted in the *People's Daily News* in Peking on Aug. 6, 1951.

Students at Szechuan University must have been especially confused. The paper went on to tell us that their campus had been borrowed for the purpose of holding meetings for four solid weeks. "Dormitories, classrooms and mess halls were occupied. Students had to move to other places or else double up and live in the library." I'll admit that that is one thing we were spared at Peita.

The publication of this report was a signal that it was safe for other places to complain about conditions in their schools too. In certain localities of East China, the Peking *People's Daily News* reported in the same story, the situation was "even more serious" than in the Southwest. "From data gathered in Fukien, Chekiang and South Anhwei and North Anhwei it is seen that instances frequently occur where students have been dragged off to participate in 'rush work,' receptions, farewell parties, the setting up of meeting halls, or drum dances to send off collective taxpayers [merchants] or collective grain-levy payers [peasants]. . . . They [the Party and political organs] consider educational cadres as shock cadres, and mobilize educational workers at will, even leading school work into a total collapse. Serious duplication in leadership is seen in schools when the school administration, the trade union, the students' association, the Party, the Youth League, the Women's Federation, the China Peace Committee, and the Sino-Soviet Friendship Association each has its own arrangements for the school, plunging the teachers and students into a multitude of duties, conferences, and social activities, as a result of which the hitherto best students show the worst record and the more progressive the teachers, the more meetings they have to attend, and the poorer they become in teaching. This has seriously affected the health of both students and teachers."

With the official spokesman of the Central People's Government taking up the somewhat belated cry, provincial newspapers hastened more details into print. The Hankow *Chang Chiang Daily News* reported on August 14th that "confusion" also existed in the tri-city area of Wuhan (Hankow, Wuchang, Hanyang). "Last term the First Municipal Middle School and eight other schools, because of participation in all kinds of activities, often suspended teaching. Up to 1,100 hours of regular classes were lost. According to a preliminary check-up fourteen different institutions demanded work from them. In the week from April 23rd to April 28th the Second Municipal Middle School took part in fourteen meetings. In Hsing-Mein Girls' Middle School, teachers and students heard the same speeches from returned representatives of the People's Volunteers three times, the first day at the order of the Student Union, the second day at the order of the Women's Association, and the third time at the order of the Educational Workers' Union. The Ninth Primary School, Second District, joined 56 outside meetings and activities of 33 different kinds from April 1st to April 26th."

The same issue of the paper summed up the results of this policy. "Before the Liberation there were 140,000 middle-school students in the province of Hunan. In the first term of 1951, there were only 62,368." The September 11th issue cited one more statistic. "The universities and technical institutions of Central South China planned to accept 16,557 students; but only 8,727 students applied to take the uniform entrance examination for this area."

The same kind of news was printed in Peking, Tientsin, Canton, Shanghai, Nanking, and other cities. The Peking *People's Daily News* admitted, "The drop in the number of students in schools above the senior middle-school level is a nation-wide problem." This did not prevent Liu Shih, head of the Supervisory Department of the Ministry of Education, from writing in *People's China* on October 1, 1951, that "great advances" had been scored in education and that "with the educational path mapped out by Mao Tse-tung . . . and with the aid of the Soviet Union's advanced educational experiences and the help of Soviet educators, we are going ahead in great strides." Of course it happens that *People's China* is published in English to carry Peking's propaganda abroad. No one in Hankow or Chungking is likely to read a copy.

For the leaders in Peking the solution was easy: blame their subordinates and issue directives "for the adjustment of the confusing state of educational work in schools." Perhaps the directives have worked. At least there has not been a second nation-wide outbreak of publicity on the subject.

A few mistakes still happen, however. About a year after the campaign to end confusion in educational work, the Hankow *Chang Chiang Daily News,* on September 2, 1952, broke the story of a deviation which had occurred at the Hupei Provincial Normal

School at I-Chang. (I-Chang is a river port with about 100,000 people along the Yangtze.) To be honest, if I had read about the case in anything except an official Chinese newspaper I would have dismissed it as anti-Communist propaganda, and crudely fabricated propaganda at that.

As reported by the Hankow paper, here is what happened in I-Chang. On June 19th students in a short course at the Normal School had been scheduled to go to the Second Municipal Primary School to gain some experience in practice teaching. For unexplained reasons the expedition was called off. Some of the students grumbled at the change in their plans, and the school authorities apparently overheard the grumbling.

The next day the vice principal, Wang Su, a veteran Party member who actually directed school affairs, announced during morning drill that classes would be suspended to investigate the thoughts of the disgruntled students. Among these young people training to be teachers were supposed to be backward elements of dubious family background who had undoubtedly carried ideas over from the old society. Then he named more than ten students who he thought needed especially searching examination.

One of the three questions we must find the answer to, he told the students, is "Who is blocking the way to learning?"

The "examination" started. Among the students who were compelled to admit their mistakes were a girl named Chang Kwang-ya and a boy named Hsiang Pei-ch'u. They were subjected to the mild torture of progressive fatigue induced by relentless and incessant questioning. After a dose of this, with classmates shouting questions and threats at them in "small meetings" to "squeeze out their secrets" and then calling "big meetings" to "crush" and intimidate them, the two victims wilted. The girl Chang admitted that she had been a member of the old Kuomintang Youth Corps. The boy had a better story; he admitted that he "had organized eight reactionaries in the countryside and plotted to murder the peasants." Wang Su now believed Hsiang to be a real *t'e-wu,* or "special agent," and put him under custody.

During the preliminary investigation a photograph turned up which the boy and girl had had taken with two other students. Naturally, the other two were accused too—Liu Hsing-kwang and

Huang Te-ch'ung. Vice Principal Wang now drafted more students into service to continue the investigation. After repeated "trials by fatigue" of the four young conspirators, Wang Su finally concluded the girl Chang was the ringleader. The interrogation went on.

On June 23rd and 24th the four accused admitted a plan to murder the principal of the school and lead the students in an armed uprising against the authorities. They named more than ten other students as being in on the plot. So Wang Su, the vice principal, chose nineteen politically reliable students from another division to carry on the investigation and put the girl and others "under control."

As the questioning went on, Wang Su announced on June 28th that all students and teachers were prohibited from leaving the school, and that all letters coming in or going out were subject to censorship. On the same day, which was sunny and warm, the school sent some students fifteen *li* (five miles) away to bring back a supply of rice. When the tired working party returned, they ate a hasty supper. Some time after the meal more than ten of the students vomited up their supper and had to get emergency treatment from the school doctor. Wang Su now suspected poisoning. The school sent the sick students to the People's Hospital to have them examined. The doctors could find no trace of poison, but Wang Su did not give up.

He started questioning the suspects again. The examiners trussed up the girl Chang with ropes, hung her up by her hands, and beat her. She confessed that her friend Hsiang had poisoned his fellow students. When Hsiang was beaten, he confessed that another student, Chu, had actually done the poisoning. Chu, who was dragged out of bed, tied up, and beaten for two hours, admitted that Huang Te-ch'ung, one of the four students in the photograph, was also in the plot.

Members of the investigation team hung Huang up and ordered two students to hit and kick him, and Huang implicated Liu Hsing-kwang. With their own hands Tang Lu-hua, the teacher in charge of the student studies, and Lu Wei-chun, acting chairman of the division, hung Liu up and strapped a carrying pole on his back. Then students hung from each end of the pole to put a weight on his arms and shoulders which must have been almost unendurable. Finally Liu admitted that he had put poison in the school's *shwei-kangs*, or water vats.

To feed the fire still more, Wang Su discovered eight other students whom he suspected of complicity, and he declared them under custody. On the morning of the 30th, fourteen special investigating teams consisting of more than fifty students were formed to carry on the examination of the criminals. The school was now in an uproar. The student security section went through the kitchens pouring the water out of all the *shwei-kangs*, kettles, and bottles. They saved three cups of it, however, to test for poison by chemical analysis. The water samples were tested, but revealed no trace of poison.

Nevertheless Wang went on to call all the teachers and students out on "urgent mobilization," and announced the crimes the young *t'e-wu* had committed. Meanwhile the examiners hung Huang Te-ch'ung up by the feet, tied his hands behind his back to a table, and wrapped a towel around his mouth to silence any outcry. Teacher Tang Lu-hua kicked him and some of the students beat him. Although the torture lasted into the afternoon, they did not get any more information.

Then the examiners wrote a statement setting forth the details of the fourteen arrested students' participation in a counter-revolutionary organization. They put the girl Chang's chop on it and showed it to her accomplice, Huang. Then they made him read it aloud, and took down what he read as his confession of guilt. Then they showed his confession to Chu, and tortured Chu again. Chu admitted the crime too, and was led out to find the poison they had used. Somewhere he found some lime used to make plaster, which he handed over to his torturers.

On the same morning the principal of the school, Li Ti-wen, went to report the case to the area government. He got in to see the general secretary, Li Han-jo, and told him that the murder plot had been discovered and that the would-be murderers had been detained. The general secretary tested the packet of lime the principal had brought along as evidence, and declared that it was not poison. Section Chief Ying of the Public Security Bureau (police) was called in and insisted that Miss Chang was not a special agent. The general secretary told the principal that he had better return to school and let the students go. But back at the school Wang Su ignored this instruction and freed only five of the fourteen, dismissing them as "accomplices under coercion."

Torture of the others was increased. On July 3rd Wang Su announced a new rule: no student could even move from room to room inside the school unless he was accompanied by two others. On July 5th Wang Su asked the detained students to write detailed confessions, setting down their personal histories, school activities, and family background. These confessions, he said, must lay special emphasis upon the poisons and the credentials they possessed. On the 6th Wang Su went back to see the general secretary with new evidence—two packages of what he thought was poison. However, Mr. Li said that the Public Security Bureau had already checked up on one of the students involved and that he was not a special agent. He warned the vice principal that if he didn't release the students soon, he might get into trouble if someone reported the case to the newspapers.

But when Wang returned to school he asked the "progressive" students to "help" their accused fellow students write the confessions and particularly to make sure that evidence was found that murder by poison had been attempted. One of the accused, Yen, managed to find wrapped in his quilt a package of foot powder which he had been using to cure his eczema. He handed it over as evidence of his guilt. The girl Chang handed in some more lime, which she had found in the girls' toilet; but because Hsiang couldn't find any suspicious-looking powder, he was hung up again and beaten periodically for two days and two nights.

On the 7th three students were released, although this naturally must have cost Wang some loss of face. The other detained persons he kept busy writing their confessions. Yen, the student who had been cleared by the Public Security Bureau, used more than 100 sheets of ten-line paper to get down all the details of the confession he was told to write. Finally, on the 11th, all of the detained students were released.

A few days later, when news of the curious goings-on at the I-Chang Provincial Normal School got around, an inspector and a clerk from the Government Educational Bureau dropped in to look into the case. They, however, told the students and teachers that it

was better to err on the side of "severity" than on the side of mildness in dealing with possible counter-revolutionaries.

After the inspector and his clerk had departed, three brave
teachers took a chance and on July 13th wrote to the Hupei Provincial People's Government and to the *Chang Chiang Daily News.*
The Provincial Bureau of Education thereupon telegraphed the
I-Chang Government demanding investigation, and the latter hastily
dismissed Principal Li, who had been a puppet all the time. Wang
Su stayed on.

In August more investigators visited the school. They found
out the truth and published it in the *Chang Chiang Daily News* on
September 2, 1952. The paper reported that "under the encouragement and with the personal participation of Wang Su," from June
29th to July 9th every one of the fourteen students "under control"
had been hung up and beaten. Altogether, the paper said with a
meticulous care for statistics, forty-seven different kinds of torture
had been applied to the students.

Student Yen had suffered sixteen kinds.

Student Chen Lung-fang had suffered nine. His brain had
been severely injured.

Others had suffered five to seven kinds. None had escaped with
less than two.

Student Chu Chen-yun had had two fingers badly injured.

But the boy Hsiang Pai-ch'ung, who had been unable to find
any "poison" to convict himself with, had suffered the most. The
newspaper reported: "Hsiang Pai-ch'ung's left arm has become dis-
abled. The wristbone is broken. His right arm is paralyzed so that
he cannot move it. His brain has also been seriously injured."

The teachers responsible for inflicting these injuries were
brought to justice and received some measure of punishment.
Charged on ten counts, including cheating his superiors, violating
government policy by dismissing classes without authorization, tor-
turing students, and creating a bad impression upon the people,
Wang Su, who had lost so much face when he couldn't convict his
charges of poisoning, was sentenced to three years in prison and dismissed from his post. Mr. Tan, the teacher in charge of student
studies, who had kicked a trussed-up student while others beat him,

was dismissed from his post. The acting chairman of the division, who had assisted in the beatings, received demerits. I hope that Hsiang Pai-ch'ung's broken wrist is healing.

But why publish such cases at all? I think that one of the reasons is that the Communists realize that sometimes things get out of hand and are impossible to hide. I-Chang is a good-sized city and a communications center. Because the news of what had gone on in the Normal School would have spread whether or not it was published, it was probably decided that the best alternative was to make the case public and blame the incident on a "deviation" committed by junior officials. In effect the authorities admitted the facts, but not the basic reasons for the facts. This technique is hard on minor officials who shoulder the blame; but Mao Tse-tung and the men who surround him cannot afford to be wrong.

Our former teachers at Peita learned this lesson when the government called them back to school in the fall of 1951 to reform their thoughts in the great ideological remolding movement which started in Peking and Tientsin in September and spread all over China in the next six months. Because there is room here only for a sketchy glimpse of the story, I shall limit myself to what the Communist press says happened at Peita.

Why did the campaign happen in the first place? Hadn't our professors helped as much as anyone else to bring the new regime into being? They had always prided themselves on being liberal or progressive; many of them had turned their backs on the old political leadership years before the Liberation. Our new leaders had publicly told them that their wisdom and experience were needed to build the new nation we had been promised. What was wrong now? In effect, the Communist press accused them of one major crime—of wanting to go on believing in the ideas they had believed in, and of wanting to go on teaching what they had always taught.

By 1951 this had become unrealistic, however. The reason for the existence of any Chinese university had changed. Pure education was not desirable any more. What the Chinese university existed to do now had been set down in blunt words at the Fifteenth All-China Students' Representatives Congress. This congress resolved that it was the responsibility of all universities in China to turn every student into "a superior cadre, upright, capable, and healthy, and possessed of a lofty degree of Communist consciousness." *

Professors in the universities obviously had to change what they thought and what they taught in order to accomplish this assignment. The reluctance of teachers to let go of the old and embrace the new during the first two years of the Liberation obviously agitated the Communist leaders. After the campaign to reform the intellectuals got under way, the Vice Minister of Education, Ch'ien Chun-ju, explained why it was necessary: "the slow rate and limited scope of change attained by the great majority of professors during the past two years." † And, Chien explained, if teachers stuck to their "personal individualism, objectivism, and sectarian point of view," then such things as true progress in the reorganization of faculties and departments, curriculum reform, reform in teaching methods, and so on, could not be achieved.

This statement of Ch'ien's was the signal for other attacks on a nation-wide front against the "erroneous old democratic ideology of the bourgeoisie" that too many teachers still clung to, and the allied sins of "liberalism" and "reformism." Our Peita president, Dr. Ma Yin-ch'u, fired off a round of his own a week before. In an article published on October 23, 1951, in the Peking *People's Daily News,* he had criticized what he called the "liberal and unorganized atmosphere" of our old university. Then, two weeks later, on November 6th, Professor Ch'ien Tuan-sheng, dean of the Peita College of Law, attacked even more vigorously what he called Peita's "traditional laxity and liberalism" and the "pedagogical philosophy of freedom of thought and freedom of study." Of course, though it was all right to let these two freedoms continue, they had led to abuses in the past.

Professor Chi'en went President Ma one step better in humbling himself and attacking his old school. In his earlier article Dr. Ma had at least recalled the "glorious revolutionary tradition" of Peita, with a history which "has been inseparable from the revolutionary career of the Chinese people." He said: "Such a close

---

* Quoted in the Peking *People's Daily News,* March 24, 1952.
† Article, "The Key to Reform of Higher Education," in *Hsueh-Hsi* (Study), Vol. 5, No. 1, Nov. 1, 1951. This magazine is the leading official "thought" journal of Communist China.

relationship as existed between Peking University and the Chinese Revolution is rare, not only in the histories of Chinese universities but also in those of universities in other parts of the world. This is the greatest glory and pride of Peking University." And perhaps he is right.

In reply Dean Ch'ien said: "People are easily deluded by the glorious tradition of Peita. Actually, except for the May 4th Movement, what has Peita to be so very proud of?" I can appreciate the circumstances which made Dean Ch'ien write this, but I think he must have been frightened indeed when he so publicly abandoned his loyalty to a great university we know he still loves and respects.

The "lax and liberal" stand of professors and such other vices as "individualism" and "objectivism," were blamed later on in the course of the thought-reform movement for the "corrosive effects of bourgeois ideology" upon Peita students. Some of these "corrosive effects" were reported in the *People's Daily News* of March 24, 1952, under charges that some Peita faculty members tried to follow a policy of "education above politics" and "pure scholarship." One teacher in Oriental Languages was accused of telling his students, "If you are competent technically, you don't have to care about politics." Other professors had said that politics was secondary but technique must not be neglected, and thus completely overlooked their students' "political consciousness." Therefore they hailed a "certain third-year student in the Department of Mechanical Engineering who expressed himself in the most absurd way" about politics as a superior student simply because he had learned more about engineering than his classmates.

Even worse, "the teachers looked askance at students whose school work suffered as a result of their active participation in other aspects of school activities" (that is, political meetings). And some exasperated faculty members even tried to talk their charges out of joining in such important political activities as the Anti-America, Aid-Korea Campaign. The chairman of the Chemistry Department, for instance, told a class, "Political activities are the work of cadres freed from production and of expert politicians."

Peita professors were also accused of interfering with the efforts of the government to encourage students to accept without too much protest the job assignments that were given them on graduation. When a student in the Physics Department was told to join the Military Cadres Training School, a professor told him, "People all agree that you are good in mathematics, so you'd better keep up your mathematical studies." Other teachers told students publicly, "Those who are good at their studies should not join the Military Cadres School." One rather bold professor in the Physics Department said to a student, "How unfortunate it is that you have to abide by the government's assignment of work after your graduation!"

After an admonition to teachers not to concentrate too much time on teaching "talented" students, the article I have been quoting from, the Number One official paper in China, ends with a sermon against a professor in the Department of Architecture. He asked his students to design a gate for the university, but he didn't like some of the drawings because they were too "simple" and "practical." Instead he praised the drawings which he called "full of imagination." Perhaps he still believed that imagination was a proper thing for a young man who wanted to be an architect. The *People's Daily News* does not think so, however. The last sentence says this about imagination: "It can only serve to beguile the students into leading an impossible life of impracticability and indulgence in beautiful 'daydreams.' "

I haven't mentioned yet how the thought-reform movement for professors really worked. It began in Peking in the fall of 1949; Peita and the other universities in the city, it appears now, were used as testing grounds for the techniques to be applied against schools in other parts of the country. Every professor and lecturer in Peita, Tsinghua, Yenching, and other universities in Peking was expected to participate. On the afternoon of September 29, 1951, they all assembled to hear Premier Chou En-lai deliver the lecture which officially launched the campaign. "Premier Chou talked for five hours," President Ma of Peita writes in the article I have already quoted from. "Although the lecture was long, the audience did not feel tired."

Then, for the next four months, the 3,000 professors and lecturers settled down to perform the tasks mapped out for them. (According to a New China News Agency report, the number of college teachers participating in the program had grown to 6,188 by November 12th.) Their first job was to study Premier Chou's speech (which has never been published in the newspapers) and examine the problem of "stand, attitude, whom we serve," and so on. In the following three stages the professors (or students, as they really were now) were supposed to study the current reports of government officials on current questions and policies as well as the "basic concepts of Marxism-Leninism and Mao Tse-tung's theory of the Chinese Revolution" and the "mistaken thoughts of the bourgeois class and the petty bourgeoisie."

These documents would not teach the teachers anything new; after all, they had had to study the same things several times before. But now they had to discuss them again and again, to parrot them in front of their colleagues, and then listen while their colleagues repeated them. But it was the fifth stage of the movement which I think was intended to push them into conformity. The fifth stage called for "the general summary of personal ideology." In practice this meant nothing but the familiar technique of "self-criticism" designed to humble a professor in front of his colleagues and his students by forcing him to criticize his beliefs and his ideals and to renounce all of the things he had believed in and tried to teach. In front of his friends, who faced the same shame themselves, he had to confess that he had been selfish, arrogant, loyal to reactionaries, corrupt, contemptuous of the working class, a worshiper of "Western imperialism," and a skeptic about the great USSR, that he had tried to suppress the patriotism of his students, and that he had poisoned them with filthy bourgeois doctrines. Then he had to "bow before the people," and promise with a show of humility that he would repent from now on and faithfully follow the leadership of the Party. Most professors had to endure this "self-criticism" at least twice before the Party functionaries in charge of the meetings would let them go. By submitting thus to public shame, the teachers we had admired so much surrendered the integrity they had cherished and fought for all their lives.

That is strong language. But any graduate of Peita who has read the public repentances published in the Communist press by China's most respected teachers in the spring and summer of 1952 must feel the same helpless pity for the scholars and thinkers who had made Peita great. Listen to what Dean Ch'ien Tuan-sheng of the College of Law said in the Peking *Kuang Ming Daily News* on July 1, 1952, under the heading "The Communist Party Educated Me." Confessing that he has been guilty of "arrogance and self-importance," he admits that before the Party began to educate him, "I shamelessly took myself to be a professor of the people and a working member of the People's Government." But thought reform showed him how his "arrogance and self-importance"—words which he repeats three times, like a charm—had cut him off from "the masses" and infected him with "the disease of bureaucratism." But, as he says, "the blessings of Chairman Mao and the Communist Party are infinite." He remarks that after his self-criticism he has been washed clean:

"All thanks are due to Chairman Mao and the Party for curing my disease, saving my soul, and giving me the education to enable me to serve the people. I shall reform myself incessantly and thoroughly, make a faithful study of Marxism-Leninism and the thoughts of Mao Tse-tung, and serve the people with all my heart—at the present, to make a success of readjusting the colleges and departments—in order to pay back the Party and Chairman Mao.

"Long live the mighty, glorious and correct Communist Party of China.

"Long live our great Chairman Mao."

For some suggestion of why respected scholars and educators groveled so before the Communist Party, look at the Hankow *Chang Chiang Daily News* of March 24, 1952. For the benefit of teachers in the Central South Area entering thought reform, the president of Hunan University describes what happened to teachers in Peking during the "resolute struggle against bourgeois mentality" during the "three-anti" campaign:

"In this struggle they [teachers, students, clerks, and workers in Peking] exposed grave infringements upon national construction and the people's interests inflicted by leading authorities and teachers, so that the latter had to forget about their 'prestige' and make self-criticism. Many presidents, deans of colleges, department heads, professors, lecturers, and assistants have made self-criticisms in the presence of the masses, criticizing their own bureaucracy, factionalism, departmentism, selfish conduct, or pro-American sentiments."

And how did these respected educators fare during their public ordeal? "Those who made thorough and profound criticism were accepted by the masses, while those who did not were asked to make two or three self-criticisms over. Some professors had to criticize themselves five times," he adds with quiet relish.

Listen to one more story, this time from a girl from Yenching who finally managed to escape to Hong Kong later in 1953. She no longer has an alma mater; the name of Yenching University was abolished in 1952 and its staff and students were dispersed among other schools. (Other foreign-subsidized universities, like St. John's in Shanghai and Lingnan University in Canton, also received their death sentence about the same time.)

Like other Yenching students, this particular girl was drafted into the Three-Anti Movement in the winter of 1951. The school authorities, in fact, canceled final examinations at the end of the term so that students and teachers could concentrate on the campaign to expose the "three vices" of "corruption, waste, and bureaucracy." Clerks and other petty employees of the school were the first victims. Everyone had to participate; those who escaped more serious charges had to confess to such crimes as using bricks that belonged to the school to build bathtubs for themselves or failing to remove a fallen tree.

Meanwhile, you remember, a campaign to reform thought, to "establish firmly a new standard of morals, of studies and patriotism" in the schools was already under way. The most popular and respected professors were chosen as the first targets.

To provide the right setting, the authorities put on an "Exhibition of American Imperialist Cultural Aggression" which every class was taken to see. Theses written by graduate students, books written by professors, and official and private letters to foreign universities were on exhibition to prove that the writers of these documents were guilty of "bourgeois ideology" or "counter-revolutionary thoughts." Guides led the students around, pointed at the documents with their sticks, and made excited speeches about the shortcomings of individual professors. Next, some of the accused teachers were led to the exhibition and publicly insulted. Professor Chang Tung-sun, the philosopher, had written ten years ago, "If I were offered a choice between Fascism and Communism, I would feel it to be a choice between being shot and being hanged." This sentence was copied in enormous characters on a long streamer and hung on the wall in the hall. Professor Chang was compelled to stand under it to be shouted at by fanatic Youth Corps members and their followers.

Mass meetings were then called to permit teachers to make public confessions of their sins. The accused first faced an all-university assembly to hear charges made by "activist students" and to make preliminary confessions. Then, while they were confined in small rooms equipped with a bed, a desk, a chair, and much writing paper, the cadre members held small meetings to distribute "evidence" to selected students to bring up at the next big meeting. The students presented these new charges at the second public meeting after the professor had read his second confession, and back he went to write a third, until his young judges were convinced that he had sufficiently humiliated himself.

The respected president of Yenching, Dr. Lu Chih-wei, was not very much worried about the campaign. Then a friend secretly tipped him off that arrangements were being made to bring him to trial. He telephoned his clerk to send all of his office files to his home only to discover that the cadre members had already taken over his office. But because he had always been treated with deference and courtesy by the Communists, when the meetings got going and the cadre members asked him to sit on the platform as an example he appeared quite at ease and even slightly amused. Perhaps he thought that it was some kind of formal ceremony which he had to preside over for the sake of appearances. He was too familiar with the stage of the Yenching assembly hall to realize that it was going to be his gallows.

When his turn to speak came, he confessed, good-humoredly, that he had also committed offenses against the people. "I borrowed two bowls of flowers from the office for my son's wedding and I forgot to return them. Thus I took something that belonged to the people for my own private use." This, of course, amused the students, which was the worst thing that Dr. Lu could have done.

Quickly, the cadre members in control of the meeting sent several staff members who had been his friends or protégés up to the stage to denounce him. These speakers dramatically counted the number of Yenching graduates in past years who had gone to the United States or who had served the old government, and contrasted them with the relative handful who had joined the Communists. The contrast, they shouted, proved that Dr. Lu had served as a running dog of the American imperialists, that he had "murdered" all of these students morally and mentally by sending them up the "counter-revolutionary road." And they made certain other charges which only Dr. Lu's friends could have had the knowledge to supply.

Spectators could see how the accusations hit Dr. Lu; he sat pale and silent, with his smile gone. It required the stabs of his false friends to shake his confidence that he was simply presiding over some expected ritual like the emperor sacrificing at the Temple of Heaven on behalf of his subjects. So President Lu went off into one of the little lonely rooms to go to work on his own confession.

Whatever resistance he tried to put up was soon broken. The Communists persuaded his daughter, Lu Yao-hua, to denounce him. How they persuaded her to turn on her father, I don't know; the rumor was that she yielded in exchange for an offer of protection, a membership in Youth Corps, and other temptations. Whatever the pay was, she earned it, first accusing her father at departmental meetings, weeping in front of all of her classmates as she told about his crimes against the people. Because the audience was greatly impressed, the cadre members called a big meeting to let her confront him face to face. She looked him in the eyes and called him an enemy of the people, and he gave up. Before he was through, he made his confession at four big meetings. Then he was removed from office and disappeared shortly afterward. The girl I met from Yenching doesn't know what has happened to him.

The professors safely reformed, the cadre members told the students: "Comrades, you have been strict and thorough in reforming the ideas of your professors. Now, how about yourselves? Don't you want to be frank, too?" The students were herded into groups of twelve, with each person charged with the duty of seeing that another student made a full confession, thus forming a sort of "chain-confession" movement within the circle. Cadre members told my friend and her classmates that they must also write down the offenses their relatives and friends had committed against the people. Unless the entire group approved, each confession had to be rewritten.

This campaign lasted for several months. Students went to three meetings a day, from 8:00 A.M. to 1:00 PM., from two until six, and from eight until midnight. My friend fell ill and had to ask for leave. First, her leave request was discussed by her group; then she had to apply to the student in charge of students in her department; next, she got the permission of the president of her department, then of the student leader in charge of the department group, and finally of the school office. At last she got permission to leave the campus for three hours.

Nobody was allowed to forget that the campaign was going on. Loudspeakers at various places on the campus relayed accusations and confessions from the meetings. According to my friend, several students attempted to commit suicide, while three were hospitalized with fatigue or nervous disorders.

A few students turned out to be hard cases for the Communists. During the late stage of the Three-Anti Movement, in the late spring of 1952, some honored guests came to Yenching—soldiers from the People's Volunteers who had been wounded fighting the Americans in Korea. These war heroes were billeted in one of the best buildings and left to wander about or sit in the sun. Most of these soldiers were from the country, and knew nothing about life away from the farm and the army. They did not bother with the modern facilities in their rooms and did not use the lavatories, even after they were invited to.

Consequently, excrement began to be encountered in all sorts of places, on the lawns, on benches in the garden, and in other unseemly places. A student by the name of Chiang from the Department of Foreign Languages and Literature took a walk with his girl friend in the garden one night and stopped by one of the benches. When she sat down, she sat on some excrement left on the bench.

Her lover was so indignant that he wrote a heated announcement calling attention to the fact that there was much excrement to be seen on the campus. He offered three guesses at its origin. First possibility—dogs. No, he reasoned, there weren't any more dogs than before, and it was most unlikely that the existing dog population had suddenly started to leave more excrement than before. Two —it might have been caused by Nationalist agents. But, the writer argued again, these accursed enemies of the people would have left bombs, not excrement. The third possibility—although he hesitated to suggest it—was that it might be caused by the guests.

Nobody, Chiang wrote, had the heart to blame the guests who had suffered so much for the people. But the hosts did hope that the guests would condescend to be more careful in the future. This announcement Chiang posted at night on a wall where everyone could see it. Perhaps because of its humor and literary style, almost one hundred of his fellow students signed their names below his.

The guests, as you might expect, were furious, and insisted on moving out at once since they had been so rudely insulted. The school authorities, at this point pretty well subdued, were seized with panic and fervently entreated the soldiers to stay. The students who had signed the poster, it was announced, would undergo a more thorough and more stringent thought reform. Everybody apologized, and the guests, now that their faces had been saved, were kind enough to stay on for a few more days.

One more example from the *Kuang Ming Daily News* is the confession by Lo Ch'ang-pei called "Searching Out My Decadent Bourgeois Ideology in the Light of the San Fan Movement," published on July 8, 1952. Dr. Lo, a teacher at Peita since 1934, is now director of the Institute of Linguistics and Philology of the Chinese Academy of Sciences, and one of the nation's outstanding scholars in his field. He pleads quietly to "a rightist insensible attitude of leadership and sentimentality," and adds, "My selfish individual-heroism, which prompts me to climb up, and my arrogant dictatorial urge for command are but the end result of my birth in a decaying Manchu family of the feudal ruling class and my bourgeois education and social relations."

Then come the details about his crimes.

He admits that his book *Language and Culture* was reactionary and of bourgeois composition. He confesses that he attended "meetings of a foreign-organized literature and history association." He admits that when asked to help in the Anti-America Aid-Korea Campaign he "indiscriminately quoted" Mao Tse-tung's words, "We will not attack unless attacked," because of his longing for a word that he surrounds with quotation marks, "peace." He even concedes that he recommended the Sinological writings of Catholic priests, made use of English words, and "welcomed foreigners to attend my lectures."

Then he pleads guilty to "individualism which is isolated from the masses," selfishness, arrogance, and self-importance. "Some of my greatest shortcomings are: my arbitrary willfulness, obstinacy, lack of faith in the masses, and reluctance to depend on the masses." Then he concludes, "I hate myself and am determined to reform."

Our teachers who in this manner "bowed in front of the people," as the Communists call it, were the men who failed to give us the leadership which might have helped save our generation from capture by the Communist revolution. They attacked and rejected the old, but they did little more than attack and reject. We counted on their knowledge and their wisdom, and I know now that they let us down. But it is hard to feel resentment toward them any longer after seeing their self-abasement and reading behind the lines to guess the pressures to which they have been subjected. It would be too much to ask them to resist now.

I have only scratched the surface of the materials available to us on what has happened to universities in China since I left. The events of the last two years would make a book, but it would be a book based on hearsay and published documents, not my own experience.* Besides, I'm not starting a book, but finishing one. And now the only question that remains is, What can we do about the disaster that has happened to us?

We don't have any neat or final answer for that yet. There is the basic question of leadership. One of the things which I know we younger people here lack is mature leadership. We have gone to a number of older anti-Communist leaders here in Hong Kong. We have come away full of respect for their experience and their

---

* Since the writing of these words, such a book has been published. For an objective, over-all understanding of these events, I recommend the research report "Higher Education in Communist China," published in December, 1953, by the Union Research Institute, P.O. Private Bag K-1, Kowloon, Hong Kong.

intelligence and full of disappointment at their preoccupation with private squabbles and feuds among themselves. In a few cases, too, we are sure, they think more about their personal ambitions, or their trading value as "independent leaders," than they do about winning back the mainland from the common enemy.

What about Formosa and the Nationalist Government in that stronghold? No Chinese who wants to destroy the Communists can ignore the existence of Formosa, although some groups here may have tried to do so. Old resentments and disappointments die hard on both sides, of course. Independent leaders outside the government who honestly tried to give good advice before the mainland was lost think that their advice was rejected and that they fell under suspicion for attempting to give it. Such persons are going to be hesitant to risk a second rebuff of the same sort. On the other hand, men in the government who were working hard to stop the Communist advance think that these other men shirked their duty or endangered the common effort by remaining critically aloof.

We don't want to live in the past. We are too young for that. We think that leadership which is going to be effective against the entrenched Communist regime must point in the direction of democracy, must tolerate some freedom to criticize. But criticism, if it is to build and not destroy, must be practical and up-to-date. Any review of the past must be only for the purpose of escaping any retracing of old, blundering steps. Criticism should be pertinent to what will happen in 1953 and afterward, and not so much to what happened in 1947 or 1948.

The Nationalist Government—which is the government we owe allegiance to—has made progress on Formosa. But more progress remains to be achieved. Particularly, I think, the government is going to have to find some better means of speaking with effect to young people. For it is the young who gave the Communists the energy and vitality to come to power. It is the people of my age and younger who are the most effective servants in helping the Communists to spread and maintain that power over China. It is going to take a long time to destroy the power the Communists have built in the past four years. Perhaps we are not going home this year or next year. But it is the people of my generation who will play the big role in the struggle against them.

I have met some older people here in Hong Kong who acknowledge this. One of the members of our group is lucky enough to be living with older members of his family, who fled from Shanghai before the Liberation with enough money to live comfortably in Hong Kong. When I called to talk to our friend, he had just come home from playing soccer and was taking a bath, and his father had to entertain me while I was waiting. After some polite and perfunctory questions about what we were doing, he actually got interested. I told him some of the things I thought China ought to have, and we were in the midst of debating them when the son came in, full of apologies for being late.

"That's all right," his father excused him. "Your friend and I have been enjoying our talk. You young people really are working hard to try to do something, aren't you? This should really be the responsibility of my generation. We lost China, and it should be our duty to win it back. But I'm afraid that you are going to have to do most of the work."

"Yes," his son said. "With due respect to Father, older people have lost too much of their vitality and their ability to hope. Most people of the older generation do not have enough courage left. They have to be practical above everything else."

He turned aside my effort to break in on him. "And something worse. Older people don't seem to be able to get together easily to cooperate and achieve something. Each one has his own self-respect, his own enemies and benefactors. He has too much fear of defeat; he's frightened of the suspicions, the distrust experience has taught him. He is willing to be a leader; he is not so willing to be led."

I tried to make amends. "But experience is exactly what we don't have. And leadership. A few people working as we do can only chip away at what the Communists are doing. It's going to take more than a few exiled students to defeat them."

"Of course," my friend's father said. "I said only that the young will have to shoulder the hardest part of this job. I believe that we are going to overturn the Communists some time. But building up a China where the same thing won't happen again is going to be harder even than defeating Mao Tse-tung and his armies and his police. That will take a long, long time. I know that I will not live to see it finished. Even you young men and women might not. You can only do your best to get it started."

It was discouraging advice, and he realized it. He went on. "The future of China really does lie with you people. Do a good job." He turned his head to his son and said half jokingly: "And if you can cooperate with older people, you'd better do it. Don't be too obstinate, too proud. There are some older people who will treat you sincerely and honestly. Naturally, there are still politicians who want to control you to keep themselves on top as long as they can. But I believe that the politicians won't be able to use our youth as political capital any more, as they have in the past."

Walking from his house to the bus stop, I walked by the site of a new house. A small piece of clay fell at my feet, and I looked up to see two workers standing on the bamboo scaffolding, daubing mud onto the skeleton of the new building. More workers were underneath, carrying soil in baskets, breaking rocks, mixing plaster. They wore short pants and coarse cotton shirts, and they were smeared with mud and perspiration. The veins stood out on their tanned arms and bare legs, dark with pumping blood. The men with the carrying poles grunted "Unh-ah, unh-ah" as they moved around the foundation under the load of their baskets.

On any other day I would have passed the new house without noticing it. There are a great many new houses being built in Hong Kong. But now I thought about us and the house we had to build, and how we needed good plans and more help, and how small our chances were of living in it after it was built. But there was nothing else to do except try it.

The bus stop at the corner was a long way away from Peking and the dormitory in Peita where we sat four years ago waiting for the Communists to liberate our city. Too many of my friends thought then that the new house was already there and waiting for us to move in. Now, in exile in Hong Kong, we have knowledge, but knowledge acquired at considerable cost. Older people I know, who left ahead of the Communists, have given up; they want to go to America or Europe and wait "until the whole thing blows over." We don't want to go to America or Europe. Our future is in China, and we want to stay as close to our future as we can get. We didn't run away from the revolution the Communists had made. We stayed to see what it was like, and we found out. We know that we were betrayed, duped into giving away to a false cause the young idealism and hope we can't expect to recapture. But one other thing we also know: it's going to be hard to betray us again.